STATISTICAL INDICATORS

STATISTICAL INDICATORS

FOR THE ECONOMIC & SOCIAL SCIENCES

ROBERT V HORN

Published by the Press Syndicate of the University of Cambridge
The Pitt Building, Trumpington Street, Cambridge CB2 1RP, UK
40 West 20th Street, New York, NY 10011-4211, USA
10 Stamford Road, Oakleigh, Melbourne, Victoria 3166, Australia

© Cambridge University Press 1993
First published 1993

Printed in Hong Kong by Colorcraft

National Library of Australia cataloguing in publication data
Horn, R. V. (Robert Victor).
Statistical indicators for the economic and social sciences.
Bibliography.
Includes index.
ISBN 0 521 41333 8.
ISBN 0 521 42399 6 (pbk).
1. Research—Statistical methods. 2. Social indicators. 3. Economic
indicators. I. Title.
001.422

Library of Congress cataloguing in publication data
Horn, Robert Victor.
Statistical indicators for the economic and social sciences /
Robert V. Horn.
Includes bibliographical references and index.
ISBN 0-521-41333-8.—ISBN 0-521-42399-6 (pbk.)
1. Economic indicators. 2. Social indicators. I. Title.
HB137.H627 1992
330'.01'5195—dc20   92-23005
                                                              CIP

A catalogue record for this book is available from the British Library.

ISBN 0 521 41333 8 hardback
ISBN 0 521 42399 6 paperback

CONTENTS

FIGURES

TABLES

PREFACE

Forget about exports and imports and profits,
and such neoclassical notions.
Let's balance the product produced from this planet
with the waste flushed into our oceans.

How many hospital beds for each citizen?
What leave for the birth of each child?
How many bookshops? How many cinemas:
What's the street price for a smile?

Nick Horn (1990)

This book is a guide to the role of indicators in the wide world of the social sciences. It concentrates on major areas and aspects of importance, gives some others at least a brief mention, and contains a bibliography indicating recent sources for further study. Although it was written in Australia and offers a few examples taken from there, the text is applicable to Britain, North America and the Western world generally. It deals with indicators of the thrust, impact and direction of change, progressing from theoretical and technical considerations to the discussion of various practical everyday applications.

I received my introduction to the subject while working with the International Labour Office, the United Nations Educational, Scientific and Cultural Organisation (UNESCO) and other international organisations in the mid 1970s, when the social indicator movement first took root, and I have continued to watch it spread and ripen since returning to the University of New South Wales in Sydney. I am grateful for advice I received over the years from colleagues at those institutions and elsewhere, as well as for the essential information services provided by the university and Commerce Faculty libraries of the University of New South Wales and by other organisations. No adequate indicator exists that would scale, weight and aggregate their ineffable contributions to this book, as well as those by my wife and family. I thank them all.

Robert V. Horn

CHAPTER 1

FROM STATISTICS TO INDICATORS

1.1 Introduction

This book deals with applications of statistics to the social sciences, including economics and other areas usually styled as 'social', such as sociology, social policy and planning. Examples are drawn mainly from those disciplines, but some applications extend to the natural sciences. The discussion does not stretch to the higher reaches of epistemology, semantics and general philosophy; rather it looks more practically at the purpose of indicators and, from there, to their nature and construction.

Sections 1.2 to 1.4 that follow discuss the statistical derivation of indicators, their structure and typology, and their use in scientific analysis. Then Chapter 2 'Indicator techniques' outlines some of the major statistical techniques and characteristics used for indicators. This material is based on the general statistical textbook literature, to which reference should be made for further detail. In Chapters 3 to 5 particular indicator applications in various fields of economics and social analysis are discussed. There are brief descriptions of some of the major subject matter, and references to sources in the bibliography, but the main emphasis is on identification of the processes involved and on appropriate socioeconomic measurement. Finally, Chapter 6 presents a summary of the main features of indicator analysis.

The bibliography covers some classic texts but concentrates otherwise on a selection of fairly recent titles, which themselves list further references, chosen from the very large literature in the various branches of the social sciences.

1.2 Classification of indicators

The term *'statistics'* is used in the dual sense of numerical facts, which are the basic material for indicators, and of a methodology, which serves as a tool for the construction of indicators. To put it in another way, statistics are the building blocks, which can be assembled in various ways for different indicative purposes. Statisticians distinguish between data, methods and purpose:

> Statistics are numerical statements of facts in any department of inquiry, placed in relation to each other . . . [they are] used for describing and analysing groups or aggregates, too large or complex to be intelligible for simple observation. (Bowley, 1923: 1–2)

Or to quote a more recent textbook:

> By Statistics we mean quantitative data affected to a marked extent by a multiplicity of causes. By Statistical Methods we mean methods specially adapted to the elucidation of [such] data. (Yule and Kendall, 1950: xvi)

We will be concerned with the process of *social quantification*, which goes back to the work of nineteenth-century statisticians like Galton in England and Quetelet in Belgium, or even the poverty studies by Gregory King in 1688. However, it has achieved wider currency only since the 1950s through the social indicator movement. In practice it is not easy to separate the data from their content and purpose.

The word 'statistics' itself was first used in the eighteenth century in Germany, in reference to the workings of the state, and the first volume of the *Journal of the Royal Statistical Society* in 1838–39 refers to facts 'which are calculated to illustrate the conditions and prospects of society'. However, the further development of statistical methods weakened the link between statistical data and their indicative purpose, leading to a division between the work of theoretical statisticians and that of applied statistical analysts. At the Statistical Congress held in Brussels in 1853 the leading statisticians of the day semed more interested in the description of living levels than in tidy rules for the analysis of consumer expenditure. However, subsequent generations of 'Year Book' statisticians and textbook writers became more concerned with the manipulation and presentation of data than with concepts. Only in more recent times have social scientists, including socially aware economists, become concerned about policy targets expressed in statistical form with reference to welfare, environment and similar issues.

Statistical methods are described in many learned papers and textbooks pitched at various levels of comprehension. For the present purpose it will be sufficient to summarise some basic methods and to refer readers to the textbooks for elaboration. The nature of indicators is less discussed in the literature and then mainly in the context of methods. Here we will try to reverse the sequence by concentrating more on the purpose and use of indicators and only then look at methods of constructing them for set objectives. Progression *from why?* *to how?* seems such a simple logical procedure in the pursuit of knowledge that it hardly requires further justification. However, with so many protagonists of the reverse procedure of expounding methods with only casual comment on the rationale of their application, indicators have sometimes become forced into unsuitable formats that obscure their meaning.

Some prevailing perceptions about statistics that are relevant to indicators can be briefly summarised as follows:

- Numbers hold a fascination of their own for many people. They become metaphors of phenomena, and they order our thinking into a fixed frame that is seemingly objective in the rigor of its spacing. The symbolic expression of so many kilometres, years or dollars reflects to us the reality of space, time or wealth.
- We must measure to cope with our environment, with the rhythm of nature and with scarce resources.
- Many scientists are so preoccupied with the exactness of methodology that they disregard the uncertainties of underlying concepts and policies.
- Comparisons, expressed numerically, set standards of what has been and can be achieved. Our values are formed not so much by what we have as by what others have in comparison to ourselves. Socioeconomic notions such as production, poverty and work are comprehensible only in relative terms. Economics, described by Alfred Marshall in 1890 as the study of 'mankind in the ordinary business of life', is dominated by assumptions about comparative rules of behaviour such as:

> More is better than Less.
> I am more important than Thou.
> Sooner is better than Later.
> What You have got I need too.
> Rationality sanctifies the greed of Economic Man.

However, such narrow views are now being expanded into more comprehensive, more compassionate attitudes, and a wide range of indicators can help us to understand better the ordinary business of life.
- Numerical symbols set the pace for mathematical manipulation, and they can be retranslated into verbal language without much regard to the logic of the result. That is reflected in statements such as 'We are now three times better off than we were last year', or in regarding output as the equiproportional function of inputs, or in positing that $a + b - b = a$ or that $ab/b = a$. Such shortcut assumptions bypass the complexities of changing context and of synergic effects.

Socioeconomic concepts are usually described in relative or even negative terms (e.g. unemployment, work, living standards, poverty). They are identified with a state or activity within a subjective frame of reference. In economics the debate about economic thought and language, to quote the title of L.M. Fraser's analytical critique of 1937, has abated with the rise of econometric analysis, which rests on narrow, rigorously defined certainties. Statisticians' choices of what to include or exclude in their counts and how to combine subseries depend largely on practical considerations inherent in the collecting process. Economists look for unambiguous statistics, rather than unambiguous concepts, for their models and will at worst accept series that do not fit well their titles (e.g. underemployment, disposable income). In direct measurement the gap between concept and statistics is sometimes narrowed by means of explanatory footnotes, but it is not so easily bridged in the indirect measurement of welfare, utility and qualitative notions in general.

In the nineteenth century inspired statisticans in Europe (e.g. Quetelet, Engel) and Australia (e.g. Coghlan, Hayter) sometimes interpreted their collections as welfare indicators, but subsequent generations of official statisticians opted for safety when, for the sake of objectivity, they left the interpretation of their collections to other analysts. For instance, the empirical observation that the income elasticity of the demand for food is less than 1 in most countries, expressed in the Engel curve (1857), led to further mathematical analysis of consumer behaviour and contributed to the subsequent development of econometrics (see section 4.9 and Zimmermann, 1932).

Indicators are expressed mainly as:

- statistics in a time series (diachronic) or at a point of time (synchronic);
- comparisons of structural components; or
- comparisons of different entities (e.g. regions, enterprises).

A single statistical datum is not indicative by itself. When we quote a figure for income per head of $a last year, or a population totalling b million at the end of last year or a literacy rate c% at that time, the figure means nothing until we compare it with corresponding figures for other periods or elsewhere. Figure 1.1, for instance, shows the change in gross domestic product (GDP) for country A between years 1 and 2 and the size of GDP in country Á compared with country B. It also shows the structure of GDP, assumed to be made up of wages and surplus, in either country or period:

$$\text{Wages} + \text{Surplus} = \text{Expenditure}$$
$$W + S = GDP$$

The comparison need not be formal; it can rest on our knowledge of the general statistical situation; so we can at once describe an income per head of $50 000 as relatively high or a literacy rate of 10% as relatively low. Yet while it is reasonable to argue that an isolated statistical datum has no indicative meaning without being related to some reference series, it can be claimed that no event is independent of other historic or circumstantial events. A single statistic, say a population count of 1 million people, has a history of earlier population sizes and changes and is itself

Figure 1.1   GDP for two countries over two periods

Country	Year 1			Year 2		
	W	*S*	*GDP*	*W*	*S*	*GDP*
A	20	30	50	30	40	70
B	10	30	40	20	60	80

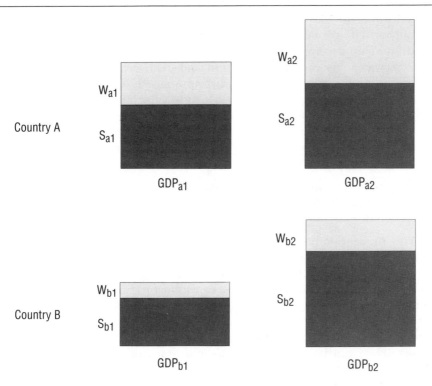

a link indicator for future counts. Yet the number by itself, 1 million, is silent; its history is impenetrable without the key furnished by other data. We need statistical series and systems to unlock its indicative content.

Indicators are intermediaries that link statistical observations with social or other phenomena. In semantic terms they are *metadata*—that is, data describing other data. This fits into a so-called *syntactic model*, as proposed by Olenski (1986) and other semiologists, from which it may be concluded that indicators acquire meaning, indeed variable meanings, in their application; they bring amorphous statistics to life.

Concepts in the social sciences are called *soft* if they cannot be defined with the precision of terms used in the physical sciences. The description varies according to the point of view of the user and the purpose to which the concepts are applied. Broad agreement about generalised meaning leaves gaps and overlaps between areas. This applies to major notions such as health, education and welfare and also to broad economic terms such as 'production', 'trade' and 'income', where precise statistical descriptions cannot hide some indeterminacy in underlying concepts (e.g. in the treatment of non-cash benefits or transfers as part of income, or of household services as production). Indicators, as neutral tools, help to clarify the specifics of concepts in a particular context. We can, for instance, extend the meaning of health statistics beyond morbidity by including the operations of pharmacies as an aspect of health service delivery.

According to Kaplan (1964: 77), specification is part of the process of enquiry itself. We begin with terms that are not specified by the context and build up a conceptual structure from empirical findings, discarding on the way some earlier information and discovering additional sources as we go along. This *instrumentalist approach* is similar to the *method of successive definition* used in physics, or to what has been called a process of *reciprocal illumination* or *successive approximation* (Ridley, 1983: 651). It involves an *iterative learning process* (De Neufville, 1975: 127) in which indicators lead to the specification of concepts. Therefore we can speak of two main functions of statistics:

1 description by summarising information;
2 induction, which involves either generalisation from samples or the formulation of laws based on repeated observation.

We can mention here the hypothesis of *sonic resonance* (Sheldrake, 1988), which suggests that, at least in the natural sciences, all systems are shaped by 'morphic fields' that represent a collective memory around them beyond the genetic encoding of individuals, in contrast to traditional assumptions about mind and matter. This can possibly be extended to the learning process as not being confined to processing statistical indicative information but subject also to the sonic resonance of universal experience. More generally, it can be claimed that no indicator can be abstracted from its historical context.

We shall return later to the conversion of statistics into indicators, but note here a caution about the process of the specification of concepts, known as *conceptualisation*, or, in related terms, of the *reification* or *concretisation* of abstract notions. The search for meaning should not be attempted by a haphazard choice of possibly related statistics fed into the computer for factorising or other complex multivariate analysis, to produce a uniform series or vector that represents the abstract notion on a single even scale. The perils of such methods have been well illustrated by Gould (1983) in chronicling attempts to create concepts of intelligence during and since the last century. They have reflected personal, political and social bias as well as the ambiguity of the statistical methods employed, in their efforts to grade persons by hereditary or environmental factors. In other words, concepts cannot be mechanically–mathematically constructed without evidence that supports the objective logic of every successive step.

The merging relation between statistics and indicators can be demonstrated with the following sequence:

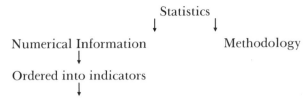

This relation can be summarised by describing indicators as *purposeful statistics*.

1.3 Operation and structure

As previously suggested, much of our thinking is anchored in comparisons. These may reflect aspirations to some ideal of virtue or harmony, but more often they are related to other people and situations in the past, present or expected future. Indicators provide a guide for expressing such comparisons in systematic scale marks. A single datum, in time or space, comes to life when related to others that indicate direction or relative magnitude. What usually matter most are simple relations, or changes in such relations, of the more-or-less type, even if expressed with mathematical precision. This relative nature of indicators calls for attention when choosing the indicator base (e.g. population of certain ages or status, production by provenience). Indicators with fixed scales are familiar in daily life (e.g. hands of a clock, markings on a thermometer, lines of a weather map). Economists use indicators to delineate the working of the economy, and other social scientists apply them to societal analysis. These examples supplement the dictionary definitions that describe an indicator as something (or somebody) that *points out*. Indicators describe what has happened, is happening or may happen; they categorise and superimpose a calculus on events. Different systems of indicators can be applied to a given set of data (e.g. metric or non-metric) or mixed bundles of indicators to abstract notions such as welfare or safety.

Pointing out can refer simply to directions (e.g. by a car trafficator, weather vane or a litmus test), or symbolically to the threat of global catastrophe (e.g. the clock on the cover of the *Bulletin of Atomic Scientists*, which stood at 10 minutes to midnight at the end of 1990), or to on-off choices of the yes-no type. More frequently, however, we are presented with a spectrum or with degrees of change where a scaled mode is appropriate for indicators. The classification of indicators can be based on various criteria of contents and objectives, and the catalogue below is directed particularly towards socioeconomic processes:

(A) Direct-objective type
    (A.1) Single variable concept
    (A.2) Combined-fixed concept
    (A.3) Combined-dynamic concept

(B) Indirect-derived
    (B.1) Binary signals
    (B.2) Complex subjective

Direct-objective indicators may be based on single series (e.g. school enrolments) or more-or-less homogeneous aggregates (e.g. value of mineral production). Sometimes they require standardisation by differential weights (e.g. calorific value of fuels). Alternatively, a fixed concept can be built up from heterogeneous components that are summed up by number or value (e.g. tonnage and value of exports). That means prior agreement on aggregation and excludes controversy (i.e. dialectical argument) about the inclusion or exclusion of any item.

For open or dynamic concepts (e.g. health, quality of life) the indicators themselves help to define the notion and acquire the dual role of specification and signal. Starting off with a vague concern, the process of selecting and testing data will show their relevance to the target notion; or to express the procedure in indicative jargon, indicators through an iterative learning process exercise a heuristic function in determining the epistemology of social–economic concerns.

Indirect-derived indicative conclusions can emerge from signals of movement or from *proxy series* that are related to the main series (e.g. economic cycles and suicides).

The distinction between subjective and objective indicators cuts across the above classification. It can be applied both to what is being measured and to how it is done. The term '*objective*' is usually applied to the mode of assessment that is based on external evidence that is independent of the reporter, such as the series published by official statistical agencies where objectivity becomes identified with factual evidence. *Subjective* indicators are judgemental, often in mode and in concept, and reflect perceptions or opinions. They can be expressed in simple yes-no terms or divided into intermediary steps of the none-little-enough-a lot type.

The indicators mentioned so far are objective in the sense of being based on circumstantial evidence that is external to and independent of the reporting person or institution. Typical here are the official statisticians' series where objectivity is identified with factual evidence. Against that we have subjective indicators based on judgemental evidence from the persons concerned. They reflect perceptions or opinions by those close to the issue in question, which yield a broader band of answers than a factual enquiry. Examples are surveys and opinion polls about perceived life values and other issues.

Subjective indicators can be formulated in simple binary terms of the more-less or better-worse signal type, and these can be further subdivided by intermediary steps (e.g. none-a little-enough-a lot), or by Maslow's hierarchical classification of five levels of human needs, or by Cantril's *self-anchoring scale* in which people express their degree of satisfaction in ten grades. From there it is only a small step to *cardinalise* such *ordinal grading* by way of assumed (not necessarily equal) step intervals, which convert them to indicators of the (A.1) type. Subjective indicators are occasionally used in economics (e.g. for housing or work satisfaction) and more widely applied in other social sciences.

The relation of subjectivity to *social facts* has been discussed in the sociological literature (e.g. Turner and Martin, 1984: part 2), as has been the link between cardinal and ordinal scaling (e.g. McKennell in Strumpel, 1973). As far as indicative measurement is concerned, the claim to objectivity for any social statistics is dubious due to the essential subjectivity of the selection and presentation process. We must also avoid confusion between *what* is being measured and *how* it is being measured:

	Mode of measurement:	
	Subjective	Objective
Concept: Subjective	(a)	(b)
Objective	(c)	(d)

For instance, we can look at the incidence of disability reflected in an outside indicator by taking the number of invalid pensioners and the cash paid to them, as per (d); or we can take the number from a census that asks people to self-enumerate their specific disabilities, as per (b); or the census can ask whether people feel themselves to be disabled in a general way, as per (a); or it can ask people in receipt of invalid pensions to grade themselves by severity of disablement, as per (c).

In a general way the objective-subjective distinction is often more a matter of form than of substance. All objective-type indicators carry a subjective value load inherent in the process of the collection, selection and presentation of statistics, and subjective-type indicators borrow objective modes of grouping, ranking and partitioning the data. For practical purposes a classification of indicators as shown in Table 1.1, on the lines of the division into objective types, will be sufficient, but it will help in understanding the nature of indicators to consider some other classifications.

We can look at interrelations within the statistical base and between components. This is important for establishing correlations within and between indicator elements (e.g. the connection between production and trade via high technology; auto-correlation between infant mortality and life expectancy; the role of elasticities of substitution in a cost-of-living index). However, such interrelations are too variable and uncertain to serve as *a priori* for classification.

Georgescu-Roegen (1971: 43) draws a distinction between *numerical* (anthropomorphic) and *dialectical* (not uniquely defined) concepts, which in many ways corresponds to our division into (A) and (B) types. In a different approach a division is drawn between *instrumental* indicators, which serve as a means to an end, and *definitive* indicators, which refer directly to their purpose. Mukherjee (1975: 89), for instance, distinguishes between statistics as the *constituent variables* of an indicator and statistics

Table 1.1   Some direct objective-type indicators

Factor	Single variable	Combined variables	
		Fixed concept	Dynamic concept
Production	Single product, houses	Factory, mine buildings	National output
Transport	Car registrations, train mileage	Motor vehicle registrations	Transport index
Trade	Product sales, export item	Group sales, total exports	Total demand, balance of payments
Transfers	Tax by type, government expenditure by type	Tax revenue, public expenditure	Tax burden, welfare spending
Finance	Bank deposits	Money supply	Flow of funds
Income	Wages, pensions	Earnings	Personal income
Labour	Employment, hours worked	Labour force participation	Labour market, time use
Population	Births, deaths	Natural increase	Market growth
Environment	Urban areas	Open space	Pollution index
Health	Hospital beds	Death rates	Healthiness index
Education	Teacher numbers	Teacher ratios	Educational status
Quality of life	Holiday length, suicides	Achievement of set goals	Multiple scale index
Culture	Attendances at concerts	Music appreciation index	Multiple scale index
Human rights	Imprisonment of protesters	Number of gaolings	Multiple scale index

as the *contingent variables* that it seeks to indicate. The contingent variables become *societal* indicators when they refer to a societal condition (e.g. state of the education system), as distinct from *social* indicators, which apply this state to differential human relationships (e.g. access to higher education). The number of persons employed/unemployed can be regarded as an instrumental or constituent indicator for the description of the labour market or the burden of unemployment, but it can also be regarded as a definite or contingent indicator.

On somewhat similar lines Johnstone (1981) distinguishes between *variables*, which particularise different facets of society, and *indicators*, which combine conceptually related variables for an overview. He describes them as basic units in theory development.

Looking beyond their internal classification, indicators can be considered as part of an information system that links observers with the dynamics of the world around them and helps them to understand it. Like language, indicators have in the first place an intermediary (instrumental) task, and again like language they rise beyond their function as a medium to that of shaping the message. With language the selection and presentation of words can carry overtones beyond their original meaning. So also the impact of indicative signposts can be varied by their size and accompanying *noise* (e.g. a government claims to have 'tightened the budget' by a spending cut of some millions when the total budget is reckoned in billions; a supermarket cuts a price 'below $5' to $4.99). The nominally equal interval spacing of numbers need not coincide with suggestive indicator breaks at decennial age points, price integers or mile-a-minute records. Also, just as language adapts itself over time to a changing environment, so must indicators evolve in response to changes in social settings and societal objectives.

The structural sequence for indicators can be depicted as follows:

observations
    organised systematically provide
data
    that contain basic information and can be ordered into
statistics
    either quantified at cardinal/fixed interval scales or non-quantified
    in ordinal ranking, further processed into
indicators
    designed to express
structure or change
    of phenomena related to
social and scientific concerns.

Systematic observations from records or surveys yield data for series that can be scaled numerically with even or variable intervals or by rank ordering without fixed intervals. The statistical database can be manipulated by means of aggregating, averaging, multivariate analysis or extrapolation to fit a framework of social concerns. The choice of data, periods and format will vary between analysts. This means that the computation of indicators, like good statistics, requires judgemental skill.

We can mention here a distinction between *social statistics* and the *social indicator movement*. Statistical interest in social conditions goes back to biblical times (Numbers 1:1-3; Luke 2:1-3), and social statistics have been used ever since as indicators of health and welfare. The social indicator movement dates only back to the 1960s, when social scientists tried a systematic translation of the language of economic indicators and models for the purposes of social planning and the study of human needs. That development was welcomed by those economists who tried to lift their eyes above the money income/wealth horizon to encompass human and environmental values. Hopes for an *holistic* approach through social indicator matrices have not been fulfilled, nor has the extension of economic measures such as gross national product (GNP) into non-monetary spheres been successful. However, much can be learnt from the debate about concepts and methods, as we shall see later.

The operational purpose of indicators is circumscribed by their reference to time or structure. Philosophers have long argued about the notions of points and flows of time, and economists have entered the debate in connection with equilibrium theory since the days of Menger, Böhm-Bawerk and Wicksell, and more recently Keynes (1930, 1936), Georgescu-Roegan (1971) and Hicks (1942: ch. 6). We may accept that time (and an indicator at a point of time) is unidirectional and irreversible. History, rather than looking back from the present to the past, when the present was unknown, looks forward from the past to the present and to the unknown future. We can regard both points and flows of time as devices superimposed on reality. As such we use them for indications of where we stand and where we are going in *cross-section (synchronic)* or *time series (diachronic)* analysis, respectively. Structurally indicators can be further divided into those that show up the forces within a system (e.g. demographic series for a labour market) and those that compare components of a larger universe (e.g. markets in different regions). Both can be extended to indicate change over time.

Some indicators have no meaningful zero level, in particular those that list attitudes on a multipoint scale from 'unhappy' to 'happy'. In this case change or difference can be expressed in points; so a change from, say, 'very dissatisfied' to 'rather dissatisfied' on a five-point scale (from 1 to 2) would be equivalent to a change from 'rather satisfied' to 'very satisfied' (from 4 to 5). However, it would be wrong to express these changes in percent as +100% and +25% respectively; on a scale from -2 to +2 similar changes would come to +50% and +100% respectively. This does not apply to objective-type indicators and others on a ratio scale, as they have a theoretical minimum level of nil, signifying the total absence of its material or satisfaction contents. It can be argued that they all have also an upper limit of total use or fulfilment. However, with many indicators this upper limit is more distant than the horizon to which we refer for production, services, income or longevity and their respective growth rates.

In some situations, however, we have definite upward bounds for indicators. One is ratios relating two or more variables to a given total, which can be a stated population for rates of employment/unemployment, literacy/illiteracy or exports by countries. Others lie between 0 and 100%, where the components relate to a stated population of people or things. As we shall see, ratios provide a convenient form for some indicators, but there are operational limits in describing their movement. There is also a subjective-type bounding of indicators in ordinal satisfaction grades at a point where the marginal utility of a further increment becomes nil. This will be discussed later in connection with poverty and living levels.

We have emphasised the interconnection between indicators and related concerns. A closer look at the latter will clarify the scope of the former. The term *'concern'* has been used by the Organisation for Economic Cooperation and Development (OECD) with reference to its scheme of social indicators under the following headings (OECD, 1982: 5):

Health
Education and learning
Employment and quality of working life

Time and leisure
Command over goods and services
Physical environment
Social environment
Personal safety.

A list of 33 indicators has been attached to the above headings. Concern here refers to areas of interest without overtones of anxiety but directed in general towards welfare. The history of the OECD program attests to its perspective of social well-being and welfare. Its purpose is stated to be:

• identifying the social demands, aspirations and problems that are, or could become, major concerns of the socioeconomic planning process;
• measuring and reporting change in the relative importance of these concerns;
• enlightening public discussion and government decision making (OECD, 1982: 7).

This framework has been designed to apply to both aggregated and disaggregated individual and national welfare.

1.4 Indicators and scientific enquiry

The analytical and interpretive role of indicators must be seen in the context of the nature and methods of scientific enquiry in general. From the large literature on this subject we will leave aside here the recent debate about the philosophy of science connected with the names of Popper, Kuhn, Lakatos and Feyerabend and just mention as references the works of Lakatos and Musgrave (1968), Georgescu-Roegan (1971), Machlup (1978), Hayek (1975) and Deane (1978).

We can start with simple statements such as: science is concerned with a judicious choice from a hierarchy of facts (Poincaré, 1913) where description and theory go hand in hand (Bridgman, 1955); science provides interesting, informative and enlightening truth (Popper, 1968), and this truth must be evident and comprehensible (Schrödinger, 1952; Heisenberg, 1959). These two last attributes in particular correspond to the general characteristics of indicators (i.e. satisfying curiosity and leading to understanding) that were mentioned at the beginning of this chapter, as was the ordering of knowledge to which Poincaré alludes.

In the long-running debate about the difference between the natural and social sciences, John Stuart Mill and many after him have held that they are in principle the same (Katzner, 1983: 20). Others have emphasised the contrast between the study of nature, where matter is silent and the behaviour of its particles is subject to strict rules, and the study of human behaviour and action, characterised by greater openness and indeterminacy (Machlup, 1978: 322; Winch, 1958: 21). Indicators have their uses in both types of science, irrespective of their identity. This applies also to another controversy about science being tied to induction by arguing from the particular to the general, while economics relies much, some say too much, on deductive *a priori* reasoning (Samuelson, 1952: 57). Here we may be more concerned with the related charge that many economic and other social models rest on a weak empirical base (Leontief, 1971: 1; Keynes, 1936: 297; Koopmans, 1957: 209). This caution about the soft sciences can be equally applied to structural indicators when they promote what Hayek (echoing Popper, see Machlup, 1978: 25) has called *scientism*, meaning an imitation of scientific methods where subjective opinions are dressed up as facts.

In the past 100 years a mathematical approach resting on a quantitative base has been developed in economics, and to a lesser extent also in other social sciences. Indeed, Schumpeter, one of its early leaders (Machlup, 1978: ch. 18), has claimed that economics is more quantitative than other social and even natural sciences. Its faith in data is often connected with a positivist outlook that looks at what was, is or will be rather than at what ought to be (Lipsey, 1963), thus fostering a value-free approach. This has not endeared the mathematical school to humanist-inclined scientists who deplore its neglect of cultural properties in economic progress and its disability to deal with dialectical concepts (Georgescu-Roegan, 1971: 341). Furthermore, there have been charges of wrongly applied statistical methods, such as the faulty logic of sometimes equating correlation with causality (Cohen, 1936: 333) or scorn for a mathematical approach that is content with formal proof without empirical verification.

Indicators are essential elements of scientific enquiries that may be labelled quantitative, empiricist, positivist or value-free. They are tools in the kit of mathematical techniques. However, they should not be identified with those approaches, nor with the shortcomings that have been admitted by some of the eminent practitioners quoted above and others. On the contrary, indicators can transcend the rigidities of closed models by going from measurable quantities to qualities (i.e. descriptive properties) for what Katzner (1983) calls *analysis without measurement*. They can incorporate non-linearities and reach into the penumbra that links, rather than divides, the categories of science, and this enables them to play a mediating role between different methodologies.

The purpose of using indicators ranges from abstract analysis to practical decision making. Stone's dictum that social indicators *serve the purposes of curiosity, understanding and action* (United Nations F/18, 1975) also applies to any other indicator. They all help us to know how things happened, why they happened and what we can do to make them happen. Their significance may vary from, say, the sporting performance of a small population group to decisions about spending billions of dollars on development aid. The basic techniques on the road from statistics to indicators that are dealt with in section 2.1 are similar for all purposes, but, as subsequently shown, they can be adapted to a great variety of applications.

Like other forms of social measurement, indicators may not have the rigour and exactitude of the methods of physical science, but they help to establish conjectural relationships that are *stochastic* in the sense of being close approximations to a sample of the ineffable truth.

Indicators can also play a part in extensions to methods of enquiry: for example, in the lateral thinking approach proposed by De Bono (1967); or in morphological research of structural interactions that attempts complete field coverage of non-numerical relationships starting from existing pegs of knowledge (Zwicky, 1969); or in the optimal resource utilisation for human settlements in *Ekistics* (Doxiadis, 1968). For the present purpose we can go back to a comment made by Keynes in his *General Theory* (1936: 297) with reference to the theory of prices and of economic thinking generally:

> The object of our analysis is not to provide a machine, or method of blind manipulation, which will furnish an infallible answer, but to provide ourselves with an organised and orderly method of thinking out particular problems; and, after we have reached a provisional conclusion by isolating the complicating factors one by one, we then have to . . . allow . . . for the probable interactions of the factors amongst themselves. This is the nature of economic thinking.

CHAPTER 2

INDICATOR TECHNIQUES

2.1 Data handling

The many textbooks dealing with economic, business or social statistics usually begin with statistical analysis without specifying the purposes of that analysis; the objective is only implicitly suggested by the examples chosen to illustrate the methods. On the other hand, the much less numerous textbooks on indicator applications (e.g. to social policy) usually concentrate on such uses rather than on methodology. This book tries to balance the two approaches by linking applications with requisite methods, on the assumption that the objectives should determine the choice of techniques, rather than heuristically manipulating neutral data to discover what information they may yield. Therefore we will look at techniques from the premises that indicators condense, classify and interpret evidence of statistical data. For a fuller treatment of techniques, reference should be made to general textbooks such as Kenkel (1989) or Mendenhall (1989), or to the more condensed volumes by Allen (1972) or Thirkettle (1981). Some of the tricks and traps in applying statistics are instructively described in the popular paperbacks by Huff (1954), Reichmann (1965) and Moroney (1951), and in Ackoff's *Art of Problem Solving* (1978).

We begin by listing some data-handling aspects of indicators that are relevant for the techniques and specification of general characteristics:

1 *Data arrangement*:
   (a) *Data selection:* Statisticians are faced by a mass of collected or collectible data from which to select and combine indicators.

(b) *Presentation:* Single or combined series must be arranged in a form likely to be comprehensible to users. This may require the translation of series that are disparate in units or timing to a common denominator.

2 *Data flow:*

(a) *Direction:* The data have to be set up according to the respective purpose of showing past, present or future directions.

(b) *Rate of change* may be expressed numerically, percentagewise or graphically.

3 *Data interconnection:*

(a) *Simple comparison* with related or unrelated other series may be made.

(b) *Indicator systems*, interconnected to show interacting societal forces, may be established.

Some basic rules for the data themselves can be stated as follows.

Aspiring to perfect *homogeneity* can become self-defeating, as no two persons or things are exactly the same. When we classify persons as wage earners or householders, we can *standardise* them by age and sex or educational and similar variables to achieve a degree of homogeneity that is sufficient for many but not necessarily all purposes. In the case of analysing consumer demand or work performance, for example, it may be necessary to look beyond age and income at ethnicity as a discriminant. Nor do the component units of production statistics for particular minerals, fibres or grains have exactly the same physical and chemical properties, and even less so do they for manufactured goods or services. Again, however, these collective indicators may be all we need for a general picture of industry and trade. In other words, the appropriate level of homogeneity depends on the indicative purpose.

The role of homogeneity is extended when two series are combined (e.g. in the form of ratios). Not only should the separate series, in the numerator and denominator, be homogeneous themselves, but so should their combination. For example, births may be related to total population if we are interested in population growth, or to females aged 15–45 years (the main reproductive ages) for the calculation of fertility rates. Furthermore, homogeneity requirements change over time. Wages, which once were the main reward for labour, are being increasingly supplemented by profit sharing and various fringe benefits, and an indicator of labour returns should include such benefits; or with changing childbearing patterns it may be appropriate to shift the reference population for fertility rates from women aged 16–50 to women aged 15–45 years. The rationale for adequate homogeneity is *consistency*. This is important in international comparisons of income or nutrition where cultural, historical and physiological norms differ.

The degree of *accuracy* of an indicator depends firstly on technical factors, such as the quality of the data and the methods used for their processing, and secondly on how they fit the indicative intent. Government statistics are usually preferred over possibly biased private sources, but they too may require consistency checks and an explanation for odd-looking figures or movements.

A false impression of accuracy can be created by quoting statistics in greater detail than is warranted by their precision or by overloading indicators with detail. Many collections that involve a large number of people or a large volume of transactions carry a margin of error caused by minor omissions, double counts or definitional uncertainties. In that case showing millions to the last digit, or even hundreds or thousands, rather than to hundred-thousands or millions, promotes the *fallacy of misplaced concreteness* by pretending unwarranted credibility for details. This sort of fussy obfuscation, often used by politicians to impress with their grasp of detail, dims the light of the broad brushstrokes of indicator trends.

Rounding up also needs a sense of proportion for significant change. If the labour force totals 1 million persons (which incidentally is so obviously rounded that one can omit saying 'about' or 'approximately' a million), a change of 1000 or less over 1 year could be ignored by rounding up to two decimals; this implies that a change of less than 1% of the total is not considered significant. In some cases the range of error from rounding (as distinct from collection errors) can be specified; for example:

    12 million to the nearest whole million
    12 345 000 correct to four significant figures
    12 million +/- half a million
    12 million +/- 10%.

Some statistical methods provide their own gauge of accuracy, such as confidence limits or chi-square tests in sampling. Beyond technical considerations the congruence of indicator statistics with concepts remains relative. If we accept that statistics serve as an intermediary language to express indicators, we must accept the risk of misinterpretation of that language. For example, it can be argued that for one particular definition of education the results of certain examinations may be a valid indicator, while for another definition it may be more valid to take an indicator based on teacher assessment of school performance.

The link between information and accuracy is discussed in decision theory (Marshak and Miyasawa, 1968), and recently decision tree models have been used to demonstrate that information from more than one source of uncertainty is not necessarily additive (Samson, Wirth and Rickard, 1989; see also section 2.5 on synergy effect).

2.2 Format

Indicators are usually presented in the form of tables or graphs. In either case the medium should clearly transmit the desired message: where do we stand, where are we going, and how can we get there? Tables are more precise than graphs mathematically, and easier for use in combination and further processing, but their blandness requires verbal explanation of their indicative content. Many users will be more interested in the general directions that can easily be read off a diagram than in struggling with the interpretation of statistical tables.

The basic requirements for the presentation of statistics are stated in all the elementary textbooks, and the popular transgressions against such precepts are discussed under titles like *Use and Abuse of Statistics* (Reichmann, 1965), *Facts from Figures* (Moroney, 1951), *How to Lie with Statistics* (Huff, 1954), and *The Data Game* (Maier, 1991). Here we will mention only some of the ground rules:

• Statistics, in whatever shape, need to be clearly described in heading and legend.
• They should not be overcrowded with detail to the point of opaqueness.
• All symbols beyond basic signs must be explained.
• Scales starting above the origin and broken scales should be avoided.
• Index numbers should show base period and, where possible, reference to actual number.
• Non-linear scaling must be clearly marked as such.

Statistical tables are condensed from a mass of information often collected in great detail over long periods. Statisticians have to select from this material whatever data they consider relevant for the purpose at hand and arrange the chosen data into such columns and rows as they think suit the purpose. In this process the objective nature of the statistics is diminished at various levels: firstly by the compiler's decision regarding what to collect under each category heading, and also by the option of substituting a sample for a complete collection; and secondly, at the level of editing, by the choice of data and of ways to present them. This means that good statistics depend on the commonsense and judgement of those who produce them and that the distinction between objective and subjective indicators is superficial.

Commonsense is also needed to strike a balance between excess and simplicity in the presentation of indicators. In Table 2.1 it is assumed that we seek information on three aspects from a datafile of population statistics: age and area composition and period change. The data are rounded to the nearest thousand and quoted in three age and two regional groups and their totals, which give a 3 × 4 table with extra rows for year 2 and its change over year 1.

For a better indication of relative size, we then convert population into proportions for age and region. This shows, for instance, that about two-thirds of the population are aged between 16 and 64, and that region A is about eight times more populous than region B. We further note that, although B has relatively more young people than A, this has little effect on the overall age distribution because of B's small share in the aggregate. We also see that between years 1 and 2 the population rose by 28 000 or 14%, and that although B contributed 18% of this rise its share in total population rose only from 11½% to 12½%.

Table 2.1   Population by region and age

Period Age group	No. by region			% by age group			% by region		
	A	B	A + B	A	B	A + B	A	B	A + B
Year 1: 0–15	41 000	9 000	50 000	23	39	25	82	18	100
16–64	117 000	13 000	130 000	66	57	65	90	10	100
65+	19 000	1 000	20 000	11	4	10	95	5	100
Total	177 000	23 000	200 000	100	100	100	88½	11½	100
Year 2: Total[a]	200 000	28 000	228 000				87½	12½	100
Change: 1 to 2	+23 000	+5 000	+28 000				+13%	+22%	+14%

[a] Detail for age and regions in period 2 not shown.

Such tabulations can be oversimplified by showing only the proportions and/or by omitting the overall distribution. The relative age distribution for (A + B) would not reveal that B is much smaller than A and has a younger population. Age differences between regions, irrespective of population size, can also be demonstrated by calculating median ages, which here (assuming fairly even distribution within the median age group) come to about 36 years for region A, 26 years for B and 34 years for (A + B).

Some of the information of Table 2.1 is shown in Figure 2.1. The first segment is based on the actual population figures and shows the relatively minor part played by region B, which is masked by the percentage base of the subsequent segments. If there are more than two groups, as there are in this example for age, the relative size of the centre group(s) is not easy to gauge visually; it is therefore shown separately in the third segment, which virtually reduces the age grouping to 16–64 and combined other groups. Other graphs could be drawn, but the scope for bar charts clearly to present detail beyond straight-out composition and aggregate time series is limited.

Tables like Table 2.1 can also be used for testing associations between characteristics such as age and location. In statistical terms we can treat the example as a 3 × 4 contingency table with two degrees of freedom. If there were no relation between age and location, the null hypothesis would apply, and the age proportions for the regions would be the same at 25%, 65% and 10% for all regions. The departure of this expected distribution, E, from the actually observed distribution, O, is summed up in terms of chi-square

$$\chi^2 = S(O - E)^2: E = 4.1$$

This corresponds to a probability ratio of 10%, which is sufficient to reject the null hypothesis. In other words, on the given data a fairly strong association is likely to exist between age and location.

Figure 2.1   Population by region and age

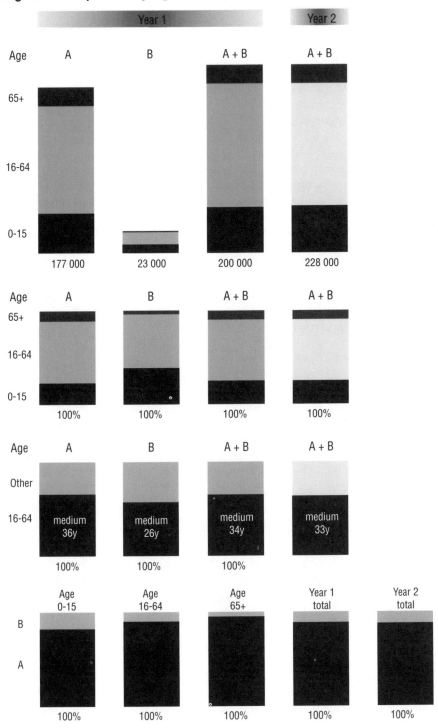

It should be noted that *age* requires further specification to the extent of dating as age at last or next birthday. Age groupings of 0–14, 15–29 and so on can be adapted to the indicator type for labour force, social units and so on. *Region* can be based on political boundaries or sometimes on equality or fairness for electoral divisions, or based on indicators such as community of interests, geographical attributes, regional homogeneity or physical conjunction and disjunction; the factors can be combined by mathematical optimising procedures (M. Horn, 1990).

The development of analytical and inductive methodology in statistics since the 1920s did not encourage the use of *graphics*. Only in recent years has more attention been given to the visual presentation of indicators. Emphasis on analysis has been extended to the communication of its results, together with an increasing application of statistics to the social sciences, including the promotion of indicators for public and business purposes. Technical progress in computer graphics has played a part in this development. Many statisticians treat graphs only as supplements to tables, but some specialised texts use them for amplification with elements drawn from cartography, computer science and communication theory (Schmid, 1983).

The general advantages claimed for graphics over tabular and textual techniques include: better and quicker communication with the user; a clearer, more emphatic and more convincing message; and greater impact. To these we can add that graphics convey the indicative content of statistics more forcefully by their concentration on directions, turning points and rates of change. Also, they lend themselves better than other formats to one of the principal purposes of indicators, namely the extrapolation of future movements on the assumption of historical consistency. They are also convenient for the presentation of a small number of series in one space for comparative or disaggregative analysis. Such analysis then becomes part of the systematic organisation for visual communication.

We can distinguish between three main types of graphical presentation:

- *graphs,* also called *curves* or *coordinate line charts*;
- *charts* in the form of separate or jointed bars or columns (*histograms*);
- *picturegrams* using pictures of attributes or scale maps.

Graphing a time series in a continuous curve is a familiar procedure for bringing out the indicative message of statistics by concentrating on the direction of trends, including turning points and rates of change. It is customary to place the independent variable, be it time or another fixed unit, on the *x*-axis (*abscissa*) and the dependent variable on the *y*-axis (*ordinate*). For flows the coordinates are centred midpoint between periods, and for stocks at the period point. Fiscal and calendar years are defined as shown in Table 2.2.

If the plot points are joined by straight lines, it is assumed that there has been steady movement between the previous and current points, unburdened by earlier history, and that the movement has been evenly spread

Table 2.2   Fiscal and calendar years

31 Dec. 1985	30 June 1986	31 Dec. 1986	30 June 1987	31 Dec. 1987	30 June 1988
1 Jan. 1986	1 July 1986	1 Jan. 1987	1 July 1987	1 Jan. 1988	1 July 1988

Calendar year 1986

Fiscal year 1986–87

Calendar year 1987

Fiscal year 1987–88

over the period. A straight line or smooth curve fitted over several periods and not necessarily touching the intermediate points seeks to establish a unique direction for a longer term trend, but the indicative value of such trend lines diminishes with increasing dispersion from the period points (see section 2.9 for trend fitting).

The visual impression of curve lines largely depends on the scales chosen for the coordinates and on their interrelations. Cartographers speak of *well-proportioned charts* that neither minimise nor exaggerate variations (Schmid, 1983: 18). This is a matter of aesthetics, efficiency and the effectiveness of visual communication, but no optimal interscalar relations exist between independent variables such as time or quantitative units, and the rightness or distortion of scales applies only in a relative sense. If we start with a scale of x (years) and y units (tonnes), both at intervals of 1 cm, an extension of the x-scale to 1+ cm intervals will reduce the angles of rises and falls, thus suggesting perhaps greater consistency of movement, while an extension of the y-scale will accentuate the changes by increasing the angles of rises and falls, and vice versa for respective reductions in scale. A proportionate increase (decrease) in both scales would magnify (reduce) the size of the picture without affecting the amplitudes of the movement. The effect of changes in scale is illustrated in Figure 2.2.

Figure 2.2   Change in scale

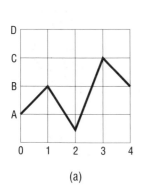

(a)

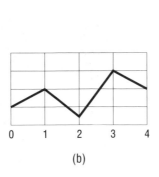

(b)

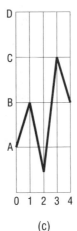

(c)

If we expect an indicator to give us a general signal for movements, up or down or sidewise, the effects of variations in the angles may not much matter because they affect the amplitudes rather than the directions between points. If we are also interested in amplitude, we must choose scales that bring out the peaks and troughs, or we may use a picturegram that graphically, even if not accurately, indicates such characteristics, as in Figure 2.3.

Deliberate distortion is sometimes used by means of broken scales for the more efficient organisation of space or as a device to heighten the effect of movements or differences. The horizontal axis can be adapted to accommodate both long term and short term movement on the same graph, for example by scaling annual figures at 1 cm intervals and quarterly data for recent years by ¼ cm. More frequently, the vertical scale is stretched by starting it well above the origin to magnify change, which has an effect similar to that of compressing the horizontal axis as in Figure 2.2(c). It is acceptable only if the presentation makes it clear, by breaks in the axis lines, that dual scales are being used.

Figure 2.4 illustrates the effect of broken and stretched scales that make movements more 'visible' than full scale presentation.

Figure 2.5 shows growth on linear and semilog scales. In (a) regular linear increments, 10–20–30–40, give a straight line using a linear scale, while in (b) exponential growth, 10–20–40–80, gives an increasing slope. Using logarithms or a semilog scale, linear growth becomes associated with a diminishing slope as in (c), while exponential growth appears as a straight line as in (d).

Figure 2.3   Change in amplitude

Relative hardness of various timbers

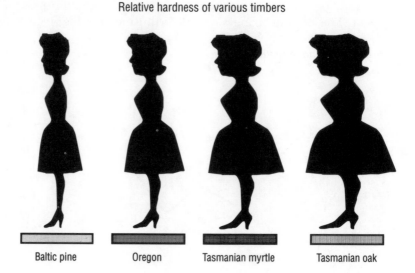

Baltic pine   Oregon   Tasmanian myrtle   Tasmanian oak

Figure 2.4   Broken and stretched scale

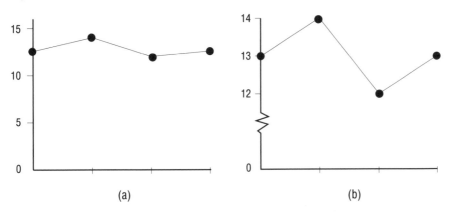

(a)   (b)

Figure 2.5   Linear and exponential series on linear and semilog scales

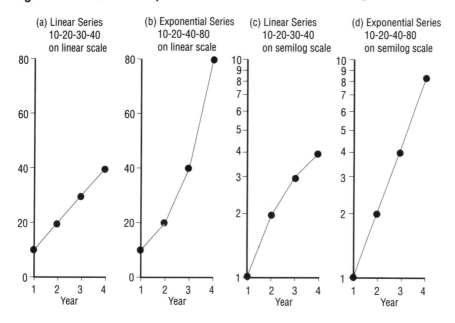

2.3 Stocks and flows

Statistics used for indicators can take the form of an historic (*diachronic*) series where time itself is a variable, or a contemporaneous (*synchronic*) series where a situation is described at a point of time, either structurally or in relation to other units. This means that we can distinguish between three major types of indicators:

- *time series*, where characteristics of people, things or notions are viewed at different, usually consecutive, points of time;
- *structural series*, where an aggregate is divided into constituent parts and ordered by size or frequency of occurrence;
- *corresponding series*, where similar kinds of statistics are shown for different locations or type groups.

The three types are illustrated in Table 2.3

Table 2.3   Vehicle exports

Export type	Period 1		Period 2	
Exports of cars:				
Small type	1000 @ $5 000 = $5 million		1500 @ $6 000 = $9 million	
Large type	1000 @ $10 000 = $10 million		750 @ $12 000 = $9 million	
		$15 million		$18 million
Other vehicle exports		$45 million		$90 million
Total exports:				
Country A	$40 million ⎫	$60 million	$80 million ⎫	$108 million
Country B	$20 million ⎭		$28 million ⎭	

Comparison between periods 1 and 2 gives a time series for exports and export components. The divisions between exports of small and large cars, and between exports of cars and other vehicles, provide structural information on the composition of exports, and the numbers of small and large cars show their relative frequency. At the same time regional information is given in the form of vehicle exports by country. The table also demonstrates that such indicators can be combined in one table, if no great detail is required.

Structural and corresponding series, which refer to a situation at a given point of time, are stock indicators, and so in a sense is each separate item in a time series. They all belong to the same category as census-style enumerations of people, things or notions that can be disaggregated by size, location or other characteristics.

Apart from such snapshots, indicators serve as signposts for movement and change in flows. Information about wealth, stocks or house numbers at a date serves as a reference base for flow statistics of income, trade or construction.

In some instances change, in the form of net flow, can be deduced by comparing stocks at the beginning and end of a period, as in Table 2.4, and in practice it is often easier to measure flows than to undertake census-type enumerations. Flow statistics (e.g. for population and housing) can be used to update census figures in intercensal years. By themselves the flow statistics tell us little about stock size beyond general observations

Table 2.4 Net flow statistics

Stock at end of year 0	Flow in year 1	Stock at end of year 1
Population	+ births and immigration - deaths and emigration	
	net flow in year 1	Population
Stock of goods	+ production and imports - local and export sales	
	net flow in year 1	Stock of goods
Games score	+ games won - games lost	
	net wins or losses	Games score

of continuous positive or negative flow, pointing to a rise or fall in stocks. They say something about the evenness of stock changes rather than the size of stock changes, and net flow by itself does not indicate the elements of inflow and outflow. However, such information can be improved by greater detail of stock and flow observations.

2.4 Ratios

Numbers by themselves have little meaning unless they are connected to other information. A statement that the number of houses in location A at date B was *x* (any whole number) does not tell us much unless it is linked with *y* applying to other dates or locations, or with related figures such as the number of inhabitants at C. Our comprehension of numbers by themselves is limited and rapidly diminishes as numerical values rise. We may be able to distinguish between 1, or 2 or 3 units, but not easily between 10 and 11 units and not at all between large numbers such as 10 001 and 10 002 or even between 100 000 and 1 000 000. We are more likely to categorise numbers in broad bands of small and large, corresponding to *ordinal* grading, as discussed below. For the present it should be noted that (*cardinal*) number statistics are often understood only in an ordinal sense of being large or small, or being larger or smaller, rather than comprehended numerically.

Apart from the conscious or subconscious grading of statistical information as such, it is frequently linked to other information by means of ratios, which are such a simple device that textbooks tend to dwell more on their potential for abuse than on their use. Structurally, a ratio divides one variable (the numerator) by a base number (the denominator). If they both belong to the same universe, the part is divided by the whole and expressed as a decimal fraction $x_1:x$, or in percentage terms as $100x_1: x$.

In relating two variables the substantive variable serves as numerator and the other, which provides the standard for comparison, goes into the denominator. Similarly, in a time comparison of like items the prior date, rather than the current date, is usually taken as the denominator, and this applies also to comparisons between independent or dependent events. The ratio $x:y$ is then expressed as n units of x per m units of y. This is illustrated in Table 2.5 using the example of Table 2.3.

For comparisons it is convenient to express two elements in the single term of a percentage or ratio, but this is achieved only at the expense of an information loss. A statement that car exports were 25% of all vehicle exports gives us the relative but not the absolute size of car exports; nor does citing exports at the rate of $5 per head of population reveal either the size of exports or that of the population. To the extent that we think in ordinal terms, the omission of actual data may not matter much. It may be a sufficient indicator for the role of the industry to say that cars made up a quarter of total exports, or for the role of exports to say that exports were equivalent to $5 per head of population. However, in other cases the omission of the numbers can give a distorted picture of relative magnitudes. A change in percentage terms or ratios can be due to a change either in the main variable or in the base to which it is related, or to both; for example, a change in the car export ratio could be due to a change either in car or in all exports. To the extent that such detail may be relevant for the interpretation of indicator movements, it is best to include some basic data with the ratios. This has the further advantage of serving as a check on the calculation and providing a basis for supplementary indicators when required.

The limitations of ratios for indicators are inherent in their structural ties to base values. While ratio changes are proportional to changes in their unit values (in either numerator or denominator or both), the significance of a unit change diminishes with rising base values; for example, $1 is a 100% rise from $1, a 50% rise from $2, and so on. Or starting from a small number, a unit increase expressed as a percentage is greater than a unit increase starting from a higher number; for example, an extra $1 on $10 is +10% but on $20 is +5%; so percentage changes from small original values can sound exaggerated. (When the original value is raised at a geometric rate, 1, 2, 4, 8, . . ., the percentage equivalent of an equal increment

Table 2.5   Vehicle exports (ratios)

Exports: cars	$15 million	0.25 = 25%
Other vehicles	$45 million	0.75 = 75%
Total	$60 million	1.00 = 100%
Population	12 million	
Exports per head		$60:12 = $5

Table 2.6   Employment/unemployment

Year		Employment		Unemployment	
1		50		50	
	Change	+10	+20%	-10	-20%
2		60		40	
	Change	+10	+17%	-10	-25%
3		70		30	
	Change	+10	+14%	-10	-33%
4		80		20	
	Change	+10	+12%	-10	-50%
5		90		10	
	Change	+10	+11%	-10	-100%
		100		0	

diminishes on an arithmetic scale, 10, 5, 2½, . . .). Taking the previous example, an increase of 25% in total exports to $75 million could be due to a rise in car exports of 100% or in other exports of 33%, or to a combination of smaller percentage changes in both components.

For the interpretation of indicators, this property of ratios to rise faster from low starting levels is particularly striking when comparing complementary series that are bounded within a range from 0 to 100%, as Table 2.6 shows. This also applies to literacy/illiteracy or cardinalised versions of satisfaction surveys where equal numerical rises mean greater proportional change in the smaller than in the larger component. As the former usually represents *unfulfilment* (e.g. unemployment, discontent), its fluctuations, expressed in ratios, will be magnified in comparison with *fulfilment*.

Problems can also arise with ratios with regard to homogeneity and consistency (see section 2.1), as well as aggregating or averaging them (e.g. for productivity or other characteristics expressed per head of population). The average ratio of a variable V (e.g income) per S (population) has to be derived from $\Sigma V : \Sigma S$ rather than from the average of unweighted microratios. Similar problems can arise in attempts to use rates for correlation or regression in cross-sectional analysis (Kuh and Meyer, 1986).

2.5   Aggregation and averages

Statistics condense descriptive information into numerical series, and in turn indicators reduce statistical series into indicative shorthand. There is little difficulty for series consisting of a single item over time or between regions (except for the changing socioeconomic environment). For series consisting of similar types of things or persons, the aggregates of the

Table 2.7   Aggregate and average of a series

Component	Year 1	Year 2	Year 3	Year 4	Mean
A	3	5	4	6	4½
B	2	1	3	2	2
A + B	5	6	7	8	6½

constituent components are often fairly representative, but they need not be so and should be tested separately if possible. In the example in Table 2.7, which could represent sales of two competing brands of a product or approval ratings of ten men and ten women, an uninterrupted upward trend in the total masks considerable fluctuations in the components. Figure 2.6 presents the same information in graphic form.

The construction of indicators leads to the general problem of progressing from *micro* to *macro*. Microvariables and microparameters represent real data (e.g. a list of firms employing so many workers for so much output, purchases of butter by so many individuals). However, aggregation in that sense is not real; it is merely a convenient arrangement to reflect the abstract notion of group endeavour or behaviour that we call production or consumption. The labour and machines used by different sorts of firms cannot be combined in a real physical sense, although their aggregates, in the shape of a production function, acquire meaning as an indicator of economic activity.

Economists have debated the relation between micro and macro theory

Figure 2.6   Aggregate of a series

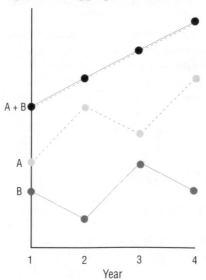
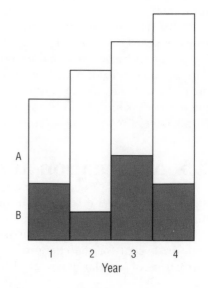

in search of *perfect aggregation* (Theil, 1954; Green, 1964; Lancaster, 1966). Take, for instance, the assumed sequence that can proceed from micro theory to macrovariables and macro theory, or vice versa. If a macroparameter is derived independently (e.g. a national demand function), it may not equal the weighted sum of microparameters when there is a *synergy effect* caused through the interplay of partly interdependent functions of supply, demand and price, or when there is over- or underspecification in a macro structural function. Such problems arise particularly in the aggregation of systems with endogenous and exogenous variables.

Averages are usually based on aggregates. Like them they reduce fairly homogeneous information into a sort of shorthand expression for the whole and its parts. They level out unit divisions, such as periods in the case of time series, or local disparities in regional series, or differences between items and reference bases in component and frequency series. The smoothing can be effected by numerical processing (e.g. adding and dividing) or by selecting a typical item to represent all items (e.g. the median). Like the aggregate the average is convenient as a single figure to serve as proxy for many, and as an indicator it helps us to relate a series to our own experience (e.g. of income, prices or hours worked).

A more scientific-sounding phrase for average is *measure of central tendency*, which suggests that individual values cluster round the centre and that values beyond are fairly evenly balanced. However, simple averaging becomes unrealistic if that well-behaved pattern of regular distribution does not apply, as in the case of skewed distributions and fluctuations. Technically there is an average for any sort of series, but its credibility depends on dispersion and skewness.

The most frequently used processed averages, known as *mean* values, are the arithmetic, geometric and harmonic means. These are illustrated in the appendix to this section, as are the *median* and *mode*, which are based on the central and most frequent values of the series respectively. *Arithmetic means* are derived by summing the items and dividing the total by the number of items, either 'unweighted' (i.e. equally weighted) or 'weighted'. Taking one \$1 coin and two \$2 coins gives an unweighted average of $(1 + 2)/3 = 1$ coin, but weighted by value this becomes $(1 + 4)/3 = \$1.67$. Arithmetic means take account of all items and smooth out the differences between them. They have the minor disadvantage that, being not *real* figures, their fractions look incongruous when people or other fixed units are involved (e.g. an average family size of 5¾ persons). Another occasional problem arises with grouped data that show open-ended top or bottom classes (e.g. less than \$2000, persons aged over 65 years), although this can usually be handled adequately with commonsense guesswork. Such minor drawbacks do not apply to the median or mode because these are based on actual figures, but they have the greater disadvantage of ignoring altogether extreme values on either side, and the median at least is deficient for irregular distributions. However, this drawback also applies to the mean when several high and low values overshadow more numerous central values.

The *geometric mean* is based on the nth root of the product of *n* values; expressed in logarithms it is a higher order application of the arithmetic mean. It is appropriate in cases of variables related to shifting bases (so it applies to growth rates, percentages and ratios), and it is also suitable for price index numbers, although there the arithmetic mean is usually employed. Because of the more even treatment of all values in the multiplicative process and its dampening effect on extreme values, the geometric mean is lower than the arithmetic mean (or the same if all variables are equal). However, that difference diminishes when the series is not very dispersed. The geometric mean is more difficult to understand and to calculate than the arithmetic mean, and its calculation becomes problematic for zero and negative values. It is therefore not often used for indicators.

The *harmonic mean* is another instance where unfamiliarity with the formula limits its application. It is appropriate for average ratios of prices, usage, speed or productivity expressed as units of a constant (e.g. for series of average prices per dollar or average speed per hour). If two teams produce an equal output of 100 units, but one does with ten men what the other does with twenty, average production or productivity per team is 13.3 units (formula in appendix), not 15, because only 1½ units are produced in a given period by the two teams.

Averaging annual rates to obtain a longer-term *growth rate* is only appropriate if the changes are fairly uniform, as shown in the example in the appendix. Otherwise the practice is no substitute for calculating the average annual growth rate, although even there the average does not tell us whether it is at all justified to claim a consistent growth/decline rate.

If a series is ranged by order of magnitude, it can be counted off at equally spaced points, taking, for instance, every tenth item for *deciles* or every fourth item for *quartiles*, where the *median* becomes the second quartile in the centre. The median is a quick indicator for a fairly regular distribution, in particular in population statistics for age or family size when extreme values are not significant.

The *mode* or most frequent value is, like the median, a positional, easily found average that ignores the other items surrounding it and thus is not useful in irregular distributions. It can be identified with typical value (e.g. in population or income series). In a *normal distribution* with a bell-shaped curve,

$$\text{mode} = \text{median} = \text{weighted arithmetic mean}$$

However, if more frequencies occur in the lower than in the upper ranges (i.e. the distribution has a *positive skew*), as is usually found in income and other economic series, the mode shifts to the left of the arithmetic mean with the median between them. In a moderately skewed distribution

$$\text{mode} \simeq \text{mean} - 3\,(\text{mean} - \text{median})$$

It is possible to make up long lists of the theoretical virtues and drawbacks of the different types of averages, but in practical terms the arithmetic mean, weighted for frequencies, is the type usually preferred for indicators. The median also is popular for a quick assessment of frequency distributions, while the others are preferred in special circumstances: the geometric mean for rates of change, the harmonic mean for performance rates, and the mode for the most typical item. The arithmetic mean and the median are the averages most easily understood by most users, and usually they are not greatly different from the other types, as will be seen from the following appendix.

Information loss through averaging occurs particularly if the average itself is used as a standard of comparison between countries. If income per head is $100 in country A, $900 in B and $2000 in C, giving an arithmetic average of $1000 or scores of –90%, –10% and +100% respectively, a change in one, say a drop to $1400 in C, would not only reduce its score to +75% of the new average ($800) but also raise the proportions attached to the unchanged amounts of the others to –87½% and +12½% respectively. This, incidentally, emphasises the effect of a *dominant series* on averaging. An even more doubtful practice is averaging the averages of several series (e.g. income and dwelling per person, doctor per population), because this assumes equal significance for growth rates in different indicators.

The use of average growth rates, as mentioned above in connection with the harmonic mean, for ratio scales does not apply to non-ratio (*non-parametric*) scales that start from an arbitrary zero point. An example is attitude scales that run from, say, 'terrible' to 'delightful', to which numbers can be attached, say in a five-point scale from 1 to 5 or –2 to +2, so that percentage change depends on the size of the base. An increase from 4 to 5 in the 1 to 5 scale can be read as +25%, but an increase from –2 to –1 in the –2 to +2 scale can be read as +100%.

An average by itself tells us nothing about the range of values it encompasses and can give a misleading impression of an even distribution. Stating the range shows us the highest and lowest values, but again nothing about the distribution, and using the interquartile range ignores the values of the first and last quarters. A better way to show *dispersion* is based on calculating the deviation of each item from the average. As the plus and minus values there cancel each other out, it is usual to use the quadratic form of taking the root of the mean of the squares of the deviations: the so-called *standard deviation*. If d stands for deviation from the average and N for the number of items, this is $\sqrt{\Sigma d^2 / N}$, as Table 2.8 illustrates.

Table 2.8 Calculation of standard deviation

Item	Frequency	Deviation from average, d	Deviation squared, d^2
A	1	-9	81
B	4	-6	36
C	5	-5	25
D	9	-1	1
E	20	+10	100
F	21	+11	121
Σ	60		364

Average = 60/6 = 10

$$\text{Standard deviation} = \sqrt{\Sigma d^2/6} = \sqrt{364/6} = 7.8$$

APPENDIX

Table 2.9 Wage rate averages

Wage rate ($)	Frequency	Weighted wage rate ($)
$x_1 = 80$	$f_1 = 20$	$(fx)_1 = 1600$
$x_2 = 100$	$f_2 = 25$	$(fx)_2 = 2500$
$x_3 = 140$	$f_3 = 5$	$(fx)_3 = 700$
$\Sigma x = 320$	$\Sigma f = 50$	$\Sigma fx = 4800$

n = no. of values = 3

Arithmetic mean = $\Sigma x/n$ = 320/3 = $106.7

Weighted arithmetic mean = $\Sigma fx/\Sigma f$ = 4800/50 = $96

Geometric mean = $\sqrt[n]{x_1 \, x_2 \, x_3}$ = $103.9

Harmonic mean = $n/(\Sigma 1/x)$ = $101.2

Median = $100

Mode = $100

Table 2.10 Income averages

Income ($)	Mid value, x ($)	Frequency	fx ($)
<1000	500	$f_0 = 30$	15 000
1000 to <2000	1500	$f_1 = 35$	52 500
2000 to <3000	2500	$f_2 = 20$	50 000
3000+	3500	$f_3 = 10$	35 000
		$\Sigma f = 95$	$\Sigma fx = 152\ 500$

Arithmetic mean (weighted) = 152 500/95 = $1605
Geometric mean = $\sqrt[4]{(500)(1500)(2500)(3500)}$ = $1601
Median position = $\frac{1}{2}\Sigma f + \frac{1}{2}$ = 48th position = 18th out of 35 in $1000 to <$2000
   group
Median = 1000 + (18/35)1000 = $1514
Modal group = $1000 to <$2000; L = lower limit of modal group = $1000; c = class
   interval = $1000
Mode = $L + c(f_1 - f_0)/(2f_1 - f_0 - f_2)$ = $1250
      $\approx$ arithmetic mean − 3(arithmetic mean − median) = $1332

Note: The mode is below the arithmetic mean with the median between them, as befits the positive leftward skew of an income distribution.

Table 2.11 Averaging growth rate

$ Growth	$ Growth	$ Growth	$	Average of % rates	Average growth rate p.a.
100 + 10%	= 110 + 11%	= 121 + 12%	= 135½	11%	8.9%
100 + 10%	= 110 + 25%	= 137½ + 70%	= 233¾	35%	33.3%
100 + 70%	= 170 + 25%	= 212 + 10%	= 233¾	35%	33.3%
100 + 10%	= 110 + 25%	= 137½ − 27¾%	= 99½	2½%	0%
100 − 27¾%	= 72¼ + 25%	= 90½ + 10%	= 99½	2½%	0%

If growth proceeds smoothly, there is no great difference between the average of annual percentage changes and the average annual growth rate, which refers to the difference between the first and last data in the year. However, the difference becomes more significant if the growth rates fluctuate from year to year, as they do in Table 2.11 (*SINET*, no. 22, May 1990, pp. 6–7). Reversing the order of percentage change makes no difference in either case.

2.6 Scaling

All measurement is based on an ordering system. This refers to a *taxonomy* of types or characteristics applied to a data set, such as the Linnæan system of classifying plants. We are not concerned here with the epistemology of statistical classification in the social sciences (see Katzner, 1983; Olenski, 1986). Nor do we need to discuss applications to the testing of hypotheses, which is explained in a multitude of statistical textbooks. Ours is the simpler task of relating measurement to indicators at the levels of component statistics and of the indicators derived from them where the classification, albeit submerged in the aggregating process, may be relevant for the interpretation of indicator movements.

Scaling reflects the relation between object (i.e. concept) and its measurement. The latter can be direct, based on a single characteristic (e.g. frequency, weight, value), or it can be superimposed on a multidimensional concept (e.g. health, welfare) and rely on an *ad hoc* scale of adequacy or satisfaction. In practical terms this is like the distinction between *cardinal* scales, based on numbers or specified items, and *ordinal* scales, based on a subjective ordering of the items ranging from good to bad, adequate to inadequate and so on. Most indicative statistics used in economics are of the cardinal type and at least nominally *value-free*. Some of these are used in other social sciences also (e.g. for the accoutrements of health or cultural services), but ordinal grading is often preferred for the *a priori* assessment of impact, worth, perception or attitudes.

A simple form of the cardinal mode is *nominal scales*, where an empirical data set is graded by number of persons, types or other such categories and is presented in the form of a statistical table. The category labels of age or other codes cannot be used for numerical operations such as addition or division by themselves, but the respective numbers of items can be expressed as percentages for convenient proportionate interpretation.

Some general features of data sets, such as homogeneity and consistency, have been mentioned in section 2.1. Here we will briefly discuss three other requirements for equivalence relations of data sets on nominal scales:

- *Reflexibility* means that elements with a common characteristic are interchangeable and occupy equal utility positions on indifference curves.
- *Symmetry* implies reversibility between elements so that $xy = yx$.
- *Transitivity* applies when elements belong to the same set $x>y$; $y>z$; $x>z$.

Such conditions apply to linear equal-interval scales rather than to non-linear ordinal ordering.

The example in Table 2.12 takes employment by industry and its location by region as variables. Using the conventional format, industry type is arranged vertically as the independent variable and the region horizontally. The industrial structure of each region, in terms of percentage of total, is given in columns 2, 5 and 8 and summarised in column 11, which gives a size order of tertiary–primary–secondary. This is close to the size order

Table 2.12 Employment by region and industry

Industry	Region A			Region B			Region C			All regions		
	Persons ('000) (1)	Industry (%) (2)	Region (%) (3)	Persons ('000) (4)	Industry (%) (5)	Region (%) (6)	Persons ('000) (7)	Industry (%) (8)	Region (%) (9)	Persons ('000) (10)	Industry (%) (11)	Region (%) (12)
Primary	200	20	7	2000	40	74	500	33	19	2700	36	100
Secondary	400	40	21	1000	30	53	500	33	26	1900	25	100
Tertiary	400	40	14	2000	40	69	500	33	17	2900	39	100
All industries	1000	100	13	5000	100	67	1500	100	20	7500	100	100

of region B, which with two-thirds of total employment predominates and imposes its industry pattern on the aggregate. Rotating the table to scale regions by industry, in columns 3, 6, 9 and 12, confirms the dominance of region B.

It is often convenient and economical to combine two proportionalised aspects (e.g. industrial and regional composition of employment) in one table, but differences in their indicative significance must be respected. To some extent *parsimony* of detail is desirable for indicators designed to show only general directions. For example, for percentages the first and subsequent decimals (e.g. 0.1%, 0.01%) are rarely significant and may give a false picture of the accuracy of underlying statistics; that would be an *error of mistaken concreteness*. In the Table 2.12 example the rounded figures for both units and percentages are probably quite adequate. However, parsimony goes too far when the presentation of percentages is not accompanied by the actual figures, or at least by their aggregate from which the detail can be reconstructed. If the numbers in the table were omitted, the dominance of region B would not be immediately visible. An alternative to the use of percentages is expression of the variables in the form of ratios, where the relation for total primary to secondary employment in Table 2.12, 2700: 1900 = 36%:25%, would be written as 1.4. Ratio bases can be modified more easily than percentages for convenient scaling. Many popular indicators take this form, such as the productivity ratio of output to employment and the various per capita figures of income, consumption and so on (see also section 1.4).

If measurement units are expressed in a numbers system rather than in nominal classes, we speak of *interval* scales, such as in frequency distributions that list population in a hierarchy of sizes. Such scaling can be used with equal or unequal intervals, group ranges or a single item representing a range, open- or close-ended ranges, discrete or cumulative variables, and so on. With any type, care has to be taken to avoid indeterminacy of boundaries, overlap and unnecessary information loss.

Table 2.13   Monthly income: householders in one region

Income range[a] ($)	Midpoint ($)	Number	Income × number ($)	% income earned
100 or less	50	20	1 000	1
101–250	175½	200	35 100	35
251–1000	625½	70	43 785	44
1000+	2 000	10	20 000	20
Sum	2 851	300	99 885	100
Average	713		333	

[a] Region A, year 0.

The example in Table 2.13 is typical for an income distribution to the extent that, while there are more low income than high income earners, the latter earn a greater proportion of total income. This is reflected in that the unweighted average income of $713 is about twice the weighted average of $333. The distribution is open at both ends. This is not important in the lower range; if all twenty of those earning $100 or less earned nothing, the overall average would drop from $333 to $330; and if they all earned $100, it would rise only to $336. However, in spite of their small number, the situation of top earners has a considerable effect, lifting the overall average of $333 for an assumed top-bracket midpoint of $2000 by $33 for any additional $1000. The effect of distribution within classes, and of interclass partitioning, can be shown by taking the first three ranges (omitting the top earners), which average $275 weighted on midpoints, as against from $130 to $421 if all earners were at the lowest and highest range points respectively. Against such large margins of uncertainty due to the range structure, only relatively minor distortions can be ascribed to rounding or to overlaps between ranges.

Relative proportions of total income earned are shown in the last column of Table 2.13. However, unlike in the preceding employment example (Table 2.12) the scales are real rather than nominal, and therefore the table cannot be rotated, or would only yield a 4 × 4 matrix with three empty cells in each column and row if that were attempted. Frequency distributions, cardinally arranged in tables or graphs, do not lend themselves easily to comparison over time or between regions. For applications as indicators they are usually reduced to an aggregative shorthand of averages and other measures of central tendency, dispersion, and their relation to normal distributions.

In *ordinal scaling* the numeral certainty of cardinal intervals is replaced by more blurred divisions of *ad hoc* adequacy. The less authoritative subjectivity of such ordinal grades has given them a somewhat lower status.

Over the past 100 years national and international statistical bureaux have taken pride in the objective base of their collections by sticking to the facts of numerical counting in cardinal terms (De Neufville, 1975: 22). Although more recently government statisticians have acknowledged the growing demand for social enquiries about attitudes and so on by including some such questions in population surveys, they remain suspicious when respondents in seemingly similar situations give varying replies because of different perceptions. At the other end some social scientists may have overstated their claim for cardinal rectitude in ordinal measurement.

Until a few years ago statistics in social research were used mainly for simple non-numerical inferences and for measurement in weak order *quasi-series* without much notion of distance (Coleman, 1964). An exception here has been scaling for attitude surveys. One of the best-known early examples is the work of psychologist *L.L. Thurstone*. This involved respondents' answering a large number of questions, which were subsequently sorted by judges into piles of what they considered to be near-equal distances of favourability, with the scale value assigned on the basis of the location of the median. This method has been simplified and further developed since (Turner and Martin, 1984: part 1). One frequently quoted version is *Guttman scales*, where answers to statements, of the yes-no type, are cross-tabulated with number of respondents, and ranged between theoretical zero frequencies of all yes or no; the consistency of replies can then be expressed as the error factor with which they depart from the Guttman model. *Likert scaling* is a simpler cardinalising process of converting replies into near-equidistant categories with consecutive ratings from which an overall score can be calculated. It should be noted that, even if there is some uncertainty about intervals in ordinal scaling, they provide flexibility for indicative relevance.

However neat the precision of cardinal measures may look, their message is ordinal for the respective beholder. Production, for example, may rise from 40 tonnes to 60 tonnes (i.e. by 50% or, in index format, from 100 to 150). Depending on the viewpoint of the producer, the user, the market analyst or whoever, this change can be regarded as of the order of normal, significant or large. Cardinal scales then become a meta-language for the ordinal expression of indicative directions. A distinction can be drawn between ordinal measurement and ordinal interpretation; ordering gives meaning to purblind cardinal data sets, but either mode can be transformed into the other.

Table 2.14 refers to income, which for an analysis of needs or welfare would have to include income from property, income from welfare agencies and perhaps an estimate of social wage. The uneven intervals of the cardinal scale reflect some ordinalising of needs on a non-linear scale to reflect the description of individual assessment in terms of adequacy and/or of a national welfare-type grading of the socially satisfactory situation. The ordinal scale can be cardinalised by turning it into a point scale (1½–3½) or index (60–140). This incidentally avoids the problem of the open top

Table 2.14 Monthly income per household

	Income ($)	Rating by adequacy	Rating by satisfactory level	Points	Index
			Indigent	0	0
(A)	0–100	Very poor			
			Unsatisfactory	1½	60
(B)	101–150	Poor			
			Minimal	2½	100
(C)	151–300	Sufficient			
			Satisfactory	3½	140
(D)	301+	Affluent			

range. Unlike given interval scales, ordinal grading has to be applied at an earlier stage to determine the scale, involving often a preview and prethink of the constituent statistics. For the aggregation of ordinal grades they must at least temporarily be cardinalised, but even so they do not lend themselves to complex forms of averaging.

Finally, there have been attempts to express social variables in money terms on the basis of utility and consumer choice theories (Fox, 1974; Van Moeseke, 1984). One such scheme assumes that individuals optimise their allocation of time among preferred uses and derives a scalar measure by expressing alternative time use in terms of dollar income forgone. Another version replaces utility functions by behaviour settings, expressed in time and money spent on different activities that make up the social status and lifestyle of the person. On that basis linear cost- and time-minimising programs can be designed. These proposals are interesting, but they are based on debatable premises and their practical applications seem very limited.

In considering the choice between ordinal and cardinal measures for health needs, Culyer (1978: 19) has drawn attention to the incertitude of the former inasmuch as, unlike with relative scales, once a number has been assigned to an entity the only constraint in ordinal scaling is that higher entities must have a greater number, and vice versa. Furthermore, with ordinal scales zero values acquire a specific meaning as signifying a complete absence of x, and there is no constraint on scaling intervals arithmetically, geometrically or in other ways.

With (cardinal) interval scales, zero points are not specially significant, but we have to distinguish between interval and ratio changes. If we compare temperature changes on the Fahrenheit (32–212°F) and Celsius (0–100°C) scales, we see that, although the ratio between 1 Celsius degree and 1 Fahrenheit degree is constant, the ratios of the levels of scale readings are not. Because the two scales do not have the same zero point (0°C = 32°F), the C/F and F/C ratios change asymptotically until at high temperature

Table 2.15 Celsius and Fahrenheit temperatures

	Scale readings				Ratios		
°C	Rise	°F	Rise	C/F	Rise	F/C	Rise
0		32		0.00		∞	
25	25	77	45	0.32	0.56	3.08	1.80
50	25	122	45	0.41	0.56	2.44	1.80
100	50	212	90	0.47	0.56	2.12	1.80
200	100	392	180	0.51	0.56	1.96	1.80
400	200	752	360	0.53	0.56	1.88	1.80
800	400	1472	720	0.54	0.56	1.84	1.80

the effect of the differing zeroes is negligible, when $C/F = 5/9 \approx 0.56$ and $F/C = 9/5 = 1.8$ (see Table 2.15).

In the example in Table 2.16 a tax of 40% is imposed on income above a threshold of $100. It will be seen that in dollar terms, the increment in income before tax doubles, from $250 to $500; so does the increment in tax, from $100 to $200, and the increment in income after tax, from $150 to $300. However, such strict linearity does not apply to ratio scales: income before tax quadrupled (+300%) from $250 to $1000, but income after tax rose less (+237%) from $190 to $640 at the same tax and tax exemption rates.

In education and other social sciences *scalogram analysis* is sometimes used to indicate the relation of persons or countries to a hierarchy of separate features of a common structure, which in a more general sense can be described as *factorial analysis of a matrix*. One such method, dating back to 1941, refers to *Guttman scales* (Johnstone, 1981). A number of features are listed horizontally in presumed order of relevance, so that the lower-rated ones are present in all the vertically listed persons or countries, with the presence of higher-rated features gradually rising until the most sophisticated person or country has all the features.

Table 2.16 Pre- and post-tax incomes

	Income before tax ($)		Tax: $100 free then 40% ($)		Income after tax ($)	
Poor	250		60		190	
	+250	(+100%)	+100	(+167%)	+150	(+79%)
Middle	500		160		340	
	+500	(+100%)	+200	(+125%)	+300	(+88%)
Rich	1000		360		640	

Table 2.17   Existing educational systems

Country	Primary schools	Secondary schools	Technical colleges	Universities and equivalents	Postgraduate institutes	Science research institutes
A	x	x	o	o	o	o
B	x	x	x	o	o	o
C	x	x	x	x	x	o
D	x	x	x	x	o	x
E	x	x	x	x	x	x

In Table 2.17, for example, the smooth hierarchical ordering of the education systems is interrupted only for country C, which has postgraduate but no science research facilities, and it could be argued that C should rank after rather than before country D. This is the sort of question that can be stimulated if the features and countries appear to follow a reasonable, though not perfect, Guttman fit. The discrepancies in larger, more elaborate tables can lead to useful discussion about the appropriateness of alternative structures, and they can be further tested and specified through factor analysis of the matrix.

2.7 Weighting and equivalence scales

The term 'weighting' is often used for internal adjustments, such as the smoothing of sample values based on their variances. Here we are concerned only with the proportional relations of the components of one or several series, as they can have a pervasive effect on indicators in aggregation, measures of central tendency and index numbers.

Any selection of variables for indicator construction involves decisions about their relative significance. This may not be so obvious when some out of a number of variables are omitted (i.e. in effect zero-weighted) or when we subsume related but not identical types under the same heading. For instance, vehicle production and registration statistics usually show categories (e.g. cars, trucks) that can be combined with equal or differential weights into a motor vehicle index. However, their relative significance for aspects such as road wear and carrying capacity varies, and the use of differential weights for different indicator purposes has to be considered. Furthermore, the total number, weighted or unweighted, has to be adjusted if there is a major shift within or between types.

Various views are held about the relevance of weighting. At the one extreme a strong case for equal weighting (i.e. no weighting) has been made for numerical taxonomies, in particular for biological systems, by Sneath and Sokal (1973: 109–13). They point to the uncertain, subjectively viewed interrelations between component features, and they also raise two points relevant to indicators. The first is that the taxonomy should be directed to its purpose; that is, a set of vehicle production data without weighting (i.e. with equal weighting) could serve well as an indicator of activity in the motor industry, but perhaps not for road use or imports/exports. Secondly, it appears that the effect of weights on the indicator diminishes with increase in the number of items. A related phenomenon is *dominance* by one or several items over others. The influence of these other items can then dwindle to the point where they become irrelevant to the aggregate, irrespective of weights.

Dividing the voting population into sectors influences the weight given to the individual. For example, many election systems are based on the principle of 'one vote, one value'; in other words, everyone's vote shall have equal weight. At once the question arises whether equality of representation should take the form of allocation by total number or by population of states, or whether an equal number of seats should be allotted to each state, which is then subdivided in equal districts to elect that number. Other divisional criteria can be applied for electoral distribution, which are tantamount to weighting (e.g. community of interest, regional homogeneity, physical or functional disjunction, contiguity or compactness). Given these parameters, then, optimal solutions can be sought at least technically by means of operations research (M. Horn, 1990).

In the usual run of demographic series, equal weight is given to persons or to major sectors determined by natural (e.g. age, gender), geographic (e.g. regions) or international codes. The population may be reduced for labour force indicators by omitting (i.e. zero-weighting) persons under the age of 15 or over 70, or it may be standardised overall in regional comparisons by the use of per capita figures. Compared with such well-established criteria the societal structure is statistically less well demarcated. Census modes vary in using terms such as 'household' and 'family unit', with some uncertainties about informal cohabitation, communal living or divided homes; so we may have to use an *ad hoc* definition of family, borrowed perhaps from government welfare agencies.

We then face the question of standardising the term for varying numbers of persons per family unit, considering that two (or more) together can live more cheaply than separately because of greater household efficiency in shared cost. This is expressed in weights known as *equivalence scales*, and is applied to the measurement of poverty as well as to the grading of social services benefits and income standards. The weights can be subjectively chosen or based on family budget or household expenditure surveys (Atkinson, 1975). The Organisation for Economic Cooperation and Development (OECD, 1982), for instance, has suggested an adjustment for disposable income in the form of factors of 0.7 for second and subsequent adults in the household and 0.5 for each child. The income needs for a family then rise from a basic $1000 as shown in Table 2.18. It will be seen that the effect of proportional weighting diminishes as income rises.

Table 2.18   Disposable family income equivalence scales

1 adult,	no children	$1000		1 adult,	no children	$1000	
2 "	"	$1700	+70%	"	1 child	$1500	+50%
3 "	"	$2400	+41%	"	2 children	$2000	+33%
4 "	"	$3100	+29%	"	3 children	$2500	+25%
2 adults,	no children	$1700		3 adults,	no children	$2400	
"	1 child	$2200	+29%	"	1 child	$2900	+21%
"	2 children	$2700	+23%	"	2 children	$3400	+17%
"	3 children	$3200	+19%	"	3 children	$3900	+15%
"	9 children	$5200	+11%	"	9 children	$5900	+9%
"	10 children	$5700	+10%	"	10 children	$6400	+8%

In a childless household a second adult adds 70% to the assumed needs of a single adult, while a third adult would add a further 41%, a fourth adult 29%, and so on. The addition of children has a lesser effect.

The *Luxembourg Income Study* (Smeeding, 1990) lists household income data for ten developed countries. It shows the wide spectrum of their equivalence factor adjustment for differences in need when estimating economic well-being. The factors affect the size of poverty groups; for example, relatively low factors overemphasise the role of single young and of older persons among the poor, while high factors accentuate families with young children.

Some recent critics have claimed that equivalence scales are not suitable for the general measurement of income inequality, because they are based on the putative needs of individual households, as expressed in their utility functions, and thus neglect the demographic composition of the population and the incidence of non-income factors. Instead these critics want to relate inequality to societal well-being (Paglin, 1975; Smeeding, 1990). One such proposal uses a *norm income* that corresponds to a socially desired minimum degree of inequality. This norm income would replace the 45° line when calculating the Gini coefficient representing inequality as discrepancy from the actual distribution. Setting the norm allows for a multivariate approach to demographic, educational and other differences, rather than the univariate weighting for dependents in equivalence scales. In practice, however, the introduction of social utility variables might create its own problems, and this approach has not, or not yet, been widely tested and accepted.

As an example for the application of equivalence weights in ranking we can take the tally of medals at the Olympic Games in Seoul in 1988 (Table 2.19). Top rankings in sports and other endeavours, designated by gold medals or similar symbols, serve as indicators of prowess. This can be extended to include second and third placings for a more generous view

Table 2.19   Medals gained at Olympic Games in Seoul, September 1988

Country	Medals				Weighted total (G1, S½, B¼)	Unweighted total per 100 million population
	Gold	Silver	Bronze	Total		
USSR	55	31	46	132	82	50
East Germany	37	35	30	102	62	600
United States	36	31	27	94	59	40
West Germany	11	14	15	40	22	65
Bulgaria	10	12	13	35	21	390
South Korea	12	10	11	33	20	85
China	5	11	12	28	14	5
Romania	7	11	6	24	14	110
United Kingdom	5	10	9	24	12	45
Hungary	11	6	6	23	15	210
France	6	4	6	16	9	30
Poland	2	5	9	16	7	45
Italy	6	4	4	14	9	25
Japan	4	3	7	14	8	12
Australia	3	6	5	14	7	95
New Zealand	3	2	8	13	6	405
Yugoslavia	3	4	5	12	6½	55
Sweden	0	4	7	11	4	140
Canada	3	2	5	10	5	40
Kenya	5	2	2	9	6½	55
Netherlands	2	2	5	9	4	65
Czechoslovakia	3	3	2	8	5	55
Brazil	1	2	3	6	3	25
Norway	2	3	0	5	3½	165
Denmark	2	1	1	4	2½	80
Finland	1	1	2	4	2	80
Other countries (27)	6	15	18	39	15	
Total	241	234	264	739	414	

of top achievement, and sometimes even to conferring the dubious distinction of runner-up or short-listed on the loser.

The Olympic Games provide an occasion for comparative listing of results between countries, as shown in Table 2.19. A few countries scored relatively more gold than silver or bronze medals, and ordinal grading by gold medals first, then silver, then bronze, would significantly improve the ranking of Kenya (from 20 to 13), Czechoslovakia (22 to 17), Hungary (10 to 6) and Italy (13 to 10), with corresponding downgrading in particular for Poland

and Sweden. However, it would not affect the three top performers nor most of the lesser ones that gained only one or no gold. On the whole, gold, silver and bronze medal gains are closely correlated. It appears that, with fairly uniform patterns, weighting does not make much difference and that a single series may be used as proxy for the aggregate.

This does not apply if there is no close relation betwen series. Relating the unweighted (or weighted) medal count to population in the last column of Table 2.19 puts prowess into the context of the role of sporting excellence within the social and cultural structure of the respective countries. The very large countries (USSR, United States and China) give way in ranking not only to countries where government promotion of sport is strong (East Germany, Bulgaria, Romania and Hungary) but also to countries where high living standards and tradition contribute to a high national sporting profile (New Zealand, Sweden and Norway). The vagaries of such ranking were demonstrated at Seoul when the Virgin Islands, an unincorporated territory of the United States with a population of about 100 000, was acknowledged as a separate competitor and won a silver medal in yachting, which put it on top of the per capita list with an equivalent of 1000 medals per 100 million. This is the obverse of the situation of dominance of a few large countries, which can be redressed with per capita population figures for socieconomic aggregates, and it shows the need for scrutinising indicator results and for care in their use in further instrumental analysis.

2.8 Index numbers

An index number shows percentage change over time or difference at a point of time. In the *simple* version it refers to a single variable and serves as an alternative expression for unit values so as to highlight interperiod and interregional differences (e.g. index numbers for the price of coal or for deaths by cancer in one or several countries). *Complex* index numbers combine different unit values by means of a weighting regimen that determines their interrelation. Apart from the indexed item, time and location also are variables, but in the different sense of predetermined modifiers with fixed intervals for years, regions and so on.

The transformation of data into an index stresses the size and direction of change, which gives it a strong indicative thrust. The base period also affects the perceived relevance of index change. Set at 100 (it can be 1 or any other number), it gives that period an aura of stability, sometimes even of good old times or of a model country with which the present situation (or other countries) are being compared. It is therefore advisable not to reach back too far and to concentrate on the indicative span of particular interest.

Index numbers have only a limited capacity for capturing changes in the environment. They can be adjusted for one factor at a time by dividing by a further indicator (i.e. *standardising*), notably for shifts in population or price but not so readily for change in the natural, living or working environment. This may not matter much for the short term indication of movement or difference, but it should be remembered that updating the format by shifting the base does not necessarily update the contents structure.

The index number problem arises with the combination of variables expressed in different units (e.g. food price items) or in categories of the same unit (e.g. petrol and diesel fuel). Apart from its own indicative purpose, the index number here serves as a means of bringing the component units to a common scale. This can be done in stages, for instance by constructing a food price index and using it as a component of a consumer price index. This standardising process is also applied to the elimination of certain change factors, in particular population or prices to result in *per capita* and/or *constant price* values. Even if not formally cast into the index number mould with a stated reference base, such a series (e.g. income per capita, rent in constant prices) becomes a sort of *hybrid* index number by its transformation from its original values.

The combination of shifting variables, especially prices and quantities, has long been debated by statisticians and economists. In 1956 the International Statistical Institute published a *Bibliography on Index Numbers*, collected under the direction of R.G.D. Allen, which quotes over 600 titles from 1707 onward, and many more papers on the subject have been published since. In the nineteenth century economists were interested in developing index numbers to determine general price levels and real economic trends. Then statisticians joined the discussion, culminating in Fisher's book on *The Making of Index Numbers* (1922), which has remained a standard reference on the subject. In the late 1920s the debate began to shift to economic interpretations and was taken up by some of the leading practitioners of the art. However, this made hardly any impact on the actual producers of index numbers, namely government and business statisticians in various fields of commerce and other social sciences. In practice it is their index numbers that are most often used as indicators and therefore interest us most here. Also, it is the technique used for their construction and adjustment, unsullied by theoretical strife, that is illustrated in the appendix to this section. This is the so-called *atomistic* approach to index numbers, and we shall refer to the alternative *functional* approach more briefly at the end of this section.

The debate usually centres on price/quantity relations in the major case of the *consumer price index* and even here it has neglected the measurement dilemma that prices are usually determined at *end* of period while quantum statistics refer to the *course* of a period, on the assumption that prices remain constant or change at a constant rate over the period. This is just one of the untidy features also inherent in the implicit volume and expenditure indexes shown in the appendix. The problems of other price index numbers (e.g. for wholesale or foreign trade or specific industries) are similar.

The appendix refers to a rudimentary consumer price index where prices of two commodities are the major variables, weighted by quantities (produced, used or sold) according to a regimen that expresses their relative sizes. The type of index most used in practice rests on base weights, which is the situation in the base year of the index. It is known as a *Laspeyre index*, named after the statistician who introduced it in 1864. It is usually juxtaposed to an index based on current weights, the so-called *Paasche index* (1874). However, this is largely a case of textbook pedantry, because in practice current volume statistics are rarely available in time and would require an annual reworking of the regimen. Among the hundreds of quantum-weighted price index statistics quoted in various publications, one rarely finds a Paasche-type current weight index.

Consumption in the example in Table 2.20 consists of two items: 2 litres of wine and 1 kg of bread (perhaps a 'Paradise index' in terms of Edward Fitzgerald's eleventh Rubai, assuming that 'books of verse' and 'Thou' are free goods there). The table assumes that the price of wine rises in the second period by 50% with a consequent fall of 20% in consumption, while the demand for bread is not so price-elastic and indeed rises by 20% following a price rise of 25% (mirroring perhaps the 'Irish Famine case' where a rise in the price of potatoes forced up its consumption because alternatives became dearer still). The base weight price index rises by 43¾% just a little more than the rise in the current weight version of 41.7%, shown in (3b) in Table 2.21. The quantum gap between the two items has narrowed, from 100:50 to 80:60, which partly offsets the greater price rise in the relatively dearer item (i.e. wine). In weighted terms, the price rise in wine contributed 78%, and that of bread 22% to the overall rise. It should be noted that neither method takes account of a change in demand over time, unless reflected in price change; both methods hold Σq_0 or Σq_1 respectively steady.

Taking the meaning of variable in a wider sense, we find that two variables can yield two indexes and their combination a third one. This is demonstrated in Table 2.21, which in addition to price index numbers (3) shows the obverse quantum index (2) and the implicit expenditure (e.g. consumption, trade, sales) index (1). The *quantum index* is the familiar indicator of real values that uses base-year prices to show what would have been the trend in income and so on if prices had not changed. Of course, that is only a guess, as are the assumptions of invariant quantities in price index numbers; perhaps even more of a guess is the extent to which the interdependence of income components is probably less than that of prices.

With the combined expenditure index (1) the problem lies not so much in shifting quantities and prices, and their interdependence, as in the concept and the aggregation process involved. We have to define consumer or other expenditure, national income and production, or the goods and services to be included in the notion of international or national trade. Once a decision has been made about the composition of this aggregate, the $\Sigma p \times \Sigma q$ can be formulated in the form of a simple index number. As it is usually impracticable to enumerate every single item of consumption and so on, statisticians concentrate on the selection of a representative sample of items and prices, so that any omissions would have no significant effect on the price index. Also, they avoid showing the $\Sigma(p \times q)$ index separately lest it be confused with a complete estimate of consumer spending, such as is shown in the national accounts, although comparison with that is of interest for determining index coverage.

Normally a base weight index is greater than a current weight index, although the difference may be only small. Neither of them passes two tests applied to show the validity of price index combinations, or indeed of any multifactor index, namely the *time reversal* and *factor reversal* tests, shown as (6) and (7) respectively in Table 2.21. These require that reversals of p or of q respectively between periods 0 and 1 should yield the same index; for example, a rise of 50% in the index between years 0 and 1 would have to be matched by a fall in the index of 33% between periods 1 and 0. Neither the Laspeyre nor the Paasche indexes pass these tests.

The *Marshall-Edgeworth* test and *Fisher's Ideal Index Number*, shown as (4a) and (4b) in Table 2.21, look more plausible because they make use of all combinations of p_0,p_1 and q_0,q_1 and the results lie between the base weight and current weight index numbers. However, the Marshall-Edgeworth index does not meet the factor reversal test; and although Fisher's index does meet both tests, it is rarely used in practice except in the form of *Divisia* and *Tornquist* indexes (Köves, 1983: 136), which are applied not so much to price measurement as to multifactor productivity for a chain index based on geometric averages. This applies where comparisons are sought for recent periods (e.g. this year with last year), related to a more remote past by assumed price vectors for the components.

Some economists have rejected this approach to index number construction as being *atomistic* (i.e. as a ritual with form rather than measurement), and they have attacked in particular Fisher's claim 'that the purpose to which an index number is put does not affect the choice of formula' (1922: 229). Bowley asked in 1928 (p. 223), 'What change in expenditure is necessary, after a change in prices, to obtain the same satisfaction as before?', and others have tried to introduce utility functions, with indifference and welfare considerations, consistent with the theories of consumer behaviour and neoclassical economic thought. The impressive list of participants, starting with the Russian economist A. Könus (1924/ 1939), includes at least four Nobel Prize winners (W. Leontief, R. Frisch, P.A. Samuelson and R. Stone) and, more recently, S. Afriat (e.g. 1981). They have tried to replace the atomistic approach with an index based on constant utility, ideally representing persons of equal taste and equal real income. In reality, however, they seem to have got no further than confirming Fisher's view that the index is best placed between the upper and lower bounds of the base and current weight calculations.

Various statistical techniques can be used for adjusting index numbers to a new base, grafting a new series onto an old one, revising weights, replacing old items by new ones, and continuously updating a base weight index with current weights by means of chain-linking. These are all illustrated in the appendix. Such methods, or similar ones, are employed by government statisticians to update continuously their consumer price indexes and other price indexes. This enhances their quality as indicators as far as improved use of available information is concerned, but it must always be remembered that the use of substitutions and proportioning cannot wholly remedy the inaccuracies caused by the uneven flow of prices and quantities reflecting the vagaries of the market and of consumer behaviour.

APPENDIX

The index in Table 2.20 is a standard base weight index (also calculable from p,q relatives), meaning that prices 'on average' rose by 43¾% assuming that the pattern of usage of the base year was known and did not change in year 1.

Time and factor reversal tests, illustrated in Table 2.21, show how accurately an index records the symmetry of change, inasmuch as a rise of 25% in one period and a drop of 20% in the next should bring the index back exactly to 100. Neither base weight nor current weight indexes do quite result in a product of 1, but Fisher's Ideal index (4b) is constructed so as to meet the test. A base weight index tends to have an upward bias, and a current weight index a downward bias, compared with the other, and this also is reflected in the test results.

Tables 2.22 to 2.26 illustrate techniques for adjusting the base weight price index.

Table 2.20   Base-weight price index: Laspeyre, aggregative
(base year 0, current year 1)

	Price ($)			Quantity			Weighted price ($)				Index		Factor contribution to index change	
Factor	p_0 (1)	p_1 (2)	Change (3)	q_0 (4)	q_1 (5)	Change (6)	p_0q_0 (7)	(8)	p_1q_0 (9)	(10)	p_1q_0/p_0q_0 (11)	Change (12)	$(p_1/q_0)(p_0q_0)$ (13)	(14)
Wine 2l	6	9	+50%	100	80	-20%	600 =	75%	900 =	78%	150	+50%	900	= 78%
Bread 2kg	4	5	+25%	50	60	+20%	200 =	25%	250 =	22%	125	+25%	250	= 22%
Total							800 =	100%	1150 =	100%	143¾	+43¾%	1150	= 100%

Table 2.21   Price-quantity combinations for constructing/testing index numbers (base year 0, current year 1)

Factor	Price ($) p_0	p_1	Quantity q_0	q_1	Weighted price ($) $p_0 q_0$ (A)	$p_1 q_0$ (B)	$p_0 q_1$ (C)	$p_1 q_1$ (D)	(E)
Wine 2 l	6	9	100	80	600	900	480	720	
Bread 2 kg	4	5	50	60	200	250	240	300	
Total	10	14	150	140	800	1150	720	1020	

	(A)	(B)	(C)	(D)	(E)
(1) Expenditure index: 100 D/A	100			127.5	
(2) Quantum indexes					
(a) Base year price: 100 C/A	100		90		
(b) Current year price: 100 D/B		100		88.7	
(3) Price indexes					
(a) Base weight (Laspeyre): 100 B/A	100	143¾			
(b) Current weight (Paasche): 100 D/C			100	141.7	
(4) Combined indexes					
(a) Marshall–Edgeworth: 100(B + D)/(A + C)			100	142.8	
(b) Fisher's Ideal Index Number: $\sqrt{(3a) \times (3b)}$				142.7	
(5) Weight reversals					
(a) Base weight reversed: 100 C/D			70.6	100	
(b) Current weight reversed: 100 A/B	69.6	100			
(6) Time reversal tests					
(a) Base weight: (3a) × (3aa) [× (0.0001)]					1.0149
(b) Current weight: (3b) × (3bb) [× (0.0001)]					0.9860
(7) Factor reversal tests					
(a) Base weight: (3a) × (2a)/(1)					1.0147
(b) Current weight: (3b) × (2b)/(1)					0.9633

Table 2.22   Alternative changes of index base

	Year 1	Year 2	Year 3	Year 4	Year 5	Year 6
Original	160	120	40	80	160	200
Index	100	75	25	50	100	125
	133	100	33	67	133	166
	400	300	100	200	400	500
or	1.33	1	0.33	0.67	1.33	1.66

Table 2.23   Grafting new series onto old series

Year	Old series Σpq $		Index	New series Σpq $		Index	Combined series index[a]
0	$\Sigma p_0 q_0 = 50$		100				100
1	$\Sigma p_1 q_0 = 60$		120	$\Sigma p_1 q_1 =$	80	100	(120/100) 100 = 120
2	$\Sigma p_2 q_0 = 75$		150	$\Sigma p_2 q_1 =$	112	140	(120/100) 140 = 168
3	$\Sigma p_3 q_0 = 65$		130	$\Sigma p_3 q_1 =$	101	126	(120/100) 126 = 151

a Combined series = new series × 1.2.

Table 2.24   Revision of weights for items I (100 to 80) and II (50 to 60)

Year	Price ($) p_I	p_{II}	Quantity Old q_I	q_{II}	New q'_I	q'_{II}	Old series Σpq $		Index	New series Σpq $		Index	Combined series index[a]
0	6	4	100	50			$\Sigma p_0 q_0 = 800$		100				100
1	9	5	100	50	80	60	$\Sigma p_1 q_0 = 1150$		143¾	$\Sigma p_1 q'_i = 1020$		100	(143¾/100) 100 = 143¾
2	10	5	100	50	80	60	$\Sigma p_2 q_0 = 1250$		156¼	$\Sigma p_2 q'_i = 1100$		108	(143¾/100) 108 = 155
3	5	8	100	50	80	60	$\Sigma p_3 q_0 = 900$		112½	$\Sigma p_3 q'_i = 880$		86	(143¾/100) 86 = 124

a Separate series for old and new weights chain-linked by factor 1.4375 (i.e. 143¾ index in year 1).

Table 2.25   Substitution of new item III for item II

Year	Price ($) p_I	p_{II}	p_{III}	Quantity[a] q_I	q_{II}	q_{III}	Old series Σpq $		Index	New series Σpq $		Index	Combined series index[a]
0	6	4		100	50		$\Sigma p_0 q_0 = 800$		100				100
1	9	5	10	100	50	25	$\Sigma p_1 q_0 = 1150$		143¾	$\Sigma p_1 q_1 = 1150$		100	(143¾/100) 100 = 143¾
2	10		12	100		25				$\Sigma p_2 q_1 = 1300$		113	(143¾/100) 113 = 162½
3	5		18	100		25				$\Sigma p_3 q_1 = 950$		82½	(143¾/100) 82½ = 118½

a Item II superseded by item III (e.g. cotton socks by nylon socks). Assume that sock expenditure ($5 × 50) remains unchanged ($10 × 25). Substitute in year 2, and then chain-link.

Table 2.26 Base weight index updated with current weights

	Price ($)		Quantity		Base q_0 series			Base q_1 series			Base q_2 series			Combined series
Year	p_I	p_{II}	q_I	q_{II}	Σpq	$	Index	Σpq	$	Index	Σpq	$	Index	index
0	6	4	100	50	$\Sigma p_0 q_0 =$ 800		100							100
1	9	5	80	60	$\Sigma p_1 q_0 =$ 1150		143¾	$\Sigma p_1 q_1 =$ 1020		100				(143¾/100) 100 = 143¾
2	10	5	70	60	$\Sigma p_2 q_0 =$ 1250		156¼	$\Sigma p_2 q_1 =$ 1100		108	$\Sigma p_2 q_2 =$ 1000		100	(108/100) 143¾ = 155¼
3	5	8	120	25	$\Sigma p_3 q_0 =$ 900		112½	$\Sigma p_3 q_1 =$ 880		86	$\Sigma p_3 q_2 =$ 830		83	(83/100) 155¼ = 128¾

[a] Chain-linked.

2.9 Correlation and regression

Social measurement usually refers to one series over time or to a comparison of two or more series. In the first case the present serves as standard for the past, or vice versa, often for the purpose of estimating the future; and in the second case we look for interrelations between two or several series, again often for the purpose of forecasting future changes in any one of them. The many well-established techniques for these processes of correlation and regression are described in the various textbooks of statistical analysis. Here we will only briefly look at some of their basic features so as to clarify the nature of the indicators they yield. We may begin with a reminder that correlation and regression, like any other processing of statistics, can enhance their indicativeness (i.e. their usefulness for the interpretation of trends and interrelations) but by themselves do not improve the quality of the underlying statistics. If these are uncertain or otherwise unreliable, processing will cover up rather than remedy such weakness.

The reference here is mainly to the linear, straight-line relationship between two series, omitting the more complex situation of curvilinear or non-linear relations. Two variables like the radius and circumference of a circle are auto-correlated by definition through the fixed term of π; others are at least strongly related, as is the case between the height and age of children, which both reflect physical development. In most cases, however, the relation is more conjectural (i.e. stochastic), and therefore less certain and less predictable, because it is based on some common and some disparate features. For example, the so-called *Phillips curve* depicts a model of cost-push inflation with a positive relation between employment and prices, suggesting that inflation, like employment, is a function of the state of demand, but both of these variables will also depend, more or less, on other factors. More generally, then, if $x = f(d,e)$ and $y = f(d,f)$, correlation analysis can be applied to determine the relative importance of the common factor, d.

At the other extreme of high auto-correlation is the case of no, or spurious, communality between the series; for example, the establishment of any correlation between the birth rate and the nesting of storks in England would be suspect.

Correlation by itself does not prove *causal* connections; it only suggests that such a connection either way may exist. A strong correlation between, say, smoking and lung cancer could indicate either of three connections: that smokers tend to be victims of lung cancer; or that persons suffering from lung cancer are likely to become heavy smokers; or that smoking and lung cancer result from a third factor, such as a hereditary feature that separately leads to cancer-prone lungs and an urge to smoke. In this example the statistics show a *positive* correlation in that both variables move in the same direction; in others, such as demand–price relations, the variables move in opposite directions and the correlation becomes *negative*. Figure 2.7 illustrates four types of correlation.

Figure 2.7 Scatter diagrams and correlation

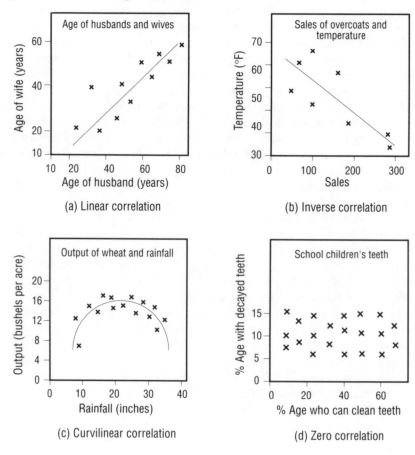

(a) Linear correlation

(b) Inverse correlation

(c) Curvilinear correlation

(d) Zero correlation

The relationship between two variables can be depicted in a *scatter diagram*, where they are plotted on the respective *x*- and *y*-axes, as in Figure 2.7. This disregards the time sequence, but the respective points of time can be marked on the diagram, which may show that correspondence is bunched or greatly scattered for certain subperiods. Overall, a close grouping or wide scatter gives a quick visual impression of the relation between the variables. This can often be expressed by drawing a line freehand, or it can be found more precisely by calculating its intercept, *a*, with the *y*-axis and the tangent value, *b*, of its angle with *x*-axis so that

$$y = a + bx$$

Along that line the +/- distances of the series *x,y* from the *line of best fit* are minimised.

Usually these deviations are squared, as in the calculation of the standard deviation, which eliminates +/- sign problems:

$$\Sigma y = na + b\Sigma x \qquad \Sigma x = na + b\Sigma y$$
$$\Sigma xy = a\Sigma x + b\Sigma x^2 \qquad \Sigma xy = a\Sigma y + b\Sigma y^2$$
$$y = a + bx \qquad x = a + by$$

This results in two regression lines whose closeness reflects the extent of correlation; they coincide in the case of perfect correlation. The geometric average of the two respective *b* values represents the *regression coefficient*, which lies between 0 (no relation) and 1 (perfect correlation between *x* and *y*).

In some cases reasonable assumptions can be made about the dominance of a series. For example, looking for the relation between price and demand for cars, it can be assumed that in the short run an inverse relation between price and demand prevails and that in the longer run the state of demand will more strongly influence price. Extrapolation of the regression line may indicate that an expected price change will lead to a corresponding change in demand, and/or vice versa, on the assumption that other factors will not greatly change (e.g. that price and car life will not be greatly affected by technological change, or that changes in highway codes will not greatly affect car use).

The *coefficient of correlation*, *r*, expresses the relation between two series, and by deduction their dependence on other independent variables within the 0-1 range. This is shown more definitely by squaring *r* to r^2 to become the *coefficient of determination*. It represents the proportion of fluctuations in one variable that are attributable to the other. With the coefficient of correlation *r* between 0 and 1, its square will be $<r$. For example, if at a given time the *r* between a rainfall measure and traffic accidents is 0.7, this indicates the relatively high linear association between the variables. To measure the strength of this association, in terms of rainfall and frequency of accidents, $r^2 = 0.49$, indicating that about half of the change in the accident rate is due to heavy rainfall.

A *rank order coefficient*, such as the *product moment* or *Spearman's coefficient*, can indicate similarities between two series. The persons or items in the series are ranked by order of size, performance or other criteria. Then if the number of items is n and the difference in ranking between pairs is $d_1, d_2, \ldots d_n$, the coefficient becomes

$$1 - 6\Sigma d^2/(n^3 - n)$$

The range is from +1 to -1, where 0 signifies perfect correlation and minus values the extent of upside-down correspondence. Ranking does not show size of difference; so a series \$1, \$2, \$3 can rank like \$100, \$101, \$1000. However, when distribution is fairly evenly and equally spaced, the device has useful indicative applications (e.g. in rating price and performance features in consumer testing, or in establishing patterns of student performance in different subjects, or in studying coincident diseases). An example is given in the appendix below.

APPENDIX

In the example in Table 2.27, the regression coefficients b, are 4.5 (for y regressed on x) and 0.18 (for x regressed on y).

The coefficient of correlation, r, varies between 0 (no association) and 1 (perfect association), 0 to +1 being positive association and 0 to -1 being negative association. The coefficient is derived from the deviations as follows:

$$r = \frac{\Sigma(x - x^*)(y - y^*)}{\sqrt{(x - x^*)\Sigma(y - y^*)^2}} = \frac{45}{\sqrt{2500}} = 0.9$$

Table 2.27   Regression: age of wine and its price

Lot	Age (years) x	Price (\$) y	x^2	y^2	xy	$(x - x^*)$	$(y - y^*)$	$(x - x^*)^2$	$(y - y^*)^2$	$(x - x^*) \times (y - y^*)$
(a)	2	10	4	100	20	-2	-5	4	25	10
(b)	3	5	9	25	15	-1	-10	1	100	10
(c)	5	20	25	400	100	+1	+5	1	25	5
(d)	6	25	36	625	150	+2	+10	4	100	20
$n = 4$	16	60	74	1150	285	0	0	10	250	45

Mean: $x^* = 4$ $y^* = 15$

Regress y on x:		Regress x on y:	
$\Sigma y = na + b\Sigma x;$	$60 = 4a + 16b$	$\Sigma x = na + b\Sigma y;$	$16 = 4a + 60b$
$\Sigma xy = a\Sigma x + b\Sigma x^2;$	$285 = 16a + 74b$	$\Sigma xy = a\Sigma y + b\Sigma y^2;$	$285 = 60a + 1150b$
$y = a + bx;$	$y = -3 + 4.5x$	$x = a + by;$	$x = 1.3 + 0.18y$

Alternatively, it can be derived from the geometric average of the regression coefficients:

$$r = \sqrt{4.5 \times 0.18} = 0.9$$

The coefficient of determination, r^2, is the proportion of total variance in the dependent variable that is explained by the independent variable; $r^2 < r$. Here

$$r^2 = 0.9^2 = 0.81$$

The difference (100 – 81) means that 81% of variations in y (price) are explained by x (age) with 19% due to other factors (e.g. imports).

In Table 2.28, based on actual test results, Spearman's coefficients were calculated for pairs of qualities, where $n = 9$, d = difference in ranking between pairs, and

$$\text{coefficient} = 1 - 6\Sigma d^2/(n^3 - n)$$

Results:

juice extraction and	juice quality	−0.08
	ease of use	−0.35
	mechanical safety	−0.32
juice quality	and ease of use	+0.45
	mechanical safety	+0.38
ease of use	and mechanical safety	+0.84
price	and overall performance	−0.23

In this example the poorly performing brand G was dearer than all the better-performing brands. In general the relation between price and performance was negative, as was the relation between juice extraction and other features. However, ease of use and safety and juice quality had positive associations.

Table 2.28 Rank order correlation: juice extractors merit-ranked by four features, weighted overall performance and retail price

Quality	Weight (%)	Rating by brand or model								
		A	B	C	D	E	F	G	H	I
Juice extraction	10	78	76	74	87	88	86	87	88	83
Juice quality	10	76	76	76	77	75	73	79	72	75
Ease of use	50	64	65	63	62	59	50	49	46	43
Mechanical safety	30	72	64	64	44	48	64	44	25	32
Overall performance	100	66	64	63	59	58	58	53	45	45
Price rank[a]		8	7	6	3½	3½	2	9	1	5

Note: Adapted from Choice, January 1991.
[a] $50 to $155; cheapest 1, dearest 9; lowest-obtainable retail price.

2.10 Time series analysis

Time series analysis seeks to discover the patterns underlying the series. We use the past to understand the present and to predict the future. Four main factors can be identified:

- *Secular trend* reflects a medium or long term movement over time that may be due to general changes in the physical, technological or social environment, including factors such as shifts in population composition, taste changes, or increases in knowledge or in information systems.
- *Seasonal trend* refers to regular changes over a fixed timespan, usually 1 year. It reflects a pattern imposed by a seasonal cycle or by a calendar cycle that flows from it (e.g. holidays, debt maturity).
- *Cyclical movements* extend over several years and differ in the depth and duration of upswing and downswing phases. Their causes and effects are much discussed in trade cycle theory, and beyond economics they manifest themselves in other recurrent natural and social changes.
- *Residual and random fluctuations* are connected with irregular and largely unpredictable changes, which may be catastrophic or may be due to irregularities in trends or cycles.

These types of fluctuations reflect the variable effects of time on statistical series. Some types overlap, and not all apply to every series, but the classification brings out some important aspects of indicative directions.

Many techniques have been developed to establish trends or random factors. Their basic approach usually relies on regression or comparison with earlier periods or averaging. With regression the process is similar to correlation analysis, in that fluctuations are smoothed to a line of best fit that minimises the deviations of the actual data from this linear (or curvilinear) trend. As an alternative, trends can be identified by making vertical rather than horizontal comparison in juxtaposition with the same period of earlier years, or by continuous averaging for January–February, February–March and so on, or for years 1-2-3, 2-3-4 and so on, which flattens out short term fluctuations.

The combination of different trend elements can be assumed to be either additive or multiplicative. If T, S, C and R stand respectively for the four types of fluctuations listed above, the *additive model* for a series A would be

$$A = T + S + C + R$$

suggesting that changes due to seasons, cycles and so on can be expressed in absolute amounts; for example, the Christmas season always adds $100 million to retail sales in December irrespective of whether sales in earlier months averaged $80 or $800, or the general trend is for sales to rise by $1 million each year. In the *multiplicative model,*

$$A = T \times S \times C \times R$$

changes are taken to be of the same proportion; for example, sales rise 10% seasonally in December, or at the rate of 4% per year.

Proceeding sequentially, we can eliminate the secular trend first to obtain

$$A - T = S + C + R$$

or

$$A/T = S \times C \times R$$

and follow on with S and C until we reach the final reduction of

$$A - T - S - C = R$$

or

$$A/(T \times S \times C) = R$$

This then not only reduces A to what it would have been without the influence of T, S, C and R, but also yields a series of indicators showing the strength of each of the factors T, S, C and R. Basic procedures of detrending are illustrated by examples in the appendix, following the brief verbal descriptions below.

Secular trend, indicated by a *trend line*, seeks to establish a consistent unidirectional movement that is independent of other factors that may also influence the series. It seeks to exclude small fluctuations and to straighten the series into a line (or other curve). The technique for this process corresponds to that used for the correlative regression of two series, as described in section 2.9, by substituting the course of time for one series. Series A is regressed on the time sequence and Σx is nullified by centring, reducing the regression formulas to

$$\Sigma y = na$$
$$\Sigma xy = \Sigma x^2 b$$

If an exponential trend line gives a better fit than an arithmetic line, the multiplicative method can be applied by using logarithms.

An alternative method for determining a trend line relies on averaging to smooth out fluctuations. In a very simple form, averages for the first and second half of the year are used to suggest the absence of a definitive straight line trend.

In a more refined version, moving averages are applied to overlapping periods of 2 and more years, which smooths the data progressively towards a straight line. However, the wider the span of the average, the fewer points it yields; that is, for a series of n items, averaging in consecutive groups of two provides $(n - 1)$ items, groups of three provide $(n - 2)$ items, and so on. It cannot be assumed that the line calculated from $\Sigma (x - x_n)/\Sigma(n - 1)$ and $\Sigma(x - x_0)/\Sigma(n - 1)$ is typical for the trend, any more than the arithmetic average $\Sigma x/n$ is necessarily representative for a scattered series. It must also be considered that averages centred on the original data reduce their timeliness. For example, if we have data for the 10 single years from 1981 to 1990, we can calculate eight 3-year averages (for 1981–83 to 1988–90), seven 4-year averages (for 1981–84 to 1987–90) and so on. This reduces the confidence that can be placed on extrapolating the line into the future. Therefore trend fitting by regression may be preferred.

It must be remembered that any such technique can produce a trend line even if there is no trend. Unlike correlation analysis, the simple methods described here carry no warning signals (e.g. correlation coefficient, standard error of estimate) for the reliability or otherwise of the results. It is assumed that changes in the series are a function of time rather than of technical, social or behavioural changes, which may not be closely linked to time. It is further assumed that the trend is unidirectional, either up or horizontal or down, or at least the chosen methods must be adjusted to cope with identifying breaks in trend. Any smoothing by regression or averaging means an information loss from the original data. However, these methods are used and can be used to advantage as long as they highlight rather than hide the indicative message: where have we been, where are we and where are we going.

Seasonal trend refers to periodic fluctuations over a year, or other set period, that are connected with the ebb and flow of economic, social and physical activities, such as occurs at the Christmas season. They are reflected mainly in monthly statistical series but can also be observed weekly (e.g. for patterns of trade) or at other periods. The evidence for such patterns in indicators is found in recurrent fluctuations of similar size in comparative periods, and must be distinguished from unidirectional trends or longer term cyclical change.

A simple way of excluding the effect of seasonal factors is to present data in the form of proportionate change over the previous year, or over an average of preceding years, rather than as direct monthly changes. This form is frequently used as the sole or auxiliary indication of current directions viewed in terms of previous years, sometimes in conjunction with deflation by a price index to calculate *real change*.

For a more refined version of deseasonalisation, a secular trend is first established, by regression or moving averages, followed by tabulation of the deviations from trend for the original figures. This shows whether there is a fairly consistent pattern of monthly or quarterly deviations over the years. The mean of the deviations for each month or quarter represents the seasonal factors, some being positive and others negative and all adding up close to nil (and preferably then adjusted to nil precisely). These factors, with reversed signs, are then added to, or subtracted from, the original data to yield a deseasonalised series, which over the year should add up to the same amount as the original series.

In this model it is assumed that peaks and troughs over the year can be evened out by additions and subtractions. Alternatively, if the seasonal effect is better expressed as proportionate change, the ratio of trend to original value can be calculated and averaged out as indicating seasonal influence, and then applied to the original series. The seasonal factors then become equivalent to +/- percentage changes; they are all positive and average out to +1.

Seasonal patterns are not constant. They shift in response to, or in connection with, general trends that may, for instance, change the relative significance of Christmas for trade. The application of computer programs for updating factors does not obviate the need for checking the consistency of the deseasonalising factors, in particular if they do not produce clearcut trends, and also because they themselves become an important indicator for seasonal impact on the respective series.

Corresponding to short term seasonal fluctuations, *long term cycles of activity* may stretch over 30 or more years. This includes the *trade cycle* as specified, for example, in the long waves of prices and production identified by Kondratieff in the 1920s and subsequently debated by economists like Wesley Mitchell, Rostov and Schumpeter. The cycles reflect the regular incidence of climatic patterns and wars, as well as of technical progress or the gestation of new investment. The causes and effects of such cycles remain subject to debate among social scientists, and their length and strength can vary considerably.

For calculating the cyclical element and removing it from long term time series, the techniques outlined previously can be used. Omitting the short term seasonal factor, T and R fluctuations are equivalent to the deviations of the trend line from the actual data:

$$C + R = A - T$$

or

$$C \times R = A/T$$

The resulting series can then be smoothed out by averaging, using, for instance, a 3 month moving average and applying this as factor to the trend values. The ratio will generally be >1 in the downswing, thus enhancing the trend values, and <1 in an upswing.

This procedure can be extended to a separation of *cyclical and random factors* by dividing the original series by the detrended decycled series to show the calculated R ratios:

$$R = A - T - C$$

or

$$R = A/TC$$

However, as R is a mix of exogenous forces (e.g. natural disasters) and endogenous elements from irregularities in trends, this might overstretch this analysis, and therefore C and R are usually combined. However, this should not prevent the analyst from drawing attention to known events that may have caused irregularities in trend or cycle movements. In summary, it should be noted that time series analysis not only refines the data by excluding trends and patterns but also shows the strengths of the various factors that influence the data.

A more advanced analysis of the interaction between cyclical fluctuations and trend is discussed by Stock and Watson (1988) using the analogy of 'random walk with drift theory' for stock prices. A 'linear' time trend rises by a fixed amount, say 1%, each quarter, as compared with a 'variable' trend that averages such an amount over a year. In any quarter the change in trend deviates from its average by a random amount, which provides a new base each quarter for future growth. It is unpredictable and turns the variable trend into a *stochastic trend*.

Growth and cyclical variations do not operate separately as the cycles continuously adjust themselves to the growth path. Isolation of the stochastic trend by regression analysis can help to assess growth policies in the short run and stabilisation policies in the long run (Stock and Watson, 1988).

APPENDIX

Table 2.29 Trend fitting: coal production in Australia 1971–79
(y, in millions of tonnes)

Year	Linear trend, 9 years					Linear trend, 6 years					Exponential trend
	y	x	x^2	xy	y_t	y	x	x^2	xy	y_t	y_t
	$y_t = 66.7 + 4.02x$					$y_t = 74.6 + 4.26x$					$y_t = 74.2 \times 1.06^x$
1971	51	–4	16	–204	50.6						
1972	54	–3	9	–162	54.6						
1973	60	–2	4	–120	58.7						
1974	59	–1	1	–59	62.7	59	–5	25	–295	53.3	55.4
1975	70	0	0	0	66.7	70	–3	9	–210	61.8	62.3
1976	69	+1	1	+69	70.7	69	–1	1	–69	70.3	70.0
1977	76	+2	4	+152	74.7	76	+1	1	+76	78.9	78.6
1978	79	+3	9	+237	78.8	79	+3	9	+237	87.4	88.4
1979	82	+4	16	+328	82.8	82	+5	25	+410	95.9	99.3
Σ	600	0	60	+241		435	0	70	+149		

Regress y on x by using formula in Table 2.26 with $\Sigma x = 0$:

Linear, 9 years: $\Sigma y = na;$ $600 = 9a;$ $a = 66.7$ $\Big\}$ $y_t = a + bx$ $= 66.7 + 4.02x$
               $\Sigma xy = b\Sigma x^2;$ $241 = 60b;$ $b = 4.02$

Linear, 6 years: $y = na;$ $435 = 6a;$ $a = 72.5$ $\Big\}$ $y_t = a + bx$ $= 72.5 + 2.13x$
               $\Sigma xy = b\Sigma x^2;$ $149 = 70b;$ $b = 2.13$

            (which centred on 0 = 1976–77 becomes $y_t = a + b + 2bx$ $= 74.6 + 4.26x$)

Exponential: $109y_t = \Sigma \log (y/n) + \Sigma(x \log y)/\Sigma x^2$ from which y_t $= 74.2 \times 1.06^x$

**Table 2.30   Elimination of trend in time series: number of births, Australia,
1980–89 (thousands)**

Semi-average method

Year	1980	1981	1982	1983	1984	1985	1986	1987	1988	1989
Number	258	276	265	248	245	233	228	227	226	223
Averages			258.4					227.4		
					242.9					

Moving average method

2 years		267	271	257	247	239	231	228	227	225
3 years		266	263	253	242	235	229	227	225	
4 years		262	259	248	239	233	229	226		
5 years		258	253	244	236	232	227			
6 years		254	249	241	235	230				
7 years		250	246	239	233					
8 years		248	244	237						
9 years		245	241							
10 years		243								

**Figure 2.8   Trend lines—moving averages: number of births, Australia,
1970–79; annual and averages for 4, 7 and 9 years**

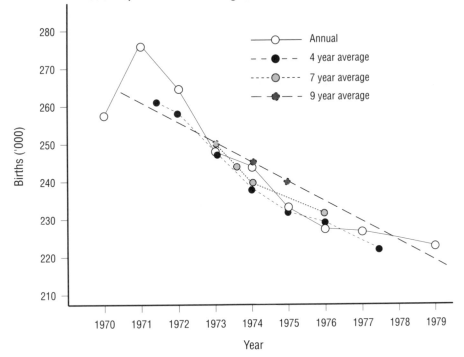

Table 2.31   Seasonal adjustment, additive model: weekly earnings ($)

A (actual), T (trend), S (seasonal), R (residual)

Year	Quarter	Actual earnings	4 quarter moving average		Seasonal difference	Seasonally adjusted earnings	Residual
			Total	Centred			
		A		T	(A - T)	S	R = (S - T)
1975/76	Sep.	157.60				156.81	
	Dec.	175.70				170.07	
			678.40				
	Mar.	165.30	705.60	173.00	-7.70	172.44	-0.56
	June	179.80	725.30	178.89	+0.91	179.08	+0.19
1976/77	Sep.	184.80	743.80	183.64	+1.16	184.01	+0.37
	Dec.	195.40	762.70	188.31	+7.09	189.77	+1.46
	Mar.	183.80	782.00	193.09	-9.29	190.94	-2.15
	June	198.70	799.10	197.64	+1.06	197.98	+0.34
1977/78	Sep.	204.10	820.40	202.44	+1.66	203.31	+0.87
	Dec.	212.50	838.00	207.30	+5.20	206.87	-0.43
	Mar.	205.10	852.80	211.35	-6.25	212.24	+0.89
	June	216.30	868.50	215.16	+1.14	215.58	+0.42
1978/79	Sep.	218.90	886.20	219.34	-0.44	218.11	-1.23
	Dec.	228.20	902.70	223.61	+4.59	222.57	-1.04
	Mar.	222.80	922.20	228.11	-5.31	229.94	+1.83
	June	232.80	942.00	233.03	-0.23	232.08	-0.95
1979/80	Sep.	238.40				237.61	
	Dec.	248.00				242.37	

Seasonal differences derived from (A - T) and averaged over period

Year	Sep.	Dec.	Mar.	June	
1975/76			-7.70	+0.91	
1976/77	+1.16	+7.09	-9.29	+1.06	
1977/78	+1.66	+5.20	-6.25	+1.14	
1978/79	-0.44	+4.59	-5.31	-0.23	
Mean	+0.79	+5.63	-7.14	+0.72	$\Sigma = 0$

A *multiplicative model* of seasonal adjustment can be calculated from the divergences from the trend line. Seasonal factors are derived in a similar way as with the additive model but take the form of divisors. For the example in Table 2.31 they work out as 0.974 for September, 1.031 for December, 0.965 for March and 1.007 for June.

2.11 Multivariate analysis

Analytical methods discussed so far rest on simple assumptions about defined patterns for one or several variables. With productivity, for example, we take it for granted that there is a close relation between production and employment at a point of time or during a period, and that there is a mutual connection if inside or outside factors change (e.g. the effect of employment on production). However, a rise in the productivity indicator could also be due to production's becoming more concentrated in efficient firms or to improved technology that reduces labour demand.

We may note that, even with the simple formula for two variables, there is a reverse indicator—in this case the labour required for one production unit with reciprocal reactions to change in structural or outside conditions. In the simple case the treatment of units, scales or weights presents no great mathematical problem, because we assume inbuilt classifications with equal interval scales taken from statistics for population, production and so on, which lend themselves to straightforward algebraic treatment. If we want to condense more complex systems with dependent and independent variables into unambiguous indicators, we must go beyond simple averaging to a more elaborate analysis of the variables.

In the previous discussion of taxonomies and their application to rank ordering, it was stated that the ordinal grading of variables de-emphasises the effect of weighting and eases the process of combining and comparing different variables (e.g. income, literacy rates). This has been extended to multifaceted indicators for economic and social concerns (e.g. development) and beyond. Cluster analysis, for instance, is used in both the natural and social sciences. Since Mahalanobis' proposals for generalised distance statistics in the 1930s, a considerable literature has appeared on multivariate analysis including standard texts by Kendall (1975) and by Sneath and Sokal (1973).

One such approach applied to indicator analysis is the so-called *Wroclaw taxonomy*, which was developed under the auspices of the United Nations Educational, Scientific and Cultural Organisation (UNESCO) by a group of Polish statisticians (Harbison et al., 1970, in particular appendix 1; Gostowski, 1972). It relates various development indicators from different countries to an ideal country, which happens to have the highest value for that variable, thus relating them in n-dimensional space. In Ivanovic's version (UNESCO Report no. 30, 1974), iterative processes are used to reduce index bias, dominance and auto-correlation. The resulting 'I-distance' measures each country's development in separate and combined rankings of economic and social factors. Similar methods resting on matrix analysis have been applied by Harbison et al. (1970) to the analysis of modernisation and development. While these methods avoid the problem of weighting, they do not bring out proportionality of changes in variables (i.e. collinearity). Also, a noted social statistician, Galtung, once described the

Table 2.32   Multivariate analysis

Analysis of dependence	Analysis of Interdependence
Variance and Covariance analysis	Component analysis
Canonical analysis	Factor analysis
Regression analysis	Correlation analysis
Confluence analysis	Cluster analysis
	Multidimensional scaling
	Association/contingency analysis
	Discriminant analysis

approach as being 'time-blind, structure-blind, uni-dimensional, arbitrary and misleading for interpretation'.

Whatever such strictures, multivariate analysis gives a more reasonable rank ordering of countries than guesses based on separate assessment. The interplay of constituent variables can be expressed through various types of multivariate analysis. As they are ancillaries rather than main instruments of indicator construction, it will suffice here to list them briefly (following Kendall, 1975; Table 2.32).

Some of the methods start with the multiple regression of a single variable on several others on which it may or may not depend. The resulting coefficient is used to reduce a large number of variables to a smaller set of components and factors that represent all or most of the variations in the given data. The components are ranked by the order of total variance of the variables they explain. Cluster analysis, for instance, groups countries (or variables) that are relatively similar to each other by using a correlation matrix that establishes indicators for likeness groupings. Discriminant analysis, rather than establishing likenesses, seeks to establish a set of variables that best differentiates between groups.

CHAPTER 3

DEVELOPMENT APPLICATIONS OF INDICATORS

3.1 Development—general

This book is concerned with indicators of the thrust, direction and impact of socioeconomic change, which can be identified with *development*. The term is often used as a synonym for growth or advancement, but it is useful to look at the distinction made by Daly and Cobb (1989: 71) between growth, seen as *quantitative expansion* in the scale of the physical dimensions of the economic system, and development, which should refer to the *qualitative change* of a physically non-growing economic system in dynamic disequilibrium with the environment.

Growth in that sense has natural limits, and it remains arguable whether such limits also apply to development as far as technology and social organisation are concerned. Both growth and development are forward looking; but as we approach the limits or potential of either, more attention is given to the reverse process of retrogression and 'de-development'.

Economic, social and technological development can be broadly distinguished, but usually these aspects interact and should preferably be considered together. Social development cannot be separated from the economic limitations imposed by scarce resources; it is often expressed in terms of manpower, equipment or budgets. Social implications of the distribution of income and wealth, or of the impact on national welfare and the environment, are never far below the surface of economic analysis.

In stressing the role of institutional and ideological adjustment, Kuznets (1971) lists six characteristics of modern economic growth:

• as *economic*-type factors, high growth rates of per capita product and population, and of productivity;

- as *structural* factors, production changes and societal shifts; and
- as *communication* factors, the expansion in their own reach as well as the performance lag of less developed countries.

Statistical constructs such as gross national product (GNP) are inadequate for comparing countries that differ in history, culture and value systems. Experts in this field (e.g. Myrdal, Balogh and Streeten) have expressed concern about the mechanical application of models that assume absolute standards of truth and validity. The selection of indicators reflects the chosen concept of development. It may give a picture of economic development defined *ad hoc*, but omit sociocultural factors because they do not fit the development concept or because such indicators are not readily available. A statistical caution can be added about the chosen period, as a high rate may be due to catch-up from a low level or a low rate to consolidation at a relatively high level where the quality of life counts more than growth.

For the current policy debate for developing countries, we refer to the various working papers by Edwards at the National Bureau of Economic Research (NBER, 1989 and previously). A narrower view, emphasising monetary management, is represented by the International Monetary Fund (IMF), which has long used objective indicators for appraising economic development and in 1986 applied them to seven major industrial countries (Crockett, 1988): GNP; domestic demand; monetary growth; interest rates; trade and current account balances; inflation; unemployment; international reserves; fiscal balances; and exchange rates.

For this conventional selection of major economic indicators no formal weighting for relative impact is applied. It is stated that international interaction is to serve as reference for domestic performance, which in turn is to be measured according to a standard set by a desirable pattern with emphasis on medium term development and consistency of domestic objectives (e.g. trade flows). The IMF has also expressed some concern about distributional effects, as mentioned in section 3.7 with reference to poverty, but apparently it has not given them high priority.

The IMF's flexible indicator framework is important for policy applications, as reflected also in its biennial World Economic Outlook series. The World Bank publishes several annual statistical surveys for more than 100 countries. *Trends in Developing Countries* shows demographic, income and industrial growth rates and distribution of household income by quintiles and top decile. *Social Indicators of Development* gives further details of human and natural resources, expenditure and investment in human capital.

A recent survey of post-1945 thoughts on (economic) development by Griffin (1988) points to the role of indicators in the analysis of trends. It distinguishes three phases for third-world countries:

1 *Brave new world of high theory* (1945 to 1950s): Priority to economic growth and the elimination of poverty through trickle-down effect; capital

formation as engine of growth; planning and industrialisation; modest foreign aid to accelerate growth; protectionist trade policies.

2 *Golden age of global expansion* (1960s to early 1970s): Rapid growth in advanced countries and world trade; growth taken for granted; less belief in trickle-down; concern about employment, income distribution and basic needs; emphasis on human capital resources; reliance on market rather than planning; interest in agriculture (green revolution) and informal sector; scepticism about aid and multinational investment; for export-led development, revival in the theory of comparative advantage.

3 *Rude awakening* (from late 1970s) in the face of famines, debt crisis and recession; falling living standards; less faith in growth; economic reform in third-world and socialist countries; human resource programs in health; better opportunities for women; decentralisation; questioning the role of state; shift from commodity fetishism to capabilities; international financial system in disarray; default and debt forgiveness; trade barriers up.

As mentioned in section 1.3, some indicators have an upper limit in the sense of operating within a range from nil to full satisfaction or maximum utility. During the third phase listed above, some development analysts, led by the group known as the Club of Rome, have stressed the *limits to growth* through finite resources, which put all development indicators within bounds. Development planners on those lines have tried to determine desirable rather than feasible targets for growth and resource use. This is different from *optimal levels* for, say, protein consumption, rainfall or sunshine, where an excess turns a positive indicator into a negative one; nor is it the same as *natural limits* with, say, full employment or full literacy, where the indicators are bound by the 100% point of target achievement.

Limits to growth refer more to a subjectively determined upper limit, where an excess would be harmful and untenable in the longer run. We need here only mention the titles of some of the books by writers concerned with overdevelopment to the point of calling for *de-development: How Much Is Lagom (Enough)?* (Backstrand and Ingelstam, 1975), *Can Sweden Be Shrunk?* (Akerman, 1979) or *Abandon Affluence* (Trainer, 1985). Something of this approach to development is also implied in models that measure satisfaction or happiness in terms of the degree of unhappiness.

Finally, to quote a more optimistic and more 'holistic' view of development, which incidentally defies statistical description, we may quote from a workshop paper issued by the Australian organisation Community Aid Abroad which operates in conjunction with Oxfam and similar bodies:

> CAA defines development as a process by which individuals identify themselves as a community and collectively acquire the necessary knowledge, power, values and organisational skills to irreversibly share and expand the community's resources for the benefit of all its members without being at the expense of other communities or of the environment.

3.2 Gross national product (see also section 4.1)

National income, or some related notion, has long been the most popular indicator of a country's development, so much so that the terms have often been identified with each other. In the course of time statisticians, as part of the elaboration of the national accounts, have refocused their attention from national income to *gross national product* (GNP = national income +/- net income paid overseas + depreciation allowances), and since the 1970s from GNP to *gross domestic product* (GDP = GNP +/- net factor income from abroad, which some countries had previously excluded from GNP). In practice there is no great difference between GDP and GNP in a global or historical context, and we will use here GNP, which is used more frequently than GDP in the development literature.

The attractions of a single, seemingly comprehensive index to cover a variety of ill-defined notions has outweighed the many doubts about its validity. It paints the big picture in a simple structural frame that highlights the identity of the threefold stream of production = income = expenditure. (There is a fourth such identity, *national dividend*, which is less mentioned because its fountainhead, *national wealth*, is an elusive notion.) The size of production in value terms in a given period, the income stream generated by past and present production in that period, and the use of that income for consumption or saving for future consumption, are entities that represent significant indicators of a country's development, in particular in conjunction with the added information provided by their disaggregation in the national accounts. Beyond indicating a country's situation and progress, GNP is used for regional and international comparisons and in practical applications such as determining the provision or receipt of funds from international agencies.

Against such advantages for GNP as a measure of development must be held other features that reduce its significance, or at least call for caution in its application. We will mention here three of these.

Firstly, there are some drawbacks of unadjusted GNP that can at least be partly remedied. Changes in population size can be excluded by quoting GNP per capita, which is a simple but rough method because it glosses over demographic structure and compositional change. Adjustment can be attempted for inflation by applying a price index, or a number of such index series for major components of GNP, although, unlike the debate about preference shifts in conjunction with the consumer price index, the problems of national aggregative deflation are usually neglected. More attention has been given to international comparisons on the basis of exchange rates or *ad hoc* purchasing-power parities, as mentioned in section 4.5.

Secondly, there is the question of constituent items on the borderline of conventional money flows, such as the costs and benefits of production for the household and community, the costs and benefits of the use of capital and resources generally, and the valuation of public goods and services used. The treatment of subsistence and other non-market-related activities is particularly important for less developed or centrally planned economies in comparison with developed market economies.

Thirdly, we have to be aware that aggregates are structure-blind and require further indicators of distribution. The national accounts give some information about the components of production, income and expenditure, but they require separate information from surveys or taxation records to work out Lorenz curves and distributional indicators such as Gini's or Theil's. The architects of the national accounts are well aware of their limitations, but their comments are often disregarded by those who want to read more into GNP than it represents. Apart from ongoing statistical refinements and international coordination, the statisticians have tried to clarify the indicative terminology by moving from the vernacular of 'national income' and 'national product' to the more precise-sounding 'GDP' and by using 'national accounts' rather than 'social accounts'. The latter was previously used by the United Nations, following the work of Stone (1973/75), which was based on the exposition by Hicks (*The Social Framework*, 1942) and others.

The seeming self-checking persuasiveness of this economic system has been the envy of other social scientists, but they have often failed to appreciate that double entry balancing is definitional and is no protection against omissions and double-sided errors. Formal elegance by itself is not enough to extend the accounts into a wider welfare sphere that can yield more profound indicators of development than GNP.

Since the 1970s the eminence of growth, and of GNP as its indicator, have come under closer scrutiny. Two economists, Nordhaus and Tobin (1972: 1), while not the first critics, set the stage for a broader attack:

> A long decade ago economic growth was the reigning fashion of political economy. It was simultaneously the hottest subject of economic theory and research, a slogan eagerly claimed by politicians . . . and a serious objective of the policies of government. The climate of opinion has changed dramatically. Disillusioned critics indict both economic science and economic policy for blind obeisance to aggregate material 'progress', and for neglect of its costly side-effects. Growth, it is charged, distorts national priorities, worsens the distribution of income and irreparably damages the environment . . .

They tried to shift the emphasis from production to consumption through a translation of GDP into a *measure of economic welfare (MEW)*. They added imputed values for leisure, non-market activity and capital services, while deducting instrumental expenditure that is not a direct source of utility (e.g. the 'regrettable necessities' of police and defence) as well as the 'cost of disamenities' (e.g. pollution). Mainly as a result of high imputed values for leisure and non-market activities, based on opportunity costs, estimates of MEW for the United States in the 1960s were two or three times higher than GDP. The increase in the indicator would probably be greater for less developed countries and reduce the gap between rich and poor countries.

Proposals to extend GNP on similar lines have been made under the names of a *measure of net economic welfare (NEW)* (Samuelson, 1973: 145–8) or *net beneficial product* (United Nations Statistical Office, 1974), and attempts have been made in various countries (e.g. Australia, Sweden, Japan) to calculate such a measure. The focus on GNP has also been widened by proposals for a revision of the national accounts system, such as the *integrated economic accounts* of Ruggles and Ruggles (1982), Eisner's *total incomes system of accounts* (1985: 24–8) and Zolotas' book *Declining Social Welfare* (1981).

However, statistical and conceptual problems overwhelm attempts to construct GNP-based extended measures of social development, welfare or similar notions, and frustrate attempts to bridge the gap between economic and social performance by imputations and amputations. Nordhaus and Tobin (1972) themselves described their attempt at constructing a measure of what has been called *macroeconomic welfare* as 'primitive' and 'experimental'. Most commentators accept GNP as valid on its own grounds, but are doubtful about attempts to widen its base meaningfully, including, for instance, assumptions required for valuing housework and leisure time, urban disamenities, capital services and similar aspects (e.g. the comments by T.I. Juster, E.F. Singer and E.F. Denison et al. in Moss, 1973; also Holub, 1983).

One main topic in this early debate was the question of estimating leisure time and housework. It was said that GNP (or GDP) has always included non-monetary estimates for self-consumed produce and owner-occupied rent, thus setting a precedent for other such unpaid-value transactions. Home-grown produce and rent estimates are very much like market transactions; their replacement by money, while boosting GNP, would not affect the rationale of the monetary system. However, by embarking on leisure and unpaid work estimates one enters the realms of fantasy, dressed up in the clothes of might-have-been opportunity cost. It is naive, not to say blasphemous, to suggest that all human activities could or should bear a price ticket, from cooking a meal to helping an old lady cross the street or singing a song; we might leave the task of devising a suitable monetary system for that to someone with the wit of Jonathan Swift.

Since the 1980s criticism of GNP as an indicator has shifted from its neglect of unpaid labour to the area of environmental impact and use of resources, and a new type of *national resource accounting*, parallel to the national income accounts, is being developed in many countries, among them the United States, Canada, Japan, France, Norway and the Netherlands (Repetto et al., 1989). This will be further discussed in section 5.6 on environment. At the same time there has been a revival in attempts to update and improve comprehensive welfare measures of the type developed by Nordhaus and Tobin (1972), Zolotas (1981) or Uno (1988) in Japan

Table 3.1 Daly-Cobb index of sustainable economic welfare, United States

Item		$ billions			% of ISEW		
		1950	1968	1986	1950	1968	1986
(B) Personal consumption		337	634	1155	88	85	148
(C) Distributional inequality index		[109]	[92]	[113]			
(D) Weighted personal consumption (B/C)		309	689	1022	81	92	131
Add							
(E) Services: household labour	+	311	392	494	82	52	63
(F) " consumer durables	+	13	33	80	3	4	10
(G) " streets and highways	+	6	14	18	2	2	2
(H) " public expenditure, health and education	+	1	16	35	0	2	4
Sum of additions (E to H)	+	331	455	627	87	61	80
Deduct:							
(I) Expenditure: consumer durables	-	42	88	212	11	12	27
(J) " defensive health and education	-	3	23	44	1	3	6
(K) " national advertising	-	7	13	21	2	2	3
(L) Cost of: commuting	-	9	17	34	2	2	4
(M) " urbanisation	-	6	19	52	2	3	7
(N) " auto accidents	-	12	21	31	3	3	4
(O) " water pollution	-	9	14	15	2	2	2
(P) " air pollution	-	25	29	22	7	4	3
(Q) " noise pollution	-	2	4	5	1	1	1
(R) Loss of wetlands	-	10	17	21	3	2	3
(S) Loss of farmlands	-	7	19	33	2	3	4
(T) Depletion of non-renewable resources	-	21	30	62	6	4	8
(U) Long-term environmental damage	-	84	151	299	22	20	38
Sum of deductions (I to U)	-	237	445	851	62	59	109
Add:							
(V) Net capital growth	-/+	-26	50	44	-7	7	6
(W) Net change in international position	-/+	4	-1	-63	1	0	-8
Net sum of adjustments (E to W)	+/-	72	59	-243	19	8	-31
Index of sustainable economic welfare (D to W)		381	748	779	100	100	100
ISEW per capita		2488	3734	3403			
GNP per capita		3512	5272	7226	141	141	212
Average annual growth (1950–86): ISEW 2.2%, per capita 0.9% GNP 3.4%, per capita 2.0%							

Note: In billions of $US at constant 1972 prices, except for item C at base 1951 = 100 and the last four lines.
Source: Condensed and adapted from Daly and Cobb (1989: 418–9, table A).

(quoted in Pearce et al., 1989: 109). A prominent example is the *index of sustainable economic welfare (ISEW)* published by Daly and Cobb (1989), which is presented in Table 3.1 as an example of the scope and limits of such composite indicators. The authors describe the purpose of the index as 'a way of measuring the economy that will give a better guidance than GNP to those interested in promoting economic welfare' (p. 401).

The starting point for this index is *personal consumption* in the GNP sense (item B in the table), adjusted for *distributional inequality* by a Gini-type index based on the 1951 = 100 quintile distribution of consumer incomes (item C). That index dropped to 92 in the 1960s and then steadily rose to 113 in 1986, signifying rising income inequality, which is regarded as a sign of reduced economic welfare. It dampened the overall rise in the ISEW from 118% to 88% for 1951–86, or from 134% to 117% for 1950–86.

The main *additions* to personal consumption, as defined for GNP, are stated by Daly and Cobb to be 'household services, such as cooking, cleaning and child care [which] contribute to economic welfare even though they are not sold in the market at an observable price', based on estimates by Eisner (1985) and the Michigan Survey Research Center of time used valued at domestic wage rates (item E). In the earlier years this estimate was equivalent to nearly the whole of the value of personal consumption, and the ratio declined to about one-half more recently because the time spent on such work has apparently not greatly changed, in spite of more use of labour-saving devices, and because wage rates for domestic work seem to have been lagging.

Against this large amount the estimates for the value of other unpaid services (items F, G and H) are not significant if taken in conjunction with respective expenditure (items I and J). Unlike Nordhaus and Tobin (1972), Daly and Cobb do not include an estimate for leisure, because they feel uneasy about this in an environment of perpetual striving, which seems to have diminished the growth of leisure, and also because of the inadequacy of opportunity cost pricing for leisure time. Furthermore, they are sceptical about dominance by large items in an index. That uncertainty also applies to their estimation of unpaid household labour.

The additions for services (items E to H) are of the same magnitude (60–90%) compared to the total index as the thirteen types of *deductions* listed under I to U. Some of the deductions are the result of spinning out capital expenditure from the time it is incurred throughout its useful life (F/I, H/J). Others are for defensive expenditure on health and so on that does not add to economic welfare, and some others for other expenditure of a 'non-useful' type (e.g. advertising, commuting, urbanisation, auto accidents). This list is typical rather than complete, and its valuation is restricted mainly to cash costs without consideration of social implications.

In the listing of the costs of pollution (items O to Q) and land degradation (items R and S), the authors, in keeping with current thinking, have tried to look beyond immediate impact to damage to ecology, aesthetics and so on, but were hampered by the paucity of data for such studies. Their fragility is apparent in the estimates of the cost of air pollution, drawn from a number of sources, which yielded a series of a steady $25 billion in 1950–60, rising to a peak of $30 billion in 1970 and declining to settle around $22 billion in the 1980s, and the cost of water pollution, which rose from $9 billion in 1950 to $15 billion in 1970 and has remained unchanged since, and the cost of noise pollution, which rose from $2 billion in 1950 to $4.5 billion in 1983 at a steady though diminishing rate. These trends hardly reflect the popular impression of rising pollution damage in the United States, unlike the trends in loss of farmlands (item S), based on a combination of urbanisation and effects on soil quality, and loss of wetlands (item R).

The estimate for depletion of non-renewable resources (item T), as a cost borne by future generations, is based on a debatable accounting procedure suggested by El Serafy of the World Bank (in Ahmad, 1988). It takes the amount needed to be set aside from the proceeds of the liquidation of an asset to generate a permanent income stream to correspond to the receipts from the non-renewable assets consumed in the present. Another bold estimate, for long-term environmental damage (item U) in terms of ecological disruption, assumes it to be proportional to the non-renewable energy consumption of fossil and nuclear fuels, calculated as a sort of consumption tax that is credited to a non-interest-bearing fund, similar to the suggested procedure for resource depletion.

More conventional assumptions are made for the *net capital growth* (item V) required to maintain current capital per worker, as being well in excess of needs every year after 1950, and for *net change in the international position* (item W), which at $5 billion per year was relatively low until 1976 but rose to $63 billion in 1986 as a liability for future generations.

Because of the exclusion of an estimate for leisure time and the inclusion of more environmental factors, the Daly–Cobb estimate of ISEW per capita for the United States, unlike the MEW of Nordhaus and Tobin (1972), is less than GNP per capita. The gap between them has been widening, in particular after 1980, when the ISEW, unlike GDP, reached a peak; it fell slightly in subsequent years. As Table 3.1 shows, the GDP additions about doubled between 1950 and 1986; in 1950 they exceeded the deductions, which overtook them in the late 1960s, rising nearly fourfold over the whole period.

Some of the debatable features in the estimation of ISEW items have been mentioned above. Like the MEW there are also more fundamental doubts about the ISEW as an indicator. Described as a guideline to those interested in promoting economic welfare, it seeks to widen the horizon of traditional economic aims while at the same time including only some of the trappings of personal and social welfare ascribed to the quality of life; nor does it justify the label 'sustainable' in its usual meaning of continuance. In its construction the ISEW does not solve the general problem of aggregating indicators of different scales and directions by its method of adding together disparate elements on the basis of money expenditure and present and future costs of disamenities. The dollar-for-dollar equivalence is dubious, and even more so is the presumed linearity in the cost trends of, say, pollution and resource use.

Information on the environment, in particular on the use of natural resources and on the degradation of the environment, is more suitably provided by separate indicators rather than in combination with GNP. Current statistical research by the United Nations and statistical agencies in many countries is therefore directed towards the construction of satellite accounts for such aspects, which are loosely linked with but separate from the traditional system of national accounts (Peskin, 1990).

3.3 Accounts systems

National income studies originated from the search for broad aggregative indicators of the state and movement of development and allied phenomena. In the 1940s, following earlier attempts, R. Stone and others provided a structural explication through an articulated system of *national accounts*. This procedure has since been sometimes reversed by constructing other systems from which summary development indicators can be derived. These indicators may not take the format of a single major aggregate like GNP, but emerge from a collection of articulated tables, or matrices, from which interrelations are calculated in a format that lends itself to interregional analysis, though not so readily to time series comparisons. These systems and their analysis contribute to the better understanding of a process that Wolfe (1981) has called *elusive development* in a book under that title, and they remain the subject of the debate that was initiated in the 1960s by W. Arthur Lewis, Gunnar Myrdal, Raul Prebisch and others and still continues.

Just as development is a complex notion, its partial indicators offer no unambiguous explanations. Also, however impressive the detailed systems may look, the required data are often not available in most countries (e.g. data on lifecycles, time use or wealth holdings). This must be remembered when considering the practicality of the systems mentioned hereunder.

Stone and the Statistical Commission of the United Nations, after pioneering the national accounts (also known as *social accounts*), expanded the notion into the sociodemographic sphere with a *System* (later called *Framework*) *of Social and Demographic Statistics (SSDS–FSDS)* (United Nations, 1979 F/24). This extends the national accounts beyond their core of the monetary flows of economic production, to living conditions, as in the schemes by Fox (1974) and Land (1975). McGranahan and his colleagues from the United Nations Research Institute for Social Development (UNRISD; McGranahan et al., 1972, 1985) made a thorough study of the assessment of socioeconomic development. From a large list they selected the core indicators listed in Table 3.2.

Table 3.2 UNRISD development indicators

Field	Core indicators[a]
Health, demography	* Infant mortality Life expectation at birth
Nutrition	* Animal protein consumption per capita per day
Education	* Literate as % of total population aged 15+ * Primary and secondary enrolment among population aged 5-19
Housing, urbanisation	% of population with reasonable access to water supply
Communications	Newspapers (daily general interest) daily per 1000 population * Telephones per 100 000 population . Television receivers per 100 000 population
Transport, services	* Cars per 1000 population: employment in services
Agriculture	* Agricultural production per male agricultural worker Adult male agricultural workers as % of all adult male labour
Industry	* Apparent consumption of steel per capita (kg) * Energy consumption per capita (coal equivalent)
Foreign trade	Exports plus imports per capita (US$)
Investment, GDP	Annual investment per economically active person (US$) * GDP per capita (purchasers' value) of current population
Employment	Wage/salary earners as % of total economically active Professional/technical workers as % of economically active population

[a] 19 core indicators chosen from 40. For analysis, mainly those marked * are used.

The per capita figures were adjusted for age structure on various equivalence scales (e.g. for three age groups 0-14, 15-64 and 65+; birth rate 0, 1, 0; telephones 1, 3, 1; GNP per capita ½, 1, ⅔. This had significant effects on demographic indicators (e.g. in lowering the unadjusted fertility gap between more and less developed countries). Conventional adjustments for inflation and differing accounting concepts were applied. The indicators were found to be highly correlated; but rather than use standard regression analysis with its assumed static relations between the variables, UNRISD applied *correspondence analysis*, which is based on the median line of the best-fitting curve that will minimise deviations in multidimensional space. These linear or curvilinear reductions are descriptive and analytic rather than express the causal dependency assumptions of regression lines, which they formally resemble. Using an iterative procedure of curve fitting, this method produces profiles and patterns that show to what extent a country is in line with expectations and development elsewhere, and subsequent causality analysis can then try to determine the roles of particular factors in the development process.

Although the emphasis is on correspondence analysis, correlation is used at various stages (e.g. in the selection of data), on the arguable assumption that indicators of different aspects of one field (e.g. education) should be closely related to others in that field. This argument can be turned around into claims that high correlation makes inclusion superfluous and indicators overdetermined. Correlation is also used for weighting in combining indicators into a general index, but no other weighting is applied, as it is thought that the method of rescaling all data from 0 to 100 in ten consecutive steps makes it superfluous. The emphasis in this scheme is on country profiles, but some variants of general indicators were calculated in the UNRISD study that showed that weighting or not weighting the average, and excluding or including GNP, made no great difference in the ranking of 78 countries. The rank order correlation of the composite index with GDP was a high 0.95 taken overall, but this index ranked less developed countries relatively higher than GDP did.

The International Development Strategy, which was the action program of the United Nations for the Second Development Decade beginning in 1970, listed a number of development goals, such as opportunity to all for a better life, more equitable income distribution, raised employment levels, and better facilities for education, health and so on. However, its belief in the pre-eminent importance of national product growth was underlined by setting a definite target of an increase of 6% per year for the gross product of developing countries, or an average annual rise of 3½% per capita on the basis of population growth of 2½% per year.

Land (1975) has applied demographic accounts and macrodynamic social-indicator models to the evolution of social conditions in the United States in the postwar era, in a form suited to the simulation analysis of an array of social and economic conditions. His notion of the lifespace of the individual includes objective physical and social conditions, as well as a subjective value context of beliefs and life satisfaction, within a sociological lifecycle that progresses from family and schooling to employment, income and consumption. Indicators can be attached for sequential and causal analysis, using lifecycle, cohort data, regression and correlation techniques.

A fairly simple demographic system is being prepared by the Netherlands Central Bureau of Statistics (Koesoebjono et al., 1989). It takes the form of a transition matrix, which shows population in households, divided into major age groups, and follows them through from preschool to full time education into full time employment, with allowance for mortality and migration flows to balance opening and closing stocks. Socio-demographic accounts on societal participation and mobility in the Netherlands are also being developed by the Central Bureau of Statistics.

A nominal national policy model, based on a matrix of indicators of basic goals and activities, can also be constructed on the lines of Tinbergen's theory of economic policy. This requires the valuation of human capital and time use and utility assumptions of the type proposed by Fox (1974) and Van Moeseke (1985).

3.4 Ordinal evaluation

A simple but striking method to indicate development trends has been used by Zapf and his colleagues from the University of Mannheim (1977, 1987; Diewald, 1984). It is a linear additive model with ordinal scaling for comparison with previous periods in terms of +, – or = signs and with summaries covering longer periods and groups of items (see Table 3.3). The *SPES* or *Sozialpolitisches Entscheidungs- und Indikatorensystem für die Bundesrepublik Deutschland* (Diewald, 1984) in its abridged version lists nearly 200 indicators, ranging from demography and social status to income and participation. Most are based on objective-type statistics and a few on perception (e.g. complaints about noise, satisfaction with the political system). The indicators are related to desired standards, as laid down by the government or other authorities, and the indicators are attached to this goal catalogue. The scoring of +, – or = applies to changes over 5 year periods from 1950 onward, and is then described as +, – or = trend and separately evaluated as representing +, – or = welfare development. Population and social status indicators are excluded from the latter, and some indicators (e.g. unemployment, short time work, accident rates) are treated as negatives.

Table 3.3   SPES indicator tableaux, West Germany

Period	National product per capita	Victims of traffic accidents	Proportion of students from working class families	Index of health satisfaction	Participation of voters in federal elections
1950–55	+	+			
1955–60	+	+	=		+
1960–65	+	–	+		=
1965–70	+	+	+	–	=
1970–75	+	–	+	+	=
1975–82	+	–		=	=
Trend 1975–82	+	≈	+	=	
Welfare assessment:					
1950–82	++	=	++	=	=
1975–82	+	=		=	–

Source: Diewald (1984, table 2).

Simple aggregation of the signs indicates some general features: an excess of + over – signs for most goal areas in 7 year periods, with minor exceptions mainly in transport (through higher cost and stress) and health (growing accident rate). The overall score of signs was positive in every period but declined, from 41 to 26, in the early 1980s due to greater unemployment and a halt in the improvement of working conditions, as well as to greater consumption of alcohol and cigarettes.

There are obvious limitations for analysis. The directions tell us nothing about the variable intervals of ordinal scaling; for victims of traffic accidents successive movements of +, –, +, – between 1955 and 1975 mask a rise from 6.9 to 7.4 in the period. There is also the question of weighting for relative importance. Is a change in income or working hours equivalent to one in cigarette consumption or voter turnout? Various options, illustrated in Table 3.4, offer themselves: *cardinalisation*, as suggested by Drewnowski (1974):

1 Establish for each series minimum, median and optimal points and apply weights that decrease with marginal utility.
2 Less elaborately, give twice as much weight to – than to + changes so as to highlight deterioration after rising pressure over recent past.
3 Provide an even increase to both + and – signs over time to give preference to the present.
4 Use a combination of 2 and 3.

More weight to deterioration accentuates the aggregate downward trend since 1960, while priority to recent periods keeps it rising until 1975. The combination of options 2 and 3 produces a pattern close to the unweighted one. Social reporting in Germany is further discussed by Zapf and his colleagues in the journal *Social Indicators Research* (1987), and recent modifications to the domains of the SPES indicator tableaux are discussed by Wiegand (1988) in the same journal.

Table 3.4   SPES indicator tableaux: summary (+ less –) scores

Type of model	Weightings in periods										Scores in periods				
	Improvements					Deteriorations					1955/60	1960/65	1965/70	1970/75	1975/80
1 Linear additive	1	1	1	1	1	1	1	1	1	1	28	41	35	36	26
2 Linear critical	1	1	1	1	1	2	2	2	2	2	1	23	13	8	3
3 Present preference	1	2	3	4	5	1	2	3	4	5	28	82	105	144	130
4 2 and 3 combined	1	1½	2	2½	3	1	2	3	4	5	28	53	48	48	32

Source: Zapf (1978) updated with Diewald (1984).

3.5 Basic needs

Turning from general development to the situation of the most deprived sectors, the World Conference on Employment initiated in 1976 a Basic Needs Strategy for the provision of a minimum of goods and services in the context of basic human rights. This includes the participation of people in decisions affecting them and the right to employment both as a means to earn income and as an end to gain satisfaction. An overall indicator of basic needs could be attempted as a conflation of differently based component series, but on conceptual and statistical grounds it remains something like a hybrid.

This is illustrated by the example in Table 3.5 (adapted from R. Horn, 1980). Nine major areas of expenditure are listed in terms of dollars spent by individuals or families in a stated period, and direct or proxy indicators are attached to each item, which are compared with a chosen standard of respective minimal needs. Needs fulfilment is expressed as percentage of the target or on an ordinal scale. The extent of fulfilment, or shortfall, is then aggregated. A number of qualitative dimensions can also be incorporated. Weighting by urgency or qualitative standards can be applied. The scheme could also be used for interitem, interdimensional and other structural analysis.

This scheme, and others like it, amplify indicators of quantified needs with qualitative features (e.g. What good are schools or hospitals to persons who have no access to them because they are too far or too dear?), and they can be adjusted for time and place with flexible weights. However,

Table 3.5 Model of basic needs dimensions

	Food	Clothing	Shelter	Water	Fuel	Light	Health	Education	Other[a]	Total
Annual use:										
Quantity										
Cost ($)										
Basic need										
% shortfall										
Ratings:										
Quality										
Access										
Distribution										
Participation										
Self-reliance										
Public provision										
Aggregate rating										

[a] Transport, utensils, drink, smokes, leisure, ceremonial . . .

it must be remembered that they point to directions rather than provide accurate measures. The notion of poverty zones can be extended to more general ordinal grading of development and welfare measures.

Drewnowski (1974) has proposed an index for *level of living* and another one for *state of welfare* on such a basis. The former, which is suitable for historical and intercountry comparisons, divides human needs into a series of material and non-material types, similar to the example above, and attaches at least three cardinal indicators (e.g. calory intake) or ordinal grades of satisfaction. The cardinal scales are ordinalised by choosing three critical points that divide the indicator range into four zones, for example:

O point	M point	A point
No satisfaction	Minimum requirement	Full satisfaction
4 Intolerable	3 Inadequate 2 Adequate	1 Affluent

Critical points can be set with flexible dimensions. For instance, Drewnowski suggests for calorie intake to put the O point at 60%, M at 100% and A at 133% of the Food and Agriculture Organisation (FAO) norm, or for leisure to put the O point at 0–3460 hours free from work per year, M at 6336 hours and A at 6816 hours. A Gini coefficient of concentration can be attached to these values by multiplying them by (1 – Gini). Weights can be derived from the priority ratings of policy makers, or else from unfilled need by using the difference from 1 of respective indicators.

This index of level of living can be supplemented by another related to state of welfare, for which Drewnowski has suggested three major categories: somatic status for physiological development, educational status for mental development, and social status for social integration and participation. This index also is based on a combination of cardinal and ordinal measures.

Various other schemes have been devised for the analysis, planning and monitoring of socioeconomic development with the help of indicators. Among these are the proposals by Adelman and Morris (1971), Land (1975 and subsequently), Fox (1974) and Khan (1979), as well as the various contributors to the volumes edited by Baster (1972), Moss (1973) and Chenery (1974). They use different datasets, apply different multivariate techniques (e.g. factor, discriminant, taxonomical or cluster analysis), and take more or less cautious attitudes to aggregation. For the present we will look only at some types of indicative measurement for purposes related to development.

3.6 Income distribution

Classical economists like Edwin Cannan have referred to the distribution question as the major end of economic enquiry, and the distribution of income and wealth within a country and in comparison with other countries has long been a major topic in discussion about economic development and welfare. The interest in this area has obvious ideological overtones of social and political reform. It is usually directed, implicitly or explicitly, by the assumption that greater equality is preferable to inequality, and much is made of general slogans calling for justice and fairness. However, this does not specify a desirable target point for distribution indicators, as the demand for greater equality is not usually pressed to the point of equal shares for all.

Furthermore, in development the call for greater equality was given a time horizon by adherents of the *trickle-down effect,* who thought (in the 1960s, and perhaps some still do) that large income inequalities with a resultant high rate of saving are necessary for growth and will eventually justify income redistribution. Finally, in welfare economics there is debate about the relation between personal and social welfare functions and the ethical measurement of inequality (Sen, 1982).

Indicators are required to describe both the state and the direction of distribution. We refer in the first instance to money income, which can be graphed as a *bar chart* where the width of the bars is scaled according to income intervals, or by way of a *Lorenz curve,* drawn in a square with equidistant scaling for income units as a percentage of income and number of recipients. Income equality on a Lorenz curve would be expressed as a diagonal line, but usually the number of low income earners exceeds their share in total income, and so the income curve is concave. The size of the area between the Lorenz curve and the equal income diagonal indicates the extent of income inadequacy. This is the *Gini coefficient,* which varies from 0 for income equality to 1 for maximum inequality (where one person receives all income). The Gini formula is based on the number in each income class and is widely used in income analysis.

Such usage does not apply to some of the more refined versions proposed by Atkinson (1975), which express inequality in terms of the lowest rank, or by Theil (1954), based on the weighted average of inequalities, or by Van Ginneken (1980), based on the variance of logarithms. These variations have special applications in sectoral analysis, but they are all based on the same database and on *ad hoc* definitions of the monetary income of individuals, families or households, including or excluding taxes.

This approach has been criticised on the grounds of the uncertain relations of monetary changes to social welfare (Atkinson, 1975; Blackorby and Russell, 1978). There is also the question of weighting, as illustrated in Table 3.6.

In this example income per capita rises from an average of $100 for the lowest earners to $480 for the top earners. The lower half only earns a quarter of all income (a). An overall rise in (disposable) income of 10% (through growth or tax measures) would leave the distribution unchanged if it accrued proportionally to every earner, as in (b). However, if it were gained in equal amounts by each quartile (or earner in quartile), as in (c), it would lift the share of the lower half from 25% to 27% at the expense of the share of the upper half. This effect can be heightened by *poverty weighting,* which means applying greater weight for low incomes in the

Table 3.6   Income distribution by quartiles

	1st	2nd	3rd	4th	Total
Number of taxpayers	25	25	25	25	100
(a) Income total	$2 500	$4 000	$8 000	$12 000	$26 500
Income per capita	$100	$160	$320	$480	$265
(b) Income total increased by 10% per capita/quartile	$2 750	$4 440	$8 800	$13 200	$29 150
(c) Income total increased by 10% ($2650) distributed equally per capita/quartile	$3 162.5	$4 662.5	$8 662.5	$12 662.5	$29 150
Poverty weight	0.44	0.28	0.17	0.11	1
(d) Income total increased by weighted portion of 10% ($2650)	$3 666	$4 742	$8 450.5	$12 291.5	$29 150
Income share: (a) and (b)	9.4%	15.1%	30.2%	45.3%	100%
(c)	10.8%	16.0%	29.7%	43.4%	100%
(d)	12.6%	16.3%	29.0%	42.2%	100%

distribution of the increase. In the example a range of weights from 0.44 to 0.11 is applied to the increment of $2650 in (d); the two lower quartiles gain even more than from the money-equal distribution (c) and now have 12.6% and 16.3% respectively (i.e. 29%) of total income as against 9.4% and 15.1% respectively in the original situation. This means that the gap between low and high earners is reduced, though still substantial.

Of course, if it is argued that an extra dollar is worth more to the poor than to the rich, even the marginal gain of $10 for the lowest class under the proportional distribution (b) could have a greater utility value than the $48 gained by those in the top quartile. However, the slope of the utility curve is the great unknown in redistribution, and we can only say in general terms that an increase across the board is likely to be more beneficial to low than to high earners and that this effect is heightened by differential weighting.

Taking actual income distribution, a World Bank survey (Chenery, 1974) suggested that growth rates in eleven less developed countries varied from 5% to 9%. In their comparison, indexes with equal or poverty weights yielded lower growth rates than proportional weighting, suggesting that growth was strongest for high incomes, but in another four countries the reverse relation applied. Such weighting of income distribution on a reasonable base can sharpen indicative trends, but it must be remembered that the assumptions are fairly arbitrary; nor do they remedy the shortcomings that apply to any income series as sole indicator of growth.

An international project for the application of income statistics to the analysis of income inequalities was initiated in 1983 under the name of Luxembourg Income Study. It was originally for seven countries but has

Table 3.7 Distribution of net family income among quintiles of families (%)

Quintile	Australia	Canada	Germany	Norway	Sweden	UK	USA
1st (lowest)	8	8	7	10	11	9	6
2nd	11	13	13	15	16	14	13
3rd	14	18	16	18	19	18	18
4th	23	24	21	23	23	23	24
5th (highest)	43	37	43	34	31	36	39
Gini coefficient	0.31	0.30	0.34	0.24	0.21	0.27	0.33
Redistribution factor[a]	13.1	8.6	3.4	15.9	17.7	8.1	12.1
Quintile span[b]	5.4	4.6	6.1	3.4	2.8	4.0	6.5

[a] Gini gross less net income as % of gross coefficient.
[b] Highest divided by lowest quintile values.
Source: Data for 1981/82, adapted from Saunders and Hobbes (1988, table 4).

since extended to about twice that number (Saunders, 1988; Smeeding, 1990), all more or less developed market economies. The country series are standardised for family size by using an equivalence scale of 0.5 for the first unit, 0.25 for each unit from the second to the ninth, and 3 for all units with ten or more members, applied to both individual and family income, net of income tax. Table 3.7 is based on these assumptions.

Income distribution, as expressed in separate quintiles, in the difference between the lowest and highest quintile, and in the Gini coefficient, is most equal in Norway and Sweden, rather less so in the United Kingdom, Canada and Australia, and least equal in the United States. The redistribution factor, based on the difference of Gini coefficients for gross and net income, provides a similar picture whereby the most pronounced income redistribution through direct taxes occurs in the two Scandinavian countries, but it is also relatively high in Australia and the United States.

These country differences are also reflected in the source composition of income, where government cash benefits provide 29% of gross income in Sweden, as against 8% in the United States, with respective taxes equivalent to 28% and 17% (Table 3.8).

If unit records are available, the technique of *microanalytic simulation* (Orcutt, 1986) can be used to predict changes in income distribution. It involves a process known as 'static adjustment ageing' for demographic changes and has been applied with satisfactory results for projections up to 5 years ahead in the United States.

Some recent critics of income equivalence scales to measure inequality maintain that they should not be based on the utility functions of household members and their putative needs, irrespective of the demographic

Table 3.8   Income sources and taxes as % of average gross income

	Australia		Canada		Germany		Norway		Sweden		UK		USA	
Wages/salaries	70		76		63		70		65		72		76	
Self-employment/ property	<u>19</u>	89	<u>12</u>	88	<u>18</u>	81	<u>14</u>	84	<u>6</u>	71	<u>7</u>	79	<u>12</u>	88
Government cash benefits		9		9		17		14		29		17		8
Total, including Other		100		100		100		100		100		100		100
Income tax		19		15		15		19		28		14		17
Social security contribution[a]	<u>0</u>	19	<u>0</u>	15	<u>8</u>	23	<u>6</u>	25	<u>1</u>	29	<u>3</u>	17	<u>4</u>	21
Net income		81		85		77		75		71		83		79

[a] **Employees.**

Source: Data for 1981/82, adapted from Saunders (1988, table 2).

composition of the population and of the uneven incidence of non-income factors. Instead they try to relate inequality to *societal well-being* (Paglin, 1975). One such proposal uses a *norm income*, said to correspond to a socially desired minimum degree of inequality. This norm income replaces the 45° line when calculating the Gini coefficient for the discrepancy from the actual distribution. Setting the norm allows for a multivariate approach for demographic, educational and other differences, rather than the univariate weighting for dependents of equivalence scales. In practice, however, the introduction of social utility variables might create its own problems, and this approach has not, or not yet, been widely tested and accepted.

3.7 Poverty

Poverty has been recognised as a major economic and social problem for centuries. It has many aspects beyond the economic test of insufficient means to meet a set standard of needs. Here we will look at poverty mainly in the context of income structure, but note that non-monetary factors such as the political, social, cultural and psychological dimensions play a major part in this field and that, as with the assessment of basic needs, their neglect can confound intra- and intercountry comparisons. This also applies to the *social wage*, which consists of the benefits of free or subsidised public services in the fields of health, education, culture, transport and so on. For instance, we would expect the social wage to be worth more to low than to high earners, or to add more to all incomes in poorer than in richer countries.

Let us first consider a current view on poverty, in the context of development programs, which can perhaps be regarded as successor to the trickle-down theory. Heller (1988), a staff member of the International Monetary Fund (IMF), has looked at the effect on the poor of seven IMF-supported adjustment programs in America, Africa and Asia with respect to exchange rates, taxes, public spending, wage restraint, deregulation, and prices and monetary policy. The impact of the programs on the poverty situation varied so much between countries and between the short and long terms that no definite conclusions can be drawn. This is not surprising, seeing that the IMF's mandate objective is to help member countries to maintain or restore internal and external financial balance compatible with sustainable growth. If the economy needs adjustment to 'live within its means', distributional effects and social impact are given what the IMF calls 'proper weight', but they seem to run second to its main aim. At least it sounds like a change of emphasis from the World Bank's earlier slogan of 'redistribution with growth' (Chenery, 1974).

In 1990 the World Bank issued its *World Development Report on Poverty*, with economic and social indicators for 121 developing nations. It is oriented towards economic growth, to be promoted by more productive use of labour and greater provision for basic social services in the areas of health, education and nutrition. The report noted an overall improvement in the developing world between 1965 and 1985, at least in terms of life expectancy, child mortality and educational attainment. Comprehensive analytical reports on poverty in the United States continue to be published by the Russell Sage Foundation in New York.

The academic/political debate on poverty has focused in recent years on alternative viewpoints: *subsistence*, where poverty is determined by an absolute minimum standard (a view now often identified with Sen, 1982), as against the *relativist* notion (associated with Townsend et al., 1979), which compares the poverty situation with a country's general standards. The distinction is politically important because the subsistence view of a poverty line encourages conservative governments to restrict income redistribution to provide income support only up to that low level. This view is inherent in the writings of B. Seebohm Rowntree and Molly Orshansky, while Townsend's relativist approach is shared by Martin Rein (1970) and A.B. Atkinson (1975).

It would be simplistic to identify poverty with a fixed proportion, say the lowest decile of income recipients. This sounds like saying that the poor will always be with us or that, as history shows, a segment of the population (e.g. 10% or 5%) will always live in poverty, perhaps because of their own, or the system's, inadequacies. Income partitioning would be going too far if it were claimed that those in the lowest decile are always 'poor' and those in the top decile 'rich' and concluded that those in the lowest decile in a prosperous country are as well or badly off as their counterparts in a less developed area. Additional indicators are required to circumscribe poverty. Townsend, in his study of poverty in the United Kingdom (Townsend et al., 1979), constructed a *deprivation index*, based on a multifactorial analysis of national expectations and practices for 60 indicators of living styles ranging from diet and housing to working conditions and recreations. However, his findings that in 1979 a quarter of UK households were in poverty have thrown doubt on an indicator that mixes disparate items and dimensions such as taste.

Statistically, problems of poverty assessment extend from setting a poverty line to identifying the poor and the intensity of poverty they suffer. A number of indicators can be used for this purpose:

- The *head count* measure gives the number of persons below the poverty line as a proportion of total population. It does not show the extent of income shortfall nor of income inequality among the poor, nor relative movements of income below the poverty line.
- The *poverty gap* measure, used by the US administration, shows the percentage shortfall of the average income of the poor, related either to the poverty line or to average income. It registers when the poor become poorer, but is insensitive to changes in their proportion in the community and to income transfers from poor to less poor persons.
- Sen (1973) has proposed a *combination* of the head count and poverty gap measures with an indicator of income distribution among the poor. His complex formula would register relative deprivation at various income levels.
- Kakwani (1980: ch. 15) in another version shows the percentage of income required to lift the income of the poor. It thus centres on *redistribution* from the top down in terms of income rather than persons.
- Hamada and Takayama (discussed in Sen, 1978) have suggested a revised income-distribution statistic that uses the poverty line as a standard of *needs fulfilment* and treats all those above the line as being just on the line. The Gini coefficient then refers to poverty below this norm. While this measure would show the extent and distribution of poverty, it fails, as the head count measure does, the *monotonicity test*, 'which requires that any income reduction for the poor should increase the poverty measure'. In this case an increase in the number of those below the line but above the poverty average would reduce the (Gini) poverty index.
- Kakwani (1984) has proposed a *general deprivation curve* based on the Lorenz curve–Gini coefficient and the equiproportional principle that, if all incomes rise in the same proportion, the index will not change— or to put it otherwise, that a rise in the income of the rich, with the income of the poor remaining unchanged, would increase the poverty indicator. This is not reflected in the Sen, Kakwani, and Hamada–Takayama measures described above.
- Other poverty measures, based on welfare functions and using ordinal weighting, have been constructed in recent years, such as the *index of*

malnutrition by Kakwani (1986) or *index of undernourishment* by Sen and Sengupta (1983, described by Kakwani).

The discussion of income distribution and poverty in terms of 'welfare economics', on the lines of Sen, Atkinson and others mentioned in this and the previous sections, continues, for example, in the book *Ethical Social Index Numbers* by Chakrarty (1990). However, it requires an 'ordering' for social evaluation and the Lorenz curve, which is a theoretical construct rather than a prescription for indicator building.

3.8 Levels of living

Going beyond the minimal requirements of basic needs and poverty relief, many attempts have been made to define an *adequate level of living* or, to use the cognate term, *welfare*. This is a multifarious endeavour because it depends so much on social and cultural factors, but indicators can throw some light on broad interrelations, temporal changes and interregional patterns. The components, however disparate, fit into a matrix that may link, for example, housing needs with political freedom or friendship attachments. At the least we can list components to which indicators can be attached, which in turn will specify the concept more definitely. This can be illustrated by looking at the alternative faces of one such aspect, namely conditions of work:

• wage rate, normal working hours, incidence of and pay for overtime;
• job security, rights on dismissal, unionisation;
• perceived satisfaction with job, employer and workmates;
• physical/intellectual demands, pre- and in-training.

As a general example of levels of living components, Table 3.9 presents successive lists compiled by the United Nations Statistical Office (1954/ 1961). Johan Galtung and his colleagues from the universities of Oslo and the United Nations take a more generous view of people's needs in society (Table 3.10). Eric Allard has surveyed the dimensions of welfare in Scandinavian countries under the characteristic title of *Having—Loving— Being* (see 1976; also Erikson, 1977). He used about 4000 interviews in Denmark, Sweden, Norway and Finland, applying factor analysis and similar techniques to show differences between groups, regions and so on (Table 3.11).

Single series are often quoted to generalise on changes or differences in living conditions, notably electricity consumption, car ownership, number of telephones, number of video or television sets, house space, and number of doctors or hospital beds—or, in a more imaginative mode, days of sunshine, area of national parks, crime rates, or number of bookshops or libraries. Such indicators provide a random glimpse of aspects of the living environment, and they may or may not be considered typical of

Table 3.9   Components of levels of living

1954 version	1961 version
Health, including demographic condition	Health
Food and nutrition	Food, consumption and nutrition
Education, including literacy and skills	Education
Conditions of work	Employment and conditions of work
Employment situation	
Aggregate consumption and saving	
Transportation	
Housing, including house facilities	
Clothing	Clothing
Recreation and entertainment	Recreation
Social security	Social security
Human freedom	Human freedom
	Background items:
	Labour force
	Income and expenditure
	Communications and transportation

Source: United Nations Statistical Office (1954/1961).

Table 3.10   Basic material and non-material needs

Category	Values: Basic material and non-material needs Needs and/or rights		Goods/services
Security		Individual/collective against accident, war	Security
Welfare	Physiological	Nutrition, water, sleep, movement, air	Food, water, clothes
	Ecological	Climatic/somatic protection, health, privacy	Shelter, medical
	Sociocultural	Self-expression, dialogue, education	Schooling
Freedom	Mobility	Rights to travel, to express and impress	Transport, communication
	Politics	Rights of consciousness formation, mobilisation	Meetings, media, parties, election
	Legal	Rights of due process of law	Courts
	Work	Rights to work	Jobs
	Choice	Rights to choose, occupation, spouse, residence	

(continues)

Table 3.10   *(continued)*

Category		Values: Basic material and non-material needs	
		Needs and/or rights	Goods/services
Identity	Related to self	Need for self-expression, creativity	Hobbies, leisure
		Need for self-actualisation, realising potential	Leisure, vacation
	Individual needs	Need for well-being, happiness, joy	Vacation
		Need for sense of purpose, life meaning	Religion, ideology
	Relation to others	Need for affection, love, sex, spouse, offspring	Primary groups
	Collective needs	Needs for roots, belongingness, association	Secondary groups
	Relation to society	Need to be active, to be subject	
	Social needs	Need to understand one's life, social transparence	
		Need for challenge, for new experiences	
	Relation to nature	Need for partnership relation with nature	

Source: Adapted from Galtung and Wirak (1977).

Table 3.11   Welfare/happiness and level of living/quality of life

Category	Welfare	Happiness
Level of living	Needs for which satisfaction is defined by impersonal or material resources (e.g. *'having'* income, housing, health, education, etc.)	Subjective evaluation of individual's satisfaction with material living conditions. *Dissatisfaction attitudes:* discrimination, perceived antagonism, unjust privileges
Quality of life	Needs for which satisfaction is defined by relations to others and society (e.g. *'loving'*, family, friends, *'being'*, personal prestige, insubstitutability, doing)	Subjective evaluation of individual's satisfaction with own human and social relations. *Satisfaction attitudes:* perceived need satisfaction, perceived happiness

Source: Adapted from Allard (1976).

the whole picture. They can be useful as a shortcut to distinguish major features of suburbs and regions, but are usually less valid for comparisons between countries with different socioeconomic structures.

Some of those indicators refer to expenditure, complementary to personal income statistics. Both approaches can be combined by relating the cost of consumer goods to income received. For example, it may be claimed that in country X a bicycle or television set costs 2 months' pay for an 'average worker', while in country Y it costs 6 months' pay, suggesting that workers in X are three times better off than their counterparts in Y. Perhaps they are a lot better off, but before drawing such conclusions it is necessary to know whether the series are comparable, to what extent cash wages in either country are supplemented by a social wage of low rents, free health care or subsidised transport, and also what is the relation of prices for bicycles or televisions to prices of other consumer goods.

Another version of this approach involves pricing a shopping list for particular items for comparisons over time, between localities or even between countries. This is an improvement over selecting only a single item if the list represents a reasonable sample of consumer spending at local or regional levels. It is similar to purchasing-power-parity calculations for foreign exchange comparisons, which will be discussed in section 4.5.

3.9 Human development

Physical features have sometimes been used as historical indicators of social development. For example, human biologists have suggested that a relation exists between the height and weight of children and their social class, on the evidence of nineteenth-century records of the heights of British navy recruits (Floud, 1983). These were drawn mainly from the urban poor and were below average for their age, although their height and nutritional state greatly improved in the industrial revolution throughout the first half of that century.

Records of convict transportation of juveniles to New South Wales at that time have also been used to show that they were of relatively small size, though perhaps no smaller than British non-convict boys of a comparative low socieconomic status. Their Australian-born descendants were taller and of what has been claimed to be 'a higher mental and moral structure' than their forebears (Gandevia, 1977; Nicholas and Shergold, 1982).

For modern analysis, Morris for the Oversea Development Council has proposed an index for the *physical quality of life*, based on equally weighted life expectancy at year 1, infant mortality and literacy. This seems a *jejune* collection, partly interrelated and barely covering what is usually understood by physical quality of life.

More recently an improved version has been published by the United Nations Development Program under the title *Human Development Index*

(1990), based on a combination of life expectancy at birth, adult literacy and GDP per capita. Its rationale is stated as follows:

> Human development is a process of enlarging people's choices. The most critical of these wide-ranging choices are to live a long and healthy life, to be educated and to have access to resources needed for a decent standard of living. Additional choices include political freedom, guaranteed human rights and personal self-respect . . .
>
> The choices people make are their own concern. But the process of development should at least create a conducive environment for people . . . to develop their full potential.

It appears that health and knowledge represent the formation of such capabilities, and income the extent of choice for their application.

The index uses the range between the highest and lowest ranking from an array of 130 countries to set minimum and maximum values for life expectancy and adult literacy (Table 3.12). In the case of GDP the range lies between the lowest recorded for any country and the 'official poverty line', stated in logarithms to express diminishing returns in the conversion of income into the fulfilment of human needs. However, about one-third of the listed countries that had GDP per capita (in purchasing-power-parity terms) of over $4862 were rated 0 for deprivation (and 1 for development). Equal index steps make increments in index numbers equiproportional in absolute numbers but cause them to fall in relative weight. For example, increases in life expectancy from 42 years to 52 years and 62 years raise that partial index by 24% and 19% respectively. The mean of the three partial indexes yields the *human deprivation index* (on a scale of 0 to 1), and its difference from 1 (referred to as its inverse or reciprocal) has been called the *human development index (HDI)*. For example, out of 130 countries in 1987 Brazil had a life expectancy of 65 years, adult literacy of 78% and GDP of $4300, yielding partial indexes of 0.35, 0.26 and 0.04 respectively, giving an average of 0.216 for the deprivation index and 0.784 for the HDI, and ranking Brazil 80th on the HDI list or 5 points below its GDP ranking.

Table 3.12 Human development index: minimum and maximum values, 1985–87

Indicator	Minimum		Maximum	
	Value	Country	Value	Country
Life expectancy at birth (years)	42	Sierra Leone	78	Japan
Adult literacy rate (%)	12	Somalia	99	Many European
Real GDP per capita ($)	220	Zaire	4861	Set top value

Source: United Nations Development Program (1990).

Table 3.13   Human development index: various countries from list of 130 countries, 1987

Indicator/index	Sierra Leone	Somalia	Zaire	Sri Lanka	USA	Nether- lands	Japan
Life expectancy at birth (years)	42	46	53	71	76	77	78
Adult literacy rate (%)	30	12	62	87	96	99	99
Real GDP per capita ($)	480	1 000	220	2 053	17 615	12 661	13 125
Human development index (0 to 1)	0.15	0.20	0.29	0.79	0.96	0.98	0.996
Ranking:							
HDI	4	7	20	83	112	127	130
GDP	27	23	5	38	129	117	126
HDI – GDP	–23	–16	+15	+45	–17	+10	+4

Source: United Nations Development Program (1990).

Table 3.13 shows values for a selection of countries for 1987, in which instance the HDI ranged from 0.116 for Niger to 0.996 for Japan. The relative importance of the three component series is evident from their mutual equivalence rates (Table 3.14).

Rises in the HDI reflect attainments, and falls retrogression. By using diminishing proportional increments and logarithm values for income it presumes declining marginal gains. It neglects distribution probably because data such as Gini coefficients are not available for many countries, and paucity of data is also probably the reason for the omission of factors such as human rights, insecurity and discrimination for human development.

Apart from omissions due to non-availability of data, the index seems to suffer from other inherent weaknesses that limit its usefulness. Its first edition refers to a mixture of 1987 statistics for life expectancy and real GDP and 1985 statistics for literacy. It would be difficult to use it as a

Table 3.14   Scale equivalence ratios for the human deprivation and human development indexes

Life expectancy: (at birth)	42 years ≃	Literacy rate:	12.3% ≃	Real GDP:	$ 220
	52 years ≃		36.8% ≃	(per capita)	$1500
	62 years ≃		60.5% ≃		$2950
	72 years ≃		100% ≃		$4860

Source: Calculated from United Nations Development Program (1990).

base for a time series because in many countries literacy rates and life expectancy data are not available annually. Literacy, in spite of the coordinating efforts by UNESCO, is difficult to define in any census. More important, both literacy and life expectancy change only slowly and then usually in an upward direction, which might give real GDP the lead part in fluctuations and diminish the significance of the HDI as a separate indicator. Also, assumptions about equivalence for differently scaled components are always debatable. Here it appears that income gains progressively greater weight than life expectancy, at least up to the cut-off point of $4860, which is exceeded by about a quarter of the listed countries, and that the relative weight of life expectancy rises more rapidly than that of literacy for less developed countries. Also, in developed countries literacy is close to its peak of 99, and so perhaps is life expectancy beyond 76 years. Therefore the United States by admitting to a slightly lower literacy rate, 96/99, is ranked only 112/130, although it has the top income rate of $17 615 as against Japan with $13 125, which country tops the HDI list.

In general, the index is suitable only for ranking low development countries. However, the United Nations Development Program report also contains other tabulations on mortality, military expenditure, urban population, nutrition and child health for a large number of countries, which can be used to expand the background of the HDI.

In seeking to test the claim that the social, unlike the economic, standard of the United States declined between 1961 and 1966, Spautz (1977) constructed an index by taking five to seven series each in the categories of health, education, welfare, racial parity and morale. Using an unweighted mean and reversing ratios for poverty rates and so on, the major series in his *index of economic health* rose by up to 25% over 10 years, except for a fall in 'morale' due to rising crime, divorce and suicide rates.

3.10 Quality of life

> Quality of Life, though impossible to define to everyone's satisfaction, is a concept that elicits much interest and stimulates much research. Most people have a strong personal interest in their own life quality, and often an active concern for . . . family members and friends. Also . . . compelling involvement with the quality of life is central in the work of many professionals: sociologists, psychologists, economists, politicians . . .

With these words Andrews (1976: ix) introduced a volume on *Research on the Quality of Life*, with contributors from the Institute for Social Research at the University of Michigan and others prominent in the field. More recently the work by Michalos, as editor of and contributor (with others) to the journal *Social Indicators Research*, now restyled as an *International and Interdisciplinary Journal of Quality-of-Life Measurement*, is an indicator of the current vigorous interest and research effort in this area. We have already dealt with some allied and overlapping concepts, such as levels of living and needs fulfilment, and will restrict ourselves here to a few aspects of interest for measurement.

Consider first a *quality-of-life index* proposed by Johnston (1988). It is based on the annual percentage changes of a fairly conservative choice of 21 objective indicators in nine major areas of social concern, such as health, employment, public safety and so on, classified as being either favourable (e.g. a rise in life expectancy) or unfavourable (e.g. rise in the unemployment rate). The special feature of the index is the application of individual *multipliers* selected pragmatically to even out the observed variabilities of the indicators and to express their changes on a common scale. This scale runs from –50 to +50 but in some cases differs for favourable and unfavourable changes (e.g. 50 for plus and 100 for minus in life expectancy at birth, or 80 and 40 respectively for percentage of families intact). For 336 indicator changes in 21 domains in the United States from 1969/70 to 1984/85, positive (157) and nil (13) movements were about the same as negative ones (166); but taking into account the frequency and amplitude of changes, more weight was given on balance to negative multipliers (376) than to positive ones (300). This seems to correspond to the prevailing view on growth indicators that falls are more significant than equiproportional rises.

An analysis of mean scores in terms of average annual change shows a decline of 3% in 1969-74, a rise of 2½% in 1974-79, a drop of 10% in 1979-82, followed by a recovery of 8½% in 1982-85. The main increases right over the 16 years were in the areas of health and education, and in equality of blacks and whites, while there were major declines in family stability and public safety and rises in poverty. A comparison with disposable income series suggests that economic performance dominated the index in boom (1983/84) and recession (1973/74, 1979/80) years but not at other times when economic performance was not a good predictor for index changes.

The example quoted above, and earlier ones about living levels and needs, mainly use indicators of what people have and ought to have according to some set standards. Some of them use perceived satisfaction for some aspects as a supplement to objective-type assessment. This is in contrast to the recent work of behavioural scientists who use *multiple discrepancy theories* related to aspiration, social comparison, person–environment fit and cognitive dissonance. They relate personal satisfaction to what others have and express quality of life in terms of the gap between aspirations and reality. This is in tune with the observation made 300 years ago by Girolomo Cardono, that happiness is perhaps the state of not being unhappy.

Michalos (1985) has listed the following basic hypotheses:

H1: Net satisfaction, as reported, is a function of perceived discrepancies between what one has and wants, what others have, what was the best one has had in the past or expected to have 3 years ago or expects to have after 5 years or deserves and needs.

H2: Perceived discrepancies, except those between what one has and wants, are functions of objectively measurable discrepancies, with direct effects on satisfactions and actions.

H3: The perceived gap between what one has and wants serves as a mediator between (is a function of) all other gaps.

H4: Pursuit and the maintenance of net satisfaction motivate human action in direct proportion to expected levels of satisfaction.

H5: All discrepancies, satisfaction and action are affected by demographic and income factors, self-esteem and social support.

H6: Objectively measurable discrepancies are functions of human actions.

Applying the theory to a survey of 300 students at the University of Guelph in 1984, Michalos used an extensive questionnaire that ranged from demographic and educational data to questions designed to ascertain domain and global satisfaction from different perspectives. Questions relevant to the seven dimensions listed above under H1 were scored on a seven-point Likert scale, ranging from 1 point for 'terrible' to 7 for 'delightful' or from 'far below' to 'well above'. Mean scores for the different dimensions and domains and their aggregates were calculated as unweighted arithmetic averages and were found to be between 3 and 5 in most cases, with only satisfaction with work (part time for full time students) being a little below the halfway mark of 3½. Multiple regression was used to show the impact of global on domain scores (H3), but they did not yield impressive results as predictors for global or domain satisfaction. Michalos maintains that multiple discrepancy theories can be used to justify education and rational persuasion for raising people's satisfaction and happiness, but can be misused by manipulators who make people feel better by making comparisons with those worse off instead of by helping the latter.

The satisfaction scaling used by Michalos is one of many developed in recent years. In a survey Larsen et al. (1985) have described and compared some popular types. Some are based on single-item scales; for example (pp. 3–4):

- Andrews and Withey (1976) score replies to 'How do you feel about how happy you are?' on a seven-point scale ranging from 'delighted' to 'terrible' (see also Michalos above).
- Cantril (1965) uses a nine-step ladder, anchored at one end with 'best possible life for you' and at the other end with 'worst possible life for you', with respondents asked to place themselves on unmarked rungs between to indicate where they stand.
- Fordyce (1978) allows for eleven response choices ranging downward from 'feeling extremely happy'.
- Fordyce (1978) further asks respondents what percentage of time they feel happy, neutral or unhappy.
- Gurin et al. (1960) ask, 'Taking all things together, how would you say things are these days?' with three possible response choices of 'very happy', 'pretty happy' and 'not too happy'.

Examples of multi-item measures of subjective well-being are:

• Bradburn and Capolovitz (1965) use a ten-item true/false inventory that has separate positive and negative effect scores and a net negative *effect balance*.

• In the eight-item scale of Campbell, Converse and Rodger (1976) respondents rate their lives along dimensions like 'interesting–boring' and 'worthwhile–useless'.

• Underwood and Froming (1980) use fifteen items for a *mood* survey for one score that reflects a positive average or hedonic tone and for another that reflects emotional reactivity.

• Larsen (1985) assesses the intensity of individual emotional experience with a 40-item *effect intensity* measure that balances positive and negative emotions.

We noted before the asymmetry of indicator movements both statistically, when calculating ratios from changing bases, and analytically, when upward moves are related as more significant than downward moves, or vice versa (e.g. in development policy). A similar asymmetry has been observed by Headey and Waring (1988) inasmuch as most people rate their quality of life as being above the midpoint. They tend to believe that their own performance in major life roles is above average, reflecting high self-esteem and reluctance to admit their own poor performance. Statistically, this could be corrected by the differential weighting of subroles, but Headey and Waring suggest that such weighting would falsify the reality of the positive skew situation towards relative superiority.

The present author carried out a simple small survey in Australia early in 1990, with replies from 50 students and colleagues. As shown in Table 3.15, the questionnaire was divided into five domains, each characterised by four questions, for the self-assessment of material status, social relations, activities, achievements and concern about national and global issues. Questions were marked under five alternative headings as 'very' or 'mildly' satisfied or dissatisfied or neutral (which could indicate either no opinion or not applicable). Sampling was haphazard, ruled by convenience. Respondents were:

    19 from a meeting by the Humanist Society of New South Wales;
     6 from a group of the University of the Third Age;
    10 from a class of the Workers' Educational Association;
    15 from readers of *Tableaus* (Australian Mensa).

No personal details were collected, but it is possible to say that most respondents had received a higher education, that genders were fairly well balanced and that most of the first three groups were elderly, with more young ones among the Mensans. The survey was in the nature of an exercise, and the results may or may not be typical beyond the participants.

The results are shown in Table 3.15, first in a three-way percentage division that combines the 'very' and 'mildly' satisfied and dissatisfied responses

Table 3.15 Quality of life: Sydney survey, 1990

Question	% (total = 100)			Index[a]				All respondents[b]
	Satisfied	Neutral	Dissatisfied	Humanist Society	U3A	WEA	Mensa	
Material status: Are you satisfied with your:								
Income?	76	8	16					75
Present work?	68	18	14					70
Career?	62	24	14					40
Housing?	90	6	4					40
Average	74	14	12	75	70	40	20	51
Social relations: Are you content about your:								
Interaction with family?	84	10	6					60
Interaction with colleagues and friends?	74	20	6					60
Participation in social events?	64	24	12					35
Participation in community life?	64	26	10					45
Average	72	20	8	55	70	55	30	50
Activities: Are you satisfied with your:								
Present health?	77	13	10					55
Opportunity to take part in sport?	68	19	13					46
Opportunity to take part in leisure/hobby activity?	64	24	12					61
Opportunity to take part in holidays/travelling?	64	24	12					60
Average	68	20	12	70	66	55	25	53

(continues)

Table 3.15 (continued)

Question	% (total = 100)			Index[a]				
	Satisfied	Neutral	Dissatisfied	Humanist Society	U3A	WEA	Mensa	All respondents[b]
Achievements: Are you satisfied with your achievements of goals:								
In the way you raised your family?	64	24	12					42
In your profession or occupation?	64	18	18					28
In your contribution to the community?	70	16	14					38
In your spiritual aspirations?	56	30	14					40
Average	63½	22	14½	42	70	15	28	36
Average first four domains	70	19	12	61	69	41	26	47
National and global issues: Are you worried about:								
Protection of the environment?	22	7	71					-70
Threats to peace in third-world areas?	35	13	52					-44
Threats to Australia from other countries?	48	19	33					-12
Direction of Australian socioeconomic policies?	10	26	64					-100
Average	29	16	55	—	-25	-75	-65	-55
Average all domains	67	18	15	60	60	16	7	30

a Index weights: very satisfied +1, mildly satisfied +½, neutral 0, mildly dissatisfied -1, very dissatisfied -2. Index span from +100 to -200, midvalue -50.
b Respondents drawn from four groups as stated on the previous page.

respectively. This confirms the general experience with such surveys that people, when not under the strain of poverty or suppression, will more often than not state that they are satisfied with their life experience and situation—in this case over 60% in each of the first four domains and subdomains. The satisfaction rate was over 75% for income, housing, family interaction and health, or, in each instance, over 80% if neutrals are excluded, exceeding dissatisfaction by a factor of 4 to 5. Only in the domain of national and global issues did dissatisfaction, in the sense of causing worry, prevail, in particular about sufficient protection of the environment, threats to peace in third-world areas and the direction of national (Australian) socioeconomic policies.

The table also presents results in the form of an index with weights of +2 for very satisfied, +1 very satisfied, 0 neutral, -2 mildly dissatisfied and -4 very dissatisfied. This form of cardinalising makes gestures to the non-linearity of personal feelings, assuming them to be more strongly affected by dissatisfaction than satisfaction. Index numbers are halved, reducing their span from +200 to -400 to a span from +100 to -200; they could be rescored to run from +100 to 0, or +100 to -100, shifting the midvalue from -50 to +50 or 0 respectively. The index, as shown, is positive with an average of +50 for the first four domains and negative at -55 for the national and global issues domain, reducing the overall average to +30, with interrelations not significantly different from the simpler counting in the three percentage columns.

As to the respondent groups, the satisfaction rate was generally lower for the Mensans than for the student groups, notably for income, although even there it remained positive except for concern about the environment and local (Australian) policy issues. No relative weighting of the twenty questions was attempted. The greater weight given to dissatisfaction made no significant difference because of its comparatively rare incidence.

CHAPTER 4

ECONOMIC APPLICATIONS OF INDICATORS

4.1 Economic activity

Social scientists sometimes look with envy on economic indicators because of their seeming certainty in expressing changing phenomena in fixed and evenly spaced quantitative or value terms presented in graphs or series that lend themselves to further statistical analysis. Statistical expression and illustration are usually more concise and persuasive than verbal description. There is no denying that the multitude of statistics and graphs published in general and specialised publications, or presented on radio and television, have a major role in communicating economic changes to business people and the general public. Any criticism of their occasional inadequacies should be seen in the context of their general usefulness.

It seems to be appropriate to begin a discussion of economic indicators with this proviso in mind, because in a general textbook there is a tendency to dwell on shortcomings and limitations that are not negligible but do not vitiate necessarily the main purpose for which indicators are and can be used. This is not meant to excuse the types of errors that Huff has slated under the telling title *How to Lie with Statistics* (1954), with examples such as the sample with the built-in bias or the gee-whiz graph, nor the interpretative errors that are discovered so often on close scrutiny of comments on published tables and graphs. Our attention here is directed not to formal mistakes but rather to faults that arise from sticking inflexibly to the formal structure, by assumptions such as: the composition and cost of preparation of a meal are the same now as they were many years ago, or the introduction of credit cards had no influence on the volume and use of bank accounts, or the entry of women into the labour force depends on family income or number of children. To put it otherwise, social and technological change is continuously reflected in economic change.

We shall therefore have to keep in mind that, however useful business indicators may be in practice, they do have certain limitations, which can sometimes override their credibility.

In practice a single indicator is usually preferred to a group of several separate indicators that refer to different facets, but this procedure can hide more than it reveals. Take, for example, the *budget balance* as sole indicator of fiscal policy. In a series of working papers published by the Organisation for Economic Cooperation and Development (OECD) in April 1990 (no. 78, Chouraqui et al.; no. 80, Gramlich) it is shown that the budget balance as fiscal indicator, even when seasonally adjusted and related to gross domestic product (GDP), rests on the dubious assumption of stable or regularly oscillating unemployment. They call for additional indicators to determine the sustainability, viability and desirability of *fiscal policy*. Sustainability could be indicated by current and anticipated spending and transfers; the effects of fiscal policy on spending reflect the consumption function; and an indicator of the effect of discretionary change can be based on the estimated change in the budget balance due to changes in unemployment.

Further indicators could measure *fiscal distortion* due to the effects of the tax structure on prices and demand. However, by their nature such indicators carry a large speculative element about present and future behaviour, and such problems seem to overwhelm attempts at developing an indicator of microeconomic efficiency that could relate the excess burden of taxation and demand for labour incentives.

There is considerable interest in the application of indicators to business or economic activity. This may refer to particular items, sectors or spheres of the economy (e.g. sales of butter, dairy produce or all foods; all retail sales). Single items may be expressed in quantum units; but if items are a mixture of types (e.g. salted and unsalted butter), value series are more appropriate as a way of weighting types. This also applies more generally for the aggregation of items by sectors or activity. Problems connected with changing types and unit values have already been mentioned in connection with price index construction in section 2.8. Other questions concern indicators designed to express a country's economic strength. We will first look at a general business index and then at some economic development indicators.

The general purpose of such indicators can be paraphrased from Bauer's definition of social indicators as:

> They enable us to assess where we stand and are going with respect to our values and goals. They look at the present state of the economy in the light of past experience and of the situation elsewhere usually with the objective of forecasting the future. (1966: 1)

This can be attempted by taking one series as proxy for economic activity.

For example, freight car loading, production of steel ingots or bank clearings have sometimes been used as single business indicators, and gross national product (GNP), itself a complex aggregate, is often taken as representative for all transactions. Here, however, we will look first at economic activity as a general term used by politicians and analysts, and then at attempts by economists to reify or conceptualise it by means of aggregation or multivariate models.

The general limits to such an attempt have already been discussed in section 1.3. They are inherent in any combination of series that differ in units, timing and magnitude of response, degree of linearity and boundaries, and dependency and interaction with other factors. A rise in the rate of unemployment of $x\%$ may not be as significant at unemployment level A as it is at level B, or as significant as a similar rise in retail sales at either level. It may be regarded as favourable for the economy at times of excess demand, or as unfavourable at other times.

In a departure from customary economic writ the OECD, in its *Economic Outlook* of December 1989, said that a current account deficit is to be regarded as 'bad' only if it reflects a government budget deficit, tax distortions, government regulation or import protection. Otherwise, and this applied to some countries in 1989, it is to be regarded as 'good'.

Aggregate business indicators are usually based on the average of the indexes for constituent series, which is the average of their percentage changes. This procedure circumvents the problem of different units, but only masks questions of different directions, amplitudes and so on. In Table 4.1 are listed some of the major business economic series that, apart from their significance as individual indicators, can be so combined.

As an example of a single *index of business activity* we can take the monthly series published in the trade supplement of the UK weekly *The Economist* from October 1933 until the 1940s. The series went back to

Table 4.1 Some business/economic series used as indicators

Series	Measure[a]	Items measured
Production	q/v	Industrial, mining, rural, building
Transportation	q/v	Rail, road, air, sea transport; telephone, cable
Investment	v	Inventories, commercial/public building
Consumption	q/v	Wholesale/retail sales
Income	v	Personal income, wages, social security
Manpower	q	Employment/unemployment, participation rate, skills
Finance	v	Loans/deposits, interest rates, consumer debt
Trade	v	Wholesale/retail, import/export
Public sector	v	Income/expenditure, debt

[a] q quantity, v value, q/v both.

1924, which was also the original base year until revision to a 1935 base. *The Economist* of 25 July 1937 commented in the trade supplement:

> The index is widely accepted as a measuring rod of Britain's economic activity . . . [it] represents an attempt to measure changes in the economic activity . . . in quantitative—not monetary—units, to give an approximate idea of fluctuations in the *real national income.*

The index was constructed on a daily average basis, corrected for seasonal fluctuations by average percentage deviations from a 12 month moving average for the monthly figures over a period of 10 years. The constituent series were combined by taking a weighted geometric average, which is appropriate for averaging growth rates. In the two exceptional instances where constituent index numbers dropped to nil, during the general strike of 1926, those series were excluded, because on multiplication the whole series would have been reduced to zero, with the further odd effect of infinite growth rates. The fourteen constituent series, with their respective weights that add to 42, are shown in Table 4.2. The weights were determined by balancing four main considerations: importance of the sphere of activity, relevance as a measure of general business activity, avoidance of arbitrary movements and statistical accuracy of the data. Employment, with 10 points or 24%, was given the largest single weight, and power and transport were also highly rated in comparison with the service industries. With its emphasis on industrial inputs and trade, the *Economist* series differs from an earlier attempt at constructing an index of physical production by the London and Cambridge Economic Service in 1924 (Rowe, 1927), which aimed at comparing national income, or at least a large proportion of it, at different dates.

The *Economist* index reflected the postwar growth in the economy, with a rise from 88 in 1924 to 98 in 1929, followed by a lapse to 80 in the

Table 4.2   *The Economist*: economic series used in index of business activity, United Kingdom

Series	Weight	Series	Weight
Employment	10	Consumption:	
Power consumption		Iron and steel	2
Coal	4	Cotton	1
Electricity	2	Foreign trade:	
Transport:		Imports of raw materials	2
Railway merchandise	4	Exports of manufactures	3
Commercial vehicles in	2	Shipping	2
use		Bank clearings:	
Postal receipts	3	Metropolitan	4
Building activity	2	Country towns	1

strike year of 1926 and 84 during the great depression, and it had recovered to 100 in 1935. It was adjusted by some substitution: in power consumption from coal to electricity, in transport from railways to commercial vehicles and in foreign trade from imports to exports.

The *Economist* index used to be much quoted, but it also received some criticism from statisticians (Rhodes, 1937) questioning its coherence or, as we may now say, its implied 'reification'. It has been called an unmeasurable abstraction resting on the assumption that each constituent series reflects three aspects of change: a factor common to all series, factors affecting some but not all groups and factor-specific causes. Questions have also been raised about the conformity of externally determined factors and the validity of commonsense weighting.

Another example of this type is the monthly *index of business activity* published by the US Department of Commerce in the 1930s in its *Survey of Current Business*, being based on production, factory employment and payrolls, freight car loadings, wholesale and foreign trade, and bank debits. It was issued conjointly with the *Annalist*, the *New York Times* index of business activity, which recorded departures from normal for seven production, two consumption and one freight index.

More recently, the OECD has been publishing an *index of industrial activity* that applies differential weights to mining, manufacturing and public utilities. In Germany the IFO Institute for Economic Research in Munich issues weekly, monthly and quarterly reports on economic trends (*Wirtschaftskonjunktur*), with single and aggregate indicators, including some based on surveys of business climate and consumer sentiment. *Consumer sentiment* indexes are also issued elsewhere. The business agency Dun and Bradstreet, for instance, publishes one in several countries as a sort of *diffusion index*, on the basis of expectations for sales, profits, prices, inventories, employment and new orders.

In the United States the Survey Research Center of the University of Michigan takes sample surveys about past and expected changes in personal finances and about the expected outlook, in both the short and long term, for business, as well as about attitudes towards purchases of large consumer durables, notably motor cars. The results are related to a base year, or else expressed as numbers of favourable (above 100) or below-favourable (under 100) ratings, or as +/- percentage changes over the previous year.

With the advent of *national accounts* after the Second World War, first published yearly and then also quarterly and monthly by many countries on a uniform basis, the previous combinations of business indicators moved into the background. National accounts themselves are not an indicator but an equilibrium system from which indicators are derived. Their use leaves open major problems of *ad hoc* combinations of subseries and aggregates and of abstractions to represent business or economic activity. National accounts represent an articulated system of major economic variables that can be combined at particular points to show national income or product. Changes in the aggregates are the outcome of complex interactions of endogenous and exogenous forces that keep the economy in an ever-changing level of quasi-equilibrium that reflects the state of economic activity.

Unlike a composite index derived from a bundle of statistics that raises questions of weighting, to take account of the relative importance of each element, the interaction of the national accounts variables, and their linear or non-linear relationships, can be expressed in functions. During the 1960s this was vividly demonstrated by the construction of flow machines at Cambridge (United Kingdom) and other universities, which pumped a fluid through pipes and valves of different dimensions to demonstrate the effects of variables such as monetary or fiscal or trade policy. The strength of the flow effects of valves controlling multipliers, accelerators, spillovers and the like on the aggregates and their interperiod change could be read off the gauges. A fluid measure representing $100 of new investment, with a multiplier setting of 1½, added at the appropriate inlet, would raise the fluid in the GNP container by $150, and more elaborate adjustments for foreign trade, taxation and so on could also be built in.

National accounts can also be adjusted to allow for changes in money value by applying appropriate price indexes to main components. GNP is then expressed in real terms by a process of weighted deflation. For intercountry comparisons the use of purchasing power parities, rather than exchange rates, seems preferable, although even this can distort long term comparisons between countries.

GNP, or its near-equivalent GDP, has become generally accepted as an indicator of economic conditions. Its application to development analysis has been previously discussed, together with its limitations due to its narrow-based market scope. Such restrictions also apply to the picture it provides for business and economic conditions as far as structure, distribution and non-monetary economic transactions are concerned. GNP excludes quantitative series such as employment and production—or rather, by recording their values in wages and factor costs it reflects the monetary, rather than the real resource, aspect and so neglects unused capacity of unemployment and industry. On the other hand, it also fails to show money turnover (e.g. bank debits) and deals only inadequately with financial intermediaries.

It may be mentioned here that other economic systems, dealing with money flows (flow-of-funds), industrial flows (input–output) or socio-economic flows (System of Social Demographic Statistics, or SSDS), do not yield generalised indicators to match GNP, although they may produce more specialised series (e.g. the import content of local output by matrix inversion from an input–output statement).

4.2 Business cycles

Business cycles, or *trade cycles*, reflect fluctuations in economic activity, with recurrent periods of expansion followed by contractions, recessions and revivals over periods usually varying from 1 to 12 years.

One of the major applications of business indicators lies in the identification of such recurring patterns and of the changes that mark the ups and downs of business experience and prospects. This corresponds to an application of outwardly uncoordinated indicators to forecast the future on the basis of present and past experience. It leads to the formulation of theories of business dynamics, which in turn is applied to the discovery of leading, lagging and coincident series and their respective turning points.

Business cycle theories were much discussed by economists during the 1920s and 1930s (e.g. by Schumpeter, Haberler, Harrod and Hicks). Here we will only refer to the statistical analysis and verification developed by Mitchell and Burns in the 1930s, and discussed more recently by Moore and Shiskin (1967), Zarnowitz (1972) and Lahiri and Moore (1991).

A useful starting point is the establishment of a *reference cycle* by taking a major business index, or a composite of major series, for comparison with individual series to bring out their respective conformance, leads or lags. The indicators calculated by Moore and Shiskin were adjusted for trend and for seasonal and irregular fluctuations so as to concentrate on the cyclical factor. Following Mitchell and Burns they chose cyclical indicators that proved helpful in anticipating, measuring and interpreting short run changes in aggregate economic activity, including production, employment, income, trade and the flow of funds. The indicators were chosen for their regularity in leading or lagging the cyclical turning points over a long period, and had to fulfil the following criteria:

economic significance
statistical adequacy
consistent timing
smoothness
currency (up-to-datedness).

The indicators were divided into eight major economic groups, ranging from employment, production and trade to government activities and economic activity in other countries. About one-half, described as *narrow series* (i.e. covering a single industry or a minor component), were given a weight of 50%, while the other half, described as *broad series* (i.e. having a wider coverage), received a 75% weighting. Each series was graded according to the criteria listed above, with the score partly based on a subjective assessment of their characteristics. Finally, 87 individual or group series were listed according to their peaks and troughs back over 100 years (or less when not previously available).

The number of series classified as *leading* indicators was 36; they had an average lead time of 6 months and included business formation and new investment commitments, stock prices, profits and money flows. A further 25 series were graded as *coincident*, including job vacancies, production, income, trade and money-market interest rates. Another 11 series were described as *lagging*; they lagged by 4 months on average and included long duration unemployment, investment spending and stock, labour costs, receivables and loan rates. However, the timing of peaks and troughs cuts across the division by economic spheres. There was considerable diversity: the 36 leading series had median leads between 6 and 15 months, while the lagging indicators were fewer in number and had lesser lags between 2 and 8 months. The 25 cycles between 1854 and 1961 varied in span between troughs from 30 to 100 months, and between peaks from 17 to 101 months. The whole scheme looks like an empirical exercise based on a rather heterogeneous collection of series that defy combination.

Haberler (1945, app. I), following the work of Thorp and others of the National Bureau of Economic Research (NBER), used a subjective assessment of the cycle by constructing a *reference index* of business activity that rates the state of the economy on a six-point scale from exceptional prosperity (+3) to deep depression (–3), for comparison over time and with other countries. This index yielded fairly regular curves for the 1880–1935 period (pp. 266–7).

A more recent adaptation of this method uses a *diffusion index*, based on the number of component series that rise or fall over the previous month or year. Expressed as a proportion of the total number of series in the respective group, or total of all groups, it gives a picture of direction and timing, though not of magnitude of change. This index means that any indicator can serve as leading and lagging at various times, but it must be remembered that there are usually more leading than lagging indicators. Experience suggests that the peak of such a diffusion index will be reached before the peak of the cycle (Alexander, 1958).

In 1973 the International Economic Indicator Project (IEI Project) was established by the NBER at Rutgers University. More than a dozen countries are now participating in this scheme, which aims at promoting better understanding of economic fluctuations to assist in policy making and forecasting and to facilitate intercountry comparisons. It remains to be seen whether this project will lead to the further development of aggregates that could serve as shorthand indicators of the business climate and likely change.

In the *leading indicator approach* proposed by Lahiri and Moore and their associates (1991), following the definition quoted at the start of this section, no fixed requirement is set for duration and amplitude, which in practice vary over time. However, they found considerable consistency in lead time for at least eight major indicators in the United States for both prewar periods, going back before 1900 in some cases, and for 1948–82: lead times of 6–12 months for business failures, housing starts and stock prices, and 3–7 months for new orders for durables, average manufacturing hours, building contracts and wholesale price. A similar range of leads also applied in other industrial countries for indicators of building and other business activity.

The IFO Institute for Economic Research in Munich publishes in its *Quarterly Digest* a survey of 500 experts in 50 countries, with ratings on a 1-5-9 scale about the present economic situation, growth prospects and so on.

The technical progress in indicator construction and analysis is shown in surveys such as the one edited by Zarnowitz (1972), but it seems to be shadowed by some unease. Firstly, the track record remains unimpressive. An Australian survey (EPAC, 1985), for example, found seven peaks and seven troughs in economic activity between 1950 and 1983. The leading indicator index gave advance warning for six peaks, with lead times varying from 2 to 16 months, and five troughs, with lead times of 1-23 months. Secondly, Koopmans has attacked *Measurement without Theory* on general methodological grounds (August 1947, reprinted with rejoinders in Gordon and Klein, 1965), and some such criticism is also implicit in comments made above. Thirdly, the previous complacent, or pessimistic, assumption about the recurrence of major cycles has been shaken by the long period since the Second World War, when cycles have been much milder, giving rise to the question 'Is the business cycle obsolete?' This is usually associated with more prompt and better informed economic management by the state and has shifted the focus of the cycle debate to the instruments and effects of economic policy. However, periods of economic instability, albeit shorter and milder than before, continue to occur, and analytical effort is shifting from conformance to a cyclical pattern to the interpretation of changing local and international policy measures. It is also concentrating more on the study of national and international development.

As for aggregate business indicators, cycle analysis shows that their diversity in timing and amplitude makes the predetermination of turning points uncertain; nor is it easy to distinguish immediately between what may be short *pauses* in expansion or contraction and *definite turns* in these phases. It may be more satisfactory to take GNP as a general indicator, together with prominent items for specific groups (e.g. steel for basic production, motor vehicle registrations for transport, unemployment for the labour market).

With the spread of economic commentaries and greater public literacy about economics, or at least about economic jargon, increasing prominence is being given in the media to indicative statements that seem to indicate the approach or arrival of a boom or recession. A typical application by the prophets of doom is to say that a country has entered a period of recession when real GDP falls in two successive quarters. This may be superficially evident, but a statistical rule of thumb takes no account of the origin, depth and interdependence of factors that operate in a recession.

Rather than rely on a single indicator, the Dating Committee of the NBER in Cambridge, Massachusetts, has defined a *recession* as 'a recurring period of decline in total output, income, employment and trade, usually lasting from six months to a year and marked by widespread contractions in many sectors of the economy'. It speaks of a *growth recession* as being characterised by slow growth in these aspects, usually lasting a year or more. *Slowdowns*, marked by growth significantly below its long term rate, may occur without a recession. A *depression* is described as a recession that is major in both scale and duration (NBER statement, 1991).

The committee works by consensus of its seven members, who are drawn from different fields of economics and make statements about coming recessions after observing trends for about 6 months or longer. In the words of the present chairman, Robert M. Hall, the committee members function as 'historians rather than as chroniclers of real time action'. However, at the end of 1990 the committee issued a more advanced statement admitting that the US economy was in recession, and it has been suggested that it will identify a month between June and September 1990 as the economic peak that ushered in the subsequent decline. This admission of the economy's entry into a recession by a respected impartial body of experts may have repercussions on the policies pursued by the US administration and the Federal Reserve Bank Board, which had previously avoided the use of the word 'recession'.

4.3 Stock exchange indexes

The stock exchange indexes used in the United States, Japan, the United Kingdom and many other countries, sometimes under familiar titles (e.g. the *Dow Jones*, the *Nikkei*), are examples of popular indicators that in

Table 4.3 Characteristics of major stock-exchange indexes

Stock exchange	Index	Main characteristics
New York	Dow Jones	30 large manufacturing firms; unweighted mean
	Standard and Poor	500 stocks; market price divided by 1941–43 value
	Wall Street Journal	Number of rises less falls on the day
Tokyo	Nikkei	225 stocks; composition and weighting unchanged since 1949; based on mean of added yen value; adjusted to 50 yen
	Topix (Tokyo Stock Exchange)	Geometric average of 1108 listed issues
London	Financial Times	30 representative industrials; geometric average; also series for 500 shares and 100 largest companies
Australia	All Ordinaries (Australian Stock Exchange)	All ordinaries weighted by number of issued shares
New Zealand	Reserve Bank	61 companies weighted by number on issue
Canada	Toronto	300 out of 1208 listed companies; capital weighted
	Montreal Portfolio	Mean of 25 most heavily traded stocks; base 1962; also similar for 500 shares and 100 largest

Source: De Caires (1988).

spite of presentational and methodological failings seem to be doing an adequate job for users. The main characteristics of some major stock-exchange indexes are listed in Table 4.3.

It can be argued that this type of index:

• needs some weighting, according to size of firm or trading volume;
• needs constant review for new share and rights issues;
• should be averaged on a geometric, rather than arithmetic, average to express rates of rise and fall; and
• should be clearly related to a base that is updated periodically to ease comparisons with companion series on the same basis.

Yet, as Table 4.3 shows, most of the much quoted indicators do not comply with all these rules. Presumably, professional users are aware of differences in scales and adjust them in their heads, but the uninitiated may well wonder why a rise of 50 points in the Dow Jones should be equivalent to a rise of 750 points in the Nikkei or 40 points in the *FT30* (London), and represent in each case a rise of 2%.

It is difficult to change entrenched indicator habits. It is no secret that the Dow Jones gives greater weight to old than to new stocks, is based on stock prices rather than on their market capitalisation, and makes no proper provision for share splits. Yet it continues to be preferred, at least in the press, to the *Standard and Poor*, which is more soundly constructed. In 1988 the Tokyo Stock Exchange stopped compiling the Nikkei because its early postwar base is biased in its weighting to basic manufacturing and the consumer and commerce sectors, and is underweighted for the burgeoning financial sector. It introduced instead its own *Topix*, which is more widely based and technically superior. However, the Nikkei continues to be published by the newspaper company that previously promoted it. The rivalry between the two often-diverging indexes has political overtones, and it appears that the Nikkei, more than the Topix, lends itself to manipulation by large operators.

In an attempt at coordination the *Financial Times* (London) daily publishes a series of *FT actuaries world indices*, separately for 24 countries and eleven world regions with a summary world index covering about 2400 stocks altogether. Averages are expressed as an index on base 31 December 1986 = 100 for local currency, sterling and the US dollar, and the day's change is given as a percentage of that value. The selection of stocks, ranging from 546 in the United States and 455 in Japan down to seventeen in Ireland and thirteen in Mexico, looks comprehensive and up to date. As an economic indicator this series seems to be more soundly constructed than some of the old faithful stock-exchange indexes quoted in the press and on the air.

Stock exchange indexes not only summarise prices on the stock market. They themselves can become a price standard for that market when *share price index (SPI) futures* are traded, taking the place of the prices for individual shares. In the usual futures deal the investor sells a parcel of shares now for future delivery at or near current prices, and pays a margin deposit, in the expectation that a month hence (or at whatever the agreed due date) the price will have dropped and so the investor can buy and deliver the shares at a profit. In the SPI futures deal the investor sells a parcel of shares now, invests the proceeds in high-yielding money-market securities, and sells a contract at a price stated as $100 \times$ SPI. At due date the investor settles at the then SPI rate ($\times 100$), with a profit (loss) if the SPI has dropped (risen).

4.4 Standardised indicators

We have so far referred to business analysis by way of single statistical series, or aggregations of similar series, that represent trade, production, income and so on. Even this simple process often requires some adjustment to bring subseries to the same level. As a case in point, the subseries may be expressed in different quantum units, or some may be expressed in quantum and others in value terms; so chalk will have to be expressed in units of cheese, or cheese in units of chalk, or both in a third unit, usually their price. This sort of standardisation may not be immediately visible when the combination is not made in the terms of the original unit but is expressed as aggregated change over a period. However, it is then hidden rather than avoided, because a comparison of period change for quantities expressed in different units still requires the interposing of a common standard (Table 4.4).

Apart from the translation of different series to a common unit, economic indicators are often adjusted to a specific base. Major instances are allowance for the number of persons concerned and for changing money values. In such cases standardisation assumes structural continuity in the reference unit.

If we want to improve comparability, by expressing, say, an income statistic as *per head of population* by dividing by the population number,

Table 4.4   Weighted quantum index

Subseries	Quantity		Unit price ($)		Weighted price ($)		Index[a]		
	Q_0	Q_1	P_0	P_1	Q_0P_0	Q_1P_1	Q_1	P_1	Q_1P_1
Chalk (sticks)	100	100	2	3	200	300	100	150	150
Cheese (500 g)	60	54	3	4½	180	243	90	150	135
Total					380	543			143

[a] Period 0 = 100.

there is the question of choosing between population at the beginning, middle or end of the income period or a population average. However, this usually matters less than potential variations in the statistic due to age, sex, occupation or location, which may make it preferable to choose a section of the population rather than the whole (e.g. per head of adult or employed population). Generally, the indicative purpose should determine the choice of a particular reference population.

The general question of adjustment for price change through the application of index numbers has been discussed in section 2.8 with reference to the atomistic and functional approaches in constructing price index numbers. A variety of such indexes, moving from producer and importer to consumer and exporter, are available, and choice should be directed by the sphere of the economy being dealt with. One of the most popular is the all-items retail price index, also called *consumer price index*, which is widely accepted as mirroring changes in the general price level and thus as a proxy indicator of inflation. The technical debate about the proper formulation of this index does not seem to have diminished the faith of business people and applied economists in this convenient *deflator* for the standardisation of economic series. Strictly speaking, it should be applied only to indicators covering retail market transactions covered by the index regimen. In practice it is also used for prices beyond that (e.g. services, fees). This can be justified on two grounds:

- Price index series for wholesale, investment, government and like transactions are not as readily available as price index series for consumption.
- Their construction involves as many or more problems than occur for retail market series.

As a further justification it may also be noted that, in the long run at least, most prices move in waves in a common upward trend, if allowance is made for technical changes, substitution and so on.

The price deflation of economic aggregates can be refined by applying separate indexes for each component. For constant price estimates of GNP and national accounts generally, statisticians use reconstructed consumer price indexes, and wages and other input and output costs as well as price series for other private and public expenditure. Such a series of expenditure on the GDP at *constant purchasers' values* is published for many countries in the *Yearbooks of National Accounts Statistics* issued by the United Nations.

Division of the constant price by actual price values of GDP yields an *implicit price deflator*, which can be regarded as a more comprehensive indicator of inflation than any of its retail or wholesale components. It shares with them the general index-number problem of cardinalising utility functions; and in the case of services for which no market values are readily available, it uses proxies (e.g. teachers' wages for the value of education). It also has some practical drawbacks, such as lags in factor payments and changes in base weights. Though resting on base weighted series, it is a linked current weight index that uses harmonic means weighted by quantities (values) of the current year, each of which is compared with a fixed base year (United Nations Statistical Office, 1976: xxvi).

As with any time series for economic aggregates, there remain also doubts about whether the adjustment of separate elements will add up to a meaningful description of a concept and of changes in that concept.

A further example of standardising concepts is the extension of cash wage statistics to include the *social wage*. This term is applied to the provision of goods and services to workers as a contribution to individual well-being. In practice it is mainly represented by public expenditure on education, health, housing, culture, recreation and other community services. This can amount to a substantial addition to non-cash benefits, estimated, for example, in Australia to be equivalent to about 20% of cash wages. International comparisons of cash wages can mean a relative underestimation of wage incomes for socialist countries that provide many free or subsidised services, as against free market economies that charge full costs. It can also vitiate historical comparisons by the long term trend in the expansion of social services and this trend's more recent halt or reversal in many Western countries.

4.5 International price comparisons

International price comparisons raise questions similar to the comprehensive determination of inflation. The daily and longer term fluctuations of *exchange rates* mirror only imperfectly the state of supply and demand on international currency markets. They are influenced by trade, capital and other so-called invisible transactions, as well as by the buying and selling by the central banks to regulate rates, by capital inflow and outflow in response to rate changes, and by speculative anticipation. Yet, because of their familiarity and frequency of publication, exchange rates are often used, beyond their currency-trade function, as indicators of relative income levels and living standards between different countries.

One drawback of expressing the value of one currency in terms of another is the volatility of intercountry rates; so expressing currency A in terms of US dollars or yen should also take into account the fluctuations between US dollars and yen, and other currencies. For many purposes it is therefore preferable to relate currency A to the currencies of all its major trading partners, weighting them according to their share in trade. This procedure results in a *trade-weighted index*, from which an effective exchange rate can be derived; and this in turn can be adjusted by comparing inflation rates in country A with inflation in its trading partners to yield a *real effective exchange rate*.

Even this adjusted rate is not ideal for income/expenditure comparisons, however, because it refers to internationally traded goods and excludes non-traded goods—in particular services, which are usually more labour-intensive and use less capital than traded goods. Therefore exchange rate comparisons are unsatisfactory for assessing economic performance and policy coordination between groups of countries, or for special tasks such as determining optimal location or calculations of contributions to international organisations.

During the past 20 years a group of UK and US economists, in particular Heston, Kravis, Summers and Marris, have initiated research that has led to the International Comparison Project (ICP) of the Statistical Office of the United Nations (Kravis et al., 1978), in which over 100 countries and many research organisations now participate. The methodology and some results of the purchasing-power-parity (PPP) studies have been discussed at some length in the *Review of Income and Wealth* (March 1980 and 1988) and *Journal of Economic Literature* (Kravis and Morris, March 1984).

The project is based on the disaggregation of GDP into some 150 classes of final product, with two to twenty items selected for each class, including consumer and producers' durables as well as construction specifications. It remains arguable to what extent the carefully developed methodology has overcome the general index-number problem of weighting an average of quantities and cardinalised respective utility functions—in this case with the assumption that people within each country have similar tastes—and how far it meets the tests of transitivity, basic invariance, preference conservation and absence of bias, but distortions through not observing all such tenets are probably not very significant.

The most striking result is that exchange-rate-converted GDP is about two to three times less than PPP-converted GDP in poor countries—a difference that systematically diminishes with rising income. The *exchange rate deviation index* (Kravis, 1984: table 3), representing the deviation of PPP from the exchange rate, fell from 2.6 for a group of eight poor countries to near 1 for wealthy countries. Average GDP per capita was about ten times greater in industrialised countries than in developing market economies, but only six times as high on a PPP base. This does not mean that those countries are not poor; it means that statistically their position is not quite as bad as exchange rate comparisons suggest. One reason is that poor countries have a high services component and that services are cheap there. The relative cheapness of non-traded goods leads to a smaller productivity gap between traded and non-traded goods than applies in rich countries. On the whole, PPP ratios are a more realistic indicator of intercountry comparisons. However, it should not be forgotten that they are based on the GDP of a money economy and that 'traded goods and services' refers to money exchanges. Barter and unpaid goods and services generally play a greater role in poor than in rich countries; and if they were included in national product, the statistical income gap would presumably be further reduced.

A light-hearted simplistic version of PPP has been published annually since 1986 by the UK journal *The Economist* under the name of the *Big*

Mac index (*The Economist*, 5 May 1990). Following from the proposition that in the long run the exchange rate between two countries should equate the prices of a basket of goods and services, a single good is taken as being representative of that basket, namely a McDonald's Big Mac hamburger, which is available, in similar shape and taste, in more than 50 countries.

At the time of the May 1990 survey, a Big Mac cost about $US2.20 in the United States, Ffr17.70 in France and $S2.60 in Singapore. This is equivalent to a parity of 8.05 for $US1 in France or 1.18 in Singapore as the implied purchasing power of the US dollar. The actual exchange rates at that time were 5.63 and 1.88 respectively, suggesting that the US dollar was undervalued by 30% in France—and undervalued also to varying degrees in most other Western European countries, Japan and the Soviet Union—but overvalued by 59% in Singapore—as well as in Hongkong (by 100%), Australia (by 26%) and Canada (by 16%). (Over- and undervalued here means relative to the US dollar.)

Parities between other countries can also be determined by the Big Mac standard. For example, it was about 100 between Japan (370 yen for a hamburger) and the Soviet Union (3.75 roubles) compared with 265 by the actual exchange rate ($US1 = 159 yen = 0.60 roubles), while the Big Mac rate of DM3 per £1 happened to be quite close to the actual exchange rate between Germany and the United Kingdom. Choosing a single article as indicator for purchasing power comparisons is reminiscent of the old gold standard, where exchange rates equalled the respective prices of gold in different countries. That likeness is superficial, however, because hamburgers are not traded internationally, nor are they a mobile store of value, and their relative prices reflect only remotely, if at all, shifts in the balance of payments. However, like other single-good or mixed baskets of goods and services, the index provides a realistic indicator of relative price levels for a particular segment of the market.

Foreign exchange rates and PPPs refer to relations between different countries, while *terms of trade* describe the price relations between different goods or types of goods traded by a particular country—or more specifically, between imported and exported goods. At the simplest level we can take the case of a country importing one good and exporting one good—in Ricardo's example (1817), England importing wine from, and exporting cloth to, Portugal. The cost of wine can then be expressed in terms of the production cost of cloth. If all trade is regarded as barter, with money merely serving as an instrument for exchanging things, the wine/cloth ratio represents what J.S. Mill (1848) called the *barter terms of trade*. If P and Q refer to price and quantity for goods a and b and there is an equivalent exchange

$$P_a Q_a = P_b Q_b$$

then the barter terms of trade are

$$Q_a : Q_b = P_a : P_b$$

The practical problem is that trade consists of a great variety of goods, and some services, which must be standardised for aggregation by summing individual PQ to $\Sigma(PQ)$ for the value of all trade, or of particular types such as import and export trade. Unlike the simple case above, where it is possible to compare x quantities of the single export good and y quantities of the single import good, and to determine an exchange ratio of $x{:}y$ that is independent of prices and, over time, independent of price changes, we must now use the value figure varied by prices, as expressed in the price index numbers, usually with fixed base weights.

Terms of trade are then conventionally expressed as the ratio of the *export price index* to the *import price index*, which shows change between periods rather than a meaningful ratio at any one period. An increase in this ratio from, say, 110 to 121 means that the terms of trade have improved to the extent that an unchanged quantity of exports will now buy a 10% greater quantity of imports, or that the same imports as before will require 9% less exports to pay for them.

The terms of trade show trends in the area covered by the export and import price indexes, excluding other aspects of the balance of payments (e.g. transport, other service payments). The general problems of index-number coverage and updating reduce their accuracy, but not their usefulness, as an indicator of price changes in foreign trade.

4.6 Labour market

Labour economics is distinguished from other areas of economics by its preoccupation with human rather than material resources. For most of its indicators we can use persons, graded by demographic characteristics as the counting unit (numeraire), rather than ubiquitous money values.

National accounts follow the old-fashioned economic notions of *work* equalling paid work. Thus they omit persons doing household, community or hobby work from what they define as the labour (or work) force and ignore unpaid activities altogether, although household services are essential for, and often interchangeable with, paid work. A more comprehensive *activities approach* (R. Horn, 1983) would encompass what Illich (1981) has called *shadow work*.

For the present purpose we will accept the traditional definitions of the International Labour Office that are used by most countries, and also the codes about borderline classes such as defence forces and part time workers, and restrict comments to the relationship between main groups, with reference to their usefulness as indicators for the labour market and productivity.

Out of the total population of a country, some groups are not available for (paid) work because they are too young or too old or too sick or otherwise occupied at any one time. Their number can only be estimated, because most of them move frequently into and out of the labour force. The young leave school to continue with full time education or to enter the labour force, and may leave it temporarily later for a study course. The old often retire on reaching the statutory age, 60 or 65; this barrier is being lifted in some countries, and anyway there is usually no age limit on those working on the land or in professions. The sick may return to the labour force on recovery. Those otherwise occupied, in particular the 'housewife' category, move freely into and out of paid work. The population between the ages of 15 and 64 is usually called the *economically active population*, or sometimes the *potential labour force*, which is perhaps not quite accurate because it includes a few who cannot or will not work and omits the small number of workers below and above the set ages. So *labour force* and *employment* are somewhat fluid notions, because at any time some persons are moving in and out for personal or economic reasons.

Table 4.5 shows that, beyond the cases of people working full time for themselves or others, and of people not engaged in paid work, there are intermediate categories that may or may not be included in labour force statistics.

Technically, population figures are derived from full or sample census collections, and employment figures from special sample surveys or as a byproduct of other collections, such as those regularly undertaken by manpower or social security agencies. The three main series for indicator purposes—reference population, employment and unemployment—interact only partially. Population changes are due to external demographic factors, and economic activity is affected also by minor shifts in the numbers at work aged under 15 or over 64 or in the military. This leads to two main indicator ratios: the *labour force participation rate*, which relates the labour force to the reference population, and the *unemployment rate*, which relates unemployment to the labour force.

The main factors determining the participation rate are the extent of postschool full time studies, the provision for retirement income and the number of women in paid employment. For men the ratio typically rises

Table 4.5   Reference population for labour force: civilians aged 15–64

Category	Description
Employed	Full time or part time
Not employed	Want to work or don't want to work
	Looking for work or not looking for work
Fully employed	Working 35+ hours, or less by choice
Underemployed	Working less than 35 hours but want to work more
Unemployed	Willing and able to work and actively looking for work
Marginally attached to labour force	Discouraged job seekers
Not in labour force	Including those only marginally attached

from about 50% at age 20 to a peak of 90%+ in their mid 50s and then drops sharply to about 25% when they reach age 65. For women the ratio is generally less than for men and has a bimodal distribution, with one peak around 50% at age 25 before marriage, followed by a drop to 30%, then a second peak of some 40% near age 50 when some re-enter the labour force; but as women generally retire earlier than men, at age 65 the rate is near 10%.

Unemployment is one of the most quoted economic indicators, be it expressed in actual figures or as a proportion of the labour force. In official statistics the term is restricted to those able and willing and ready to work. It does not cover discouraged job seekers, often women, nor others who, while able, can afford to wait for a suitable job. A change in employment will result from a reciprocal change in unemployment or from a change in the labour force. This means that a rise or fall in the participation rate can affect either employment or unemployment or both.

In the example in Table 4.6 the unemployment rate can change only at the expense of employment when the labour force is fixed; but when the labour force increases, both employment and unemployment can rise simultaneously or one at the expense of the other. Changes in unemployment, and the unemployment rate, should therefore always be considered in the context of movements in the total labour force to give a fuller indication of labour market changes.

Unemployment is defined for international statistics as mentioned above, and some other specific descriptions are based on the number of persons in receipt of unemployment benefit under social security or insurance schemes. There are no corresponding firm statistical definitions of *labour demand*, but in some countries indicators have been constructed from job vacancy tabulations by public and private agencies or from the number of 'positions vacant' advertisements in the press.

We cannot discuss here the limitations and bias inherent in any such attempt to capture a fluid notion such as labour demand. If credible statistics of labour demand by occupations, and possibly also region, are available one could apply Perlman's (1969) method to disaggregate unemployment,

Table 4.6 Participation rate and unemployment rate

Reference population	Labour force	Participation rate (%)	Employment	Unemployment	Unemployment rate (%)
1000	800	80.0	750	50	6.3
			700	100	12.5
			768	32	4.0
1010	804	79.6	753	51	6.3
			750	54	6.7

U, by three major types: structural U_s, frictional U_f, and demand U_d, with vacancies, V, for each occupation equalling its $(U_s + U_f)$:

$$U = U_s + U_f + U_d$$
$$V = U_s + U_f$$
$$U_s = V - U_f$$
$$U_f = V - U_s$$
$$U_d = U - V$$

If $V \geqslant U$,

$$U_d = 0$$
$$U = U_s + U_f$$

U_d refers to the market as a whole; it is nil if total $V > U$, and such U as exists must then be of the U_s and U_f type. If $U > V$, then U_d is represented by the excess of U over V, and V consists of persons who cannot find work for structural and frictional reasons; so $V = U_s + U_f$.

U_s and U_f signify internal imbalances in the labour market. In occupations where $U < V$ (i.e. U exists in spite of excess demand), U = U_f, in those where $V > U$ (i.e. persons are unplaced in spite of jobs existing), $V = U_f$. If there is any U_d, it must be allotted to occupations with excess $U > V$. Structural unemployment is then derived as the balance, representing such unemployment as could be removed by retraining for occupations for which there is excess labour demand. This is illustrated in Table 4.7 by a simple two-occupation model where U equals V or is more or less than V. In this example the interplay of two indicators is used to disaggregate one of them.

Further to the relation of market factors, behavioural elements can be considered as in the augmented *Phillips curve* that interrelates unemployment and wage levels, or by taking attitudes to work and leisure as expressed in the shifting preference curve of the *substitution* of work for leisure to earn more and the *income effect* when leisure is preferred to work. Training, mobility, barriers, market segmentation and so on increase the complexities of the market and its indicators.

Table 4.7 Two-occupation unemployment model

Occupation		U	V	U_f	U_s	U_d		U	V	U_f	U_s	U_d
A	(i)	20	50	20			(iii)	20	30	20		
B		80	60	60	20			80	50	50	10	20
Total		100	110	80	20			100	80	70	10	20
A	(ii)	20	20	20			(iv)	20	10	10		10
B		80	80	80				80	70	70		10
Total		100	100	100				100	80	80		20

4.7 Productivity

Productivity has been described as the ratio of output to the total input of factors required to achieve it (Ducommun, 1968), and factor productivity as the ratio of factor output to factor input. The factors usually considered, either separately or together, are labour and capital. Other costs of production (e.g. power, transport), unless identified separately, are assumed to be proportional to labour and capital in what is called *multifactor productivity*. Productivity is associated with efficiency of production. It can serve as an indicator of technological progress in the long term, and over shorter periods it can also be influenced by managerial efficiency, capacity utilisation, work habits or weather conditions (Englander and Mittelstädt, 1988: 9). It is an important indicator for the planning and industrial progress of the firm and the economy as a whole.

For the measurement of productivity we have to establish the relation of production to its constituent elements, which, as so often with indicators, raises questions about the combination of disparate components with different scales of values and trends. Labour is preferably expressed in physical units of time (e.g. manhours), even if this glosses over differences in skills, quality, paid work and non-work time, and so on. For capital no corresponding measure is available, because the diffused use of equipment usually does not allow its allocation to period- or product-specific output. Therefore it is necessary to fall back on general capital-stock and flow statistics of the firm and the aggregates shown in national accounts, with unavoidable assumptions of homogeneity of capital composition and use.

As a general starting point we can take a *Cobb–Douglas-type production function*, where L = labour, K = capital, A = productivity and V = output:

$$V = A(L, K)$$
$$A = V/(L, K)$$

The variables are usually shown in index form on the basis of a common year for output and input, and these in turn can be expressed as annual percentage changes over a stated period, as, for example, in the OECD publication cited above.

There are a number of statistical variations in the construction of the index, in particular with respect to the usual assumption of a fixed relation between labour and capital factors and their combination by arithmetic or geometric averaging. It has been suggested, for instance, that instead of the conventional geometric average a so-called *Divisia Index* should be employed, which uses the weighted sum of growth rates:

$$\Delta A = \Delta L \times \Delta K$$

However, such refinements probably do not make much difference to a calculation of gradual change that cannot claim a high degree of accuracy in the estimation of its components anyhow.

For longer term analysis the trends in productivity must be viewed against the broader picture of technological progress leading to the replacement of labour by capital. The replacement of manpower by labour-saving machines, of which computerisation and robotics are conspicuous examples, is evidenced in the declining share of labour in national income. The question then arises whether the increasing use of machines means limitless growth in output and labour displacement. Some recent trends are shown in the OECD study by Englander and Mittelstädt (1988: 14).

The annual rate of output growth in OECD countries and the United States has declined by up to 50% since the 1960s. This seems to have been due only partly to a fall in demand and capacity usage and more so to the decline of labour and capital productivity in recent years. Labour productivity, reflecting technological progress, remained positive, at 1.4% and 0.6% respectively for 1979–88, but fell to less than half than the rates of 4.1% and 2.2% respectively recorded for 1960–73. Capital productivity turned negative, to about –1% per year for most countries, due probably to a slowdown in the early postwar catch-up and to deceleration in technological advances. The total factor productivity (TFP) rate remained around 1.5% in a few countries, such as Japan (down from 6% in the 1960s), but in most others was less than 1%.

Apart from general trends, productivity statistics are useful for comparing industries. Such an analysis of the OECD statistics suggests that TFP growth in manufacturing fell on average from 4% in the 1970s to 2% in the early 1980s but did still better than the service industries (trade, transport, finance and social), which declined from 2% to nil. The productivity lag in those industries has been ascribed to various factors:

- measurement problems for intangibles of unknown quality;
- overinvestment in technical hardware in the 1970s, with long lead periods to apply it efficiently; or

Table 4.8 Growth rates: business sector (average annual percentage changes)

| | OECD countries | | | | | United States | | | | |
| | | | Productivity | | | | | Productivity | | |
Period	Output	Factor input	TFP[a]	Labour	Capital	Output	Factor input	TFP[a]	Labour	Capital
1960–73	5.2	2.4	2.8	4.1	–0.4	3.8	1.3	1.5	2.2	0.3
1973–79	2.9	2.2	0.7	1.6	–1.4	2.8	2.9	–0.1	0.3	–0.9
1979–88	2.9	1.7	0.6	1.4	–1.3	2.2	2.2	0	0.6	–1.0

[a] TFP = total factor productivity; capital shares in 1985 were 32.3 for OECD countries and 32.2 for the United States.
Source: Englander and Mittelstädt (1988: 14).

- an uneven spread of new technology, which overall had more application in the manufacturing than in other industries.

Productivity indicators can be combined with wage statistics to gauge a country's competitiveness. Exchange rates do not necessarily reflect disparities in cost/price structures, and differences exist in industry and wage structures between countries. However, the following ratio probably serves best as an indicator of a country's international competitiveness:

$$\Delta \text{ Unit cost per worker index} = \frac{\Delta \text{ Output per worker index}}{\Delta \text{ Wage rate index}}$$

4.8 Performance (see also section 5.11)

In evaluating projects and subsequently monitoring their performance, planners have long used various indicators to compare costs with benefits. These methods have been considerably refined in recent years in both the public and private sectors. UNESCO, for example, has published a series of monographs on evaluation (e.g. Soumelis, 1977; Freeman et al., 1980; Weilenmann, 1980; Grabe, 1983), applicable to the projects that UNESCO supports. These deal at length with the complexities of the evaluation process, in terms of deciding the module of objectives, ranging from specific targets and patterns of goals to more general objectives and organisational purpose. The process extends to evaluative criteria based on the direct measurement of alternative systems. The close interrelation between decision-making levels and the continuous nature of the evaluation process are illustrated by charts showing progress and feedback between them. Such schemes rely heavily on social or socioeconomic indicators drawn from existing statistics and special surveys (e.g. for the performance evaluation of educational systems).

The large international finance institutions run evaluation studies of their projects at various levels. The International Monetary Fund (IMF), which promotes international monetary cooperation and alleviates disequilibria in balances of payments through short term loans, uses economic criteria (see section 3.1). The World Bank, either by itself or in conjunction with other agencies, runs a number of programs, for adjustment lending, structural and sector adjustment, and so on, the effectiveness of which is monitored by means of various indicators. As an example of the bank's check on projects, Table 4.9 presents part of its report *Project Performance Results for 1987* (1989). The elaborate assessment process relies on judgements based either on indicators collected *ad hoc* or on existing sources. Major criteria vary according to the nature of the project, but often include the economic rate of return, the sustainability of the project and the building up of local institutions. Costs and time taken for implementation can also become major considerations. The World Bank has an experienced Operations Evaluation Department, which is flexible in following changing goals and at times is critical of deficiencies in execution and supervision not only by the countries concerned but also by the bank itself.

The influence of the World Bank, in particular in developing countries, extends past the granting of loans to direct or indirect influence on economic policy, the monetary and fiscal fields, investment and trade, debt management, price setting and so on, and the project assessment process extends into those wider spheres.

Table 4.9 gives an indication of the large number and value of projects handled by the World Bank: 187 projects valued at $US7500 million in 1987, spread over major economic sectors and regions. For about one-half of the projects an *economic rate of return* has been calculated, defined as being:

> . . . based on a comparison of costs and benefits, measured using shadow prices that indicate real values to the economy. Inherent in the costs and benefits are four indicators of performance considered particularly important by the Bank: sustainability of benefits, progress with institution building and the extent of time and cost overruns. (World Bank, 1989b: 3)

It is not clear to what extent the calculation of costs and benefits may go beyond the list of narrow economic criteria applied by the IMF (see

Table 4.9   Evaluation by the World Bank of 187 projects, 1987

	Projects		Results satisfactory (%)	Economic rates of return (%)	Likely to be sustainable (%)	Objectives achieved	
	Number	$US billions				Most (%)	Some (%)
Agricultural	67	2.0	61	13.1	43	31	49
Industry/energy	42	2.2	83	10.2	58	29	59
Infrastructure/urban	49	1.9	75	21.2	43	19	32
Human/technical assistance	22	0.4	77		50	43	48
Structural adjustment	7	1.0	86		86	86	14
Region							
Africa	49	0.8	53	10.4	30	28	37
Asia	50	3.1	84	19.0	61	39	26
Europe/Middle East	49	2.2	83	8.9	61	28	61
Latin America	39	1.4	88	17.8	42	30	38
Total	187	7.5	72	13.0	49	31	46

Source: World Bank (1989b).

section 3.1). The economic rate of return is described as a relatively objective measure, calculated first at project appraisal and re-estimated at the time of completion (when it usually works out less by several percentage points). Overall assessment of the extent to which results are satisfactory and sustainable largely relies on subjective expert views.

Table 4.9 suggests that 72% of the listed projects showed satisfactory results and that 77% at least fulfilled some of the institutional aims, but only 49% were thought likely to sustain their benefits (33% marginal or uncertain and 18% unlikely). Structural adjustment projects scored best on all of these criteria. Among the regions, African projects generally did worse than those elsewhere.

Going from international assessment to the measurement of *enterprise performance*, including comparison between government and private business undertakings, the reference is usually to *allocative efficiency*. This is represented in competition by return on assets (i.e. the relation of price to marginal cost) or in monopolies by excess profits. For public goods provided with only general cost constraints, input costs and output have to be assessed using subjective criteria or by comparison with similar enterprises (Vining, 1989). Attempts to account for sociopolitical factors in the provision of public goods, and for environmental factors in the location and operation of all enterprises, create further problems in the construction of performance indicators. Perhaps a systematic methodology for performance measurement could be derived from the current experiences with transfers of public enterprises to the private sector in the United Kingdom and elsewhere, and also from the recurring takeover waves by expanding firms in industrialised countries.

The choice of indicators reflects the ambiguity of performance concepts. The generally accepted measure of *performance efficiency* in industry is the target rate of return on assets that represents the optimal allocation of resources. Applied to public enterprises, this means a rate of return that is neither so high as to overcharge the community nor too low to subsidise the service. Looking at the commercial aspects of public enterprise pricing applied to the New Zealand electricity industry, Read and Sell (1987) have suggested the notion of *avoided cost* as a short term pricing signal, equal to the savings made by customers if they were to reduce their demand by one unit:

> ... if the price were set lower, the Corporation would be selling at a loss and pass extra costs on to the consumer ... if higher, consumers would forego profitable activities for which the Corporation could profitably provide electricity ... Both better off in the long run if prices are determined by the avoided costs.

An apparent contradiction arises when the system is not in equilibrium and the replacement cost of the power station is no longer a good indicator of its value:

> . . . with surplus capacity the Corporation would have to raise prices so reducing demand even further . . . and with demand in excess of capacity it would be forced to lower prices, stimulating further demand . . . the exact opposite of the competitive situation.

This seems to point to an apparent conflict between financial performance and commercial price setting, ascribable to timing: the short term variable price is linked to the long term investment decision, and one input variable is used as sole determinant of output.

It has been further argued (Hussey, 1971; Argenti, 1980) that performance indicators should monitor and assess confidence in plans and objectives, not merely progress towards targets. This gives them a dynamic function in reappraising plans:

> . . . a set of objectives will be likely to contain aims which cannot be simultaneously satisfied and . . . may require going in different directions at the one time . . . this represents the greatest benefit from . . . setting performance indicators . . . for government and public sector management to be forced to explicitly acknowledge their priorities and have them publicly debated. (Curran in Wyatt and Ruby, 1988)

Performance tests can be subjectively applied to the coverage, progress and relevance of specific programs. Morris et al. (1988: 56–66), for example, outline a *program test* where informed raters grade every test item by importance of objective on a five-point scale and by content and appropriateness for participants each on a three-point scale. These are multiplied for each test item, and the sum of the products divided by the number of items shows which of several tests is the most appropriate for the program. Adjusted for zero values, the test yields an index of relevance ranging from 0 to 1. Note that not only is the rating subjective, but also the weighting through differential scaling.

For the evaluation of *macroeconomic performance* in the sense of Keynesian monetary and fiscal policy that seeks internal balance in output, employment and prices and external balance in trade, budget outcome is sometimes quoted as an indicator, although even a balanced budget can be expansionary or restrictive because of the differential effects of taxation and government spending. The OECD has until recently relied on the *cyclically adjusted budget balance (CAB)* for the analysis of fiscal policy, together with the *debt stabilisation gap*, equal to the budget change needed to stabilise the debt/GNP ratio through discretionary fiscal policy. It is now exploring a range of supplementary measures (Chouraqui et al., 1990: 19):

> . . . estimated budget balance had real output been on trend, or if unemployment had remained unchanged; estimation of sustainability on the basis of spending projections and assumed levels of interest and growth rates; impact of fiscal policy on aggregate demand.

Inflation affects period comparisons of performance indicators. The rate of return from assets to produce the income can be computed in various ways:

- the *historical cost* of assets at time of purchase;
- *price level accounting*, based on revaluing all assets in terms of their purchasing power;
- *relative price-level accounting*, which also considers the relative price changes of individual assets;
- *current cost accounting*, based on the replacement cost of assets (Swan, 1990).

Each of these methods is debatable. Historical cost, enshrined by tradition and often by law, overstates return in current prices, and price-level accounting and replacement cost valuation ignore technical change.

Job evaluation is another area of indicative interest. It can be applied at various stages, beginning from describing job functions and setting standards required for potential applicants, to reviews of the job structure within an enterprise in the light of changing techniques and production programs, and finally to assessing individual performances of employees in connection with their career advancement.

The grading of jobs within an enterprise can be of considerable practical importance in wage negotiations, where it is applied in the metal trades in the United States, as well as in some other industries there and elsewhere. Typically for indicators, the choice of a system lends a certain gloss of objective assessment to the process; but in reality that choice depends on subjective judgement, hopefully backed by commonsense, and on the bargaining strengths and tactics of the negotiating parties (i.e. employers and trade unions).

The example in Table 4.10, is based on a scale used by the US Metal Trades Association and adopted also for a work value enquiry for the Australian Metal Trades Award in 1966. The following steps can be distinguished:

1 agreement on the major characteristics to be taken into account;
2 agreement on their relative weights for skill and effort;
3 assessment of the required characteristics for each job;
4 ratings multiplied by weight to yield aggregate scores;
5 listing of jobs according to score;
6 'broadbanding' of scores into categories (e.g. 101–200, 201–300);
7 agreement on lowest and highest wages (e.g. 100–200 and 500+ ranges);
8 fitting progression in either a straight line or a 'bowline', where rates rise more slowly for lower than for upper grades.

In the example job A involves less skill, initiative and responsibility than job B but more physical effort and accident risk. Job B rates about 50% more points than A; but on a bowline fitting of pay rates to evaluation points, B's pay could be twice as high, or more, than A's pay.

Table 4.10 Comparative job evaluation

Job characteristic	Factor (%)	Job A Rating (max. 10)	Job A Score	Job B Rating (max. 10)	Job B Score
Education	14	3	42	7	98
Experience	22	4	88	6	132
Initiative, ingenuity	14	2	28	8	112
Physical effort	10	7	70	1	10
Mental and visual effort	5	1	5	6	30
Responsibility[a]	20	2	40	7	140
Work conditions, hazards	15	6	90	2	30
Total	100		363		552

[a] Divided in equal parts between responsibility for equipment and processes, for materials and products, for the safety of others and for the work of others.
Source: R. Horn (1975a: 156).

The advantage claimed for this system is its rational flexibility, but its application presumes a state of responsible negotiations about the work contract between parties prepared to trade off their mutual claims.

The measurement and assessment of programs are discussed in detail in a series of nine books edited by Herman of the Center for the Study of Evaluation at the University of California; for example, that by Morris et al. (1988) is entitled *How to Measure Performance and Use Tests*. More on the macro side, Carley (1981) has described the use of social indicators for social measurement.

4.9 Economic diagrams and formulas

Indicators rest on the actual or assumed continuity of statistics as expressed in trend lines. For analysis we are interested in the directions of such trends and in their turning points rather than in the details of point-to-point movements. Indicators can then be presented in diagrams to accompany, or replace, statistical tables. This applies generally to economic as well as other statistics discussed here. A brief survey of graphical methods has been given in section 2.2, and the various textbooks carry references to economic indication by way of charts, graphs and diagrams (e.g. pie charts, Gantt progress charts, break-even charts, band curves, Lorenz curves, Z charts). Here we will look only at some examples of the juxtaposition of variables that highlight their interdependence, graphically or in brief formulas and can serve as indicators.

Figure 4.1   Component charts: price index numbers

Type of goods	Value share	Year 1	Year 2	Year 3	Year 4
Imported	(20%)	100	110	130	120
Local	(80%)	100	105	110	115
All goods	(100%)	100	106	114	116

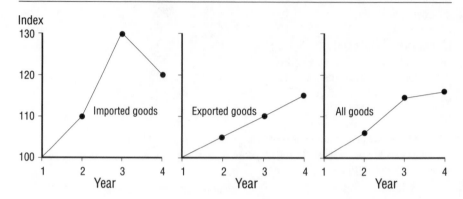

Component charts (Figure 4.1) can be used to highlight the influence, or even dominance, of one or several components. In looking at total imports, for example, the effect of variations in one class, say consumer goods, can be demonstrated as leading the trend in the total, or perhaps in swamping a contrary trend in capital goods, or a turning point in the overall trend can be attributed to a particular component.

Apart from trend, a component chart shows relative magnitudes; for example, for imports the comparative size of consumer and capital goods can be depicted. In graphs based on period change, the relative difference is glossed over when both components and totals are shown as index numbers, or when percentage changes rather than values are used. To avoid this type of ambiguity the aggregate is graphed both including and excluding a particular segment. If, for example, the rate of inflation is thought to be due to both external factors (e.g. import prices beyond the control of government) and internal factors (e.g. local prices that depend on regulation), two separate graphs could be drawn or, alternatively, one for an aggregate price index and another excluding the import or local component. Unlike the first, the second method shows the role of the component in its proper proportion.

Terms of trade (Figure 4.2) describe the price relations between different goods, or types of goods, that are imported and exported by a country. It is a somewhat narrower concept than exchange rates or purchasing power parities, which also include the relative costs of capital and other financial exchanges. In the example given by John Stuart Mill (1848), England imports

Figure 4.2   Export and import price index and terms of trade

	Year 1	Year 2		Year 3		Year 4	
Price index		Index	Change	Index	Change	Index	Change
Imports	100	110	(+10%)	130	(+18%)	120	(−8%)
Exports	100	120	(+20%)	110	(−8%)	130	(+18%)
Terms of trade[a]	100	109	(+9%)	85	(−22%)	108	(+27%)

[a] Terms of trade = 100 (Export index/Import index)

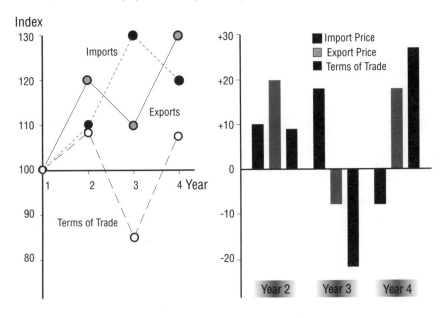

wine from and exports cloth to Spain. The cost of wine can then be expressed in terms of the production cost of cloth; and as Mill regarded all trade as barter, with money merely serving as an instrument of exchange, he called the wine/cloth ratio the *barter terms of trade*. If P and Q refer respectively to the price and quantity of goods a and b, and there is an equivalent exchange, so that

$$P_aQ_a = P_bQ_b$$

then the barter terms of trade are

$$Q_a/Q_b = -P_aP_b$$

As trade in practice consists of a variety of goods, and some services, they must be standardised for aggregation by summing up the PQ to ΣPQ for imports, exports or all trade. Instead of single barter rates and exchange ratios we have to use combined value figures, which vary with prices as indicated by a price index, which is usually constructed with fixed base weights. The terms of trade are then expressed by the ratio of the export to the import price indexes, which measures change over a given period, rather than by an absolute price ratio. An increase in this ratio from 110 to 121 means that the terms of trade have improved to the extent that an unchanged quantity of exports will buy a quantity of imports 10% greater than before, or that the same quantity of imports will now require 9% less exports to pay for them.

It is important to note that the terms of trade measure only *changes* in the price relativities of trade items. Because of their heterogeneous and shifting composition, one cannot use them to say that x units of exports are required to buy y units of imports, although one might make anecdotal comparisons to claim that at present prices x bushels of wheat will buy y number of cars. Overall, series of terms of trade are a useful indicator of trends, in particular for the distinction between price and quantity changes in traded goods. For this purpose particular attention must be given to the up-to-date weighting of price indexes.

Market penetration (Figure 4.3) is measured by the distinction between home production and foreign trade in a manner suggested by the OECD (Brodin and Blades, 1986). If L stands for local production, M for imports and X for exports (total or particular items L_i, M_i, X_i, for trading partners j_0, j_1 . . .), the following ratios can be calculated:

$$\text{Import strength} = \frac{M}{L} \qquad \text{Export strength} = \frac{X}{L}$$

$$\text{Import supply} = \frac{M}{M + L} \qquad \text{Export dependence} = \frac{X}{X + L}$$

$$\text{Import penetration} = \frac{M}{L + M - X}$$

Import penetration here is expressed as the relation of imports to home supplies, including imports, less exports, and the *penetration index* reflects the interplay of these three variables. Import strength and penetration increase with rising imports, and more so if imports replace local production. Export strength and dependence increase with rising exports, particularly if these do not rise at the expense of local supplies. If imports and exports rise by equal amounts, without change in local production, the import penetration index, as well as the other index numbers shown in the table in Figure 4.3, will rise also.

The interrelations will not be immediately clear if these variables are graphed separately. However, they can be emphasised in different ways: by contrasting diagrams of import and export strengths, to demonstrate the relative significance of local and overseas markets; or by contrasting import supply and export dependence, to bring out the importance of foreign markets on local supplies; or by graphing the import penetration index, to stress the role of imports in overall supplies.

Figure 4.3   Overseas trade indicators

Class	Local production L	Imports M	Exports X	Local supply $L + M - X$	Import strength M/L	Export strength X/L	Import supply $M/(M + L)$	Export dependence $X/(X + L)$	Import penetration $M/(L + M - X)$
Base	100	10	10	100	0.1	0.1	0.09	0.09	0.10
I	100	20	10	110	0.20	0.10	0.17	0.09	0.18
	100	30	10	120	0.30	0.10	0.23	0.09	0.25
	100	40	10	130	0.40	0.10	0.29	0.09	0.31
II	100	10	20	90	0.10	0.20	0.09	0.17	0.11
	100	10	30	80	0.10	0.30	0.09	0.23	0.13
	100	10	40	70	0.10	0.40	0.09	0.29	0.14
III	90	20	10	100	0.22	0.11	0.18	0.10	0.20
	80	30	10	100	0.38	0.13	0.27	0.11	0.30
	70	40	10	100	0.57	0.14	0.36	0.13	0.40
IV	110	10	20	100	0.09	0.18	0.08	0.15	0.10
	120	10	30	100	0.08	0.25	0.08	0.20	0.10
	130	10	40	100	0.08	0.31	0.07	0.24	0.10
V	100	20	20	100	0.20	0.20	0.17	0.17	0.20
	100	30	30	100	0.30	0.30	0.23	0.23	0.30
	100	40	40	100	0.40	0.40	0.29	0.29	0.40

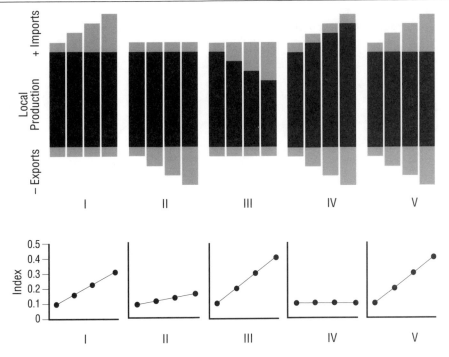

This can be done for particular items or classes of goods, although there may be a statistical problem of coordinating the respective classifications, or it can be done for aggregate GNP and gross domestic expenditure in relation to their export and import components. Corresponding market-penetration indicators can sometimes be calculated also for a particular brand of good in relation to the overall market, and in other competitive situations (e.g. for television viewing on alternative networks where L represents total possible viewing time).

Intensity of trade between countries A and B, as viewed by A, is expressed by comparing B's share in A's trade with B's share in world trade. If they are identical—that is, if the bilateral relation between A and B is about the same as for their trade with the rest of the world—the index is 1. If the bilateral relation is more (less) intense, the index is greater (less) than 1. This indicator is of particular interest for the comparative analysis of small and large trading countries.

We use the symbols M and X for imports and exports respectively, and the subscripts i, j and w for countries A and B and the world respectively. Then for country A we have as numerator of the index A's exports to B as a proportion of A's total exports, and as denominator the proportion that B absorbs of total imports not absorbed by A—and vice versa for country B (see Figure 4.4).

The intensity of trade index for country A, I_{ij}, is then calculated by

$$I_{ij} = \frac{X_{ij} / X_i}{M_j / (M_w - M_i)}$$

Figure 4.4   Trade Intensity

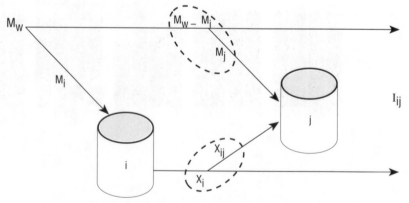

X_{ij} / X_i = proportion of i's exports captured by j; serves as a measure of importance to i of j as an importer of i's goods.

$M_j / M_w - M_i$ = proportion of all imports not absorbed by i, but by j; serves as a measure of scale of j as an importer.

Table 4.11   Intensity of trade between two countries

Trade	Country A	Country B	Others	Total
Country A exports		$X_{ij} = 60$	940	$X_i = $ 1 000
Country A imports		$M_{ij} = 50$	1 150	$M_i = $ 1 200
Country B exports	$X_{ji} = 50$		28 950	$X_j = $ 29 000
Country B imports	$M_{ji} = 60$		21 940	$M_j = $ 22 000
World exports				$X_w = $ 300 000
World imports				$M_w = $ 300 000

which comes to 0.81 in the example in Table 4.11. The corresponding index for country B, I_{ji}, is arrived at similarly:

$$I_{ji} = \frac{X_{ji} / X_j}{M_i / (M_w - M_j)}$$

At 0.40, it is lower than I_{ij} because in the larger country B trade with a smaller partner is relatively less important.

One can go further with standardising bilateral trade by size of exports by using the formulas

$$I_{ij} = \frac{M_{ij} / M_i}{X_j / (X_w - X_i)}$$

and

$$I_{ji} = \frac{M_{ji} / M_j}{X_i / (X_w - X_j)}$$

which work out at 0.43 and 0.74 respectively in the example.

The *J curve* describes a possible lag effect of a currency depreciation (Figure 4.5). Such a depreciation is usually directed towards an improvement in the trade balance. It can be expected that the consequent price rises, in domestic currency, will reduce the demand for imports and make exports more competitive on world markets. J curve analysis spells out some of the obstacles along this path.

In distinguishing between the price and volume effects of a depreciation, it is likely that the volume of import orders will not immediately change but that, as they will become dearer in terms of foreign exchange, the trade balance will worsen. An unchanged volume of exports will in the first place earn an unchanged return in foreign exchange; and gradually when that is converted into higher returns of local currency, exporters will lower their prices and be able to sell a greater volume. In the longer run imports will decline because of their higher prices; so then the depreciation will improve the balance-of-trade position because of both rising exports and falling imports.

Figure 4.5   J curve: effect of currency depreciation in year 2

	Year 1	Year 2	Year 3	Year 4	Year 5
Exports	100	100	120	140	140
Imports	120	140	120	100	100
Trade balance (J curve)	-20	-40	0	+40	+40

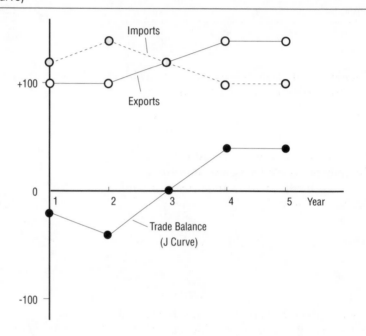

A number of general factors have to be taken into account, such as price and demand elasticities in the markets of both trading partners, the potential for import substitution, the import content of exports, freedom of exchange and trade flows, and the effects of devaluation on capital flows. The J curve points to only one set of factors, albeit the important one of market lags, but in practice these are difficult to isolate from the other changes caused by a change in the exchange rate.

It is not claimed that a reverse J curve effect applies in the rarer case of a major foreign-exchange appreciation, because the motivation, initial situation and operation of market forces are likely to be quite different from the depreciation case, but not the exact opposite.

Activity charts show the direction rather than size of economic activities. The chart in Figure 4.6, devised by Schroders Australia Limited for change between March and September 1990, places major indicators into a grid according to their cycle modes, and this gives an impression of the prevalence

Figure 4.6   Economic activity chart, March 1990

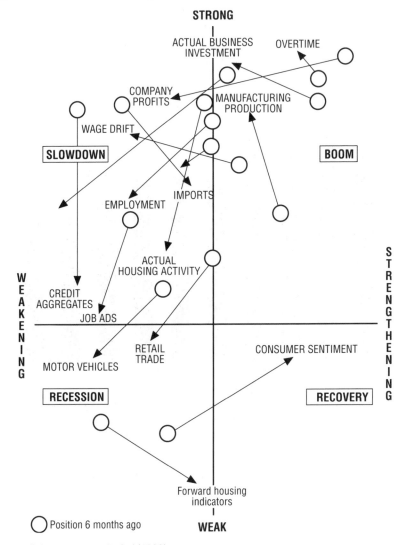

Source: Schroders Australia Ltd (1990).

of slowdown and recession over business strength indicators. Schroders, in its *Report on Economic Activity* issued in November 1990, commented:

The current position of each indicator is shown by its position in the grid. The position of the indicator six months previously is marked by the corresponding circle. Each indicator is judged by two criteria—relative strength or weakness and whether it is strengthening or weakening . . .

Over the past six months, almost all of the indicators have moved in the expected anti-clockwise position. Six months ago the indicators were suggesting that a slowdown had commenced. Currently, they are clearly indicating that the slowdown has gathered momentum to such an extent that a recession is now a clear possibility. (p. 1)

Engel curves (Figure 4.7) relate expenditure on food to total family expenditure. Not only is the observation of this relationship of intrinsic

Figure 4.7   Engel curves

(a) Food expenditure as % of household income, Australia

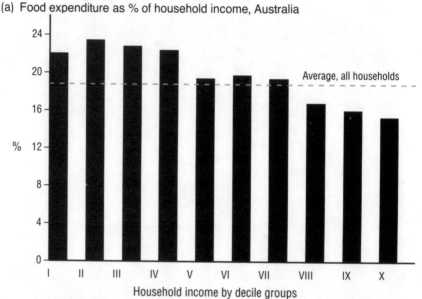

Household income by decile groups

Notes: 1988/89; income deciles for 14.3 million persons in 5.1 million households; reference to commodity and service expenditure in Australian dollars; overall average 18.7%.
Source: Australian Bureau of Statistics (Cat. no. 6528.0, 1989, table 1).

(b) Private expenditure on food and total final consumption, Australia

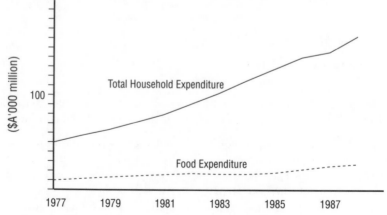

Source: Australian Bureau of Statistics (Cat. no. 5201.0, 1989, table 16).

significance for the analysis of income and expenditure; it has also been of historic importance as the early formulation of an 'economic' or 'econometric' function. The German statistician Ernst Engel maintained that the poorer the family, the greater the proportion of its total expenditure that must be devoted to food, which was later reformulated to read 'the proportion of income spent on food declines as income rises' or 'the income elasticity for food is <1 (Zimmermann, 1932).

This means that at least the direction of the demand for food is indicated by the trend in income. However, this does not apply in reverse, because a rise in food expenditure may be due to either a rise in income (e.g. between years 1 and 2 in Table 4.12) or a fall in income (e.g. between years 3 and 4).

Engel's law was formulated at the time when the application of statistics to social questions such as poverty and family budgets was first systematically applied for what we may call indicative purposes. Apart from Engel himself, investigators included Le Play in France, Quételet and Ducpétiaux in Belgium, and Wright in the United States, some of whom participated in the landmark Statistical Congress of 1853 at Brussels. Engel's law has since been confirmed by many surveys in many countries, while attempts to verify claims for similar behaviour in expenditure on housing (*Schwabe's law*) and the reverse for expenditure on clothing (*Schiff's law*) have been less successful.

The importance of the Engel curve goes well beyond its indicative role in the food and total expenditure relation. Its seeming certainty as a behavioural function contributed to the development of econometric analysis, and it can also be regarded as a forerunner of the general theory of the propensity to consume and this theory's derivation of the investment multiplier by Keynes.

The *Phillips curve* (Figure 4.8) refers to the old debate about the relation between unemployment and wage rates, which was revived in 1958 through an article by A.H.W. Phillips writing in the journal *Economica*. The statistics indicated an inverse relation between them in England over many years. At that time there was considerable theoretical and practical concern about both inflation and labour demand in Western countries. This relationship has been tested and discussed subsequently (e.g. Dornbusch and Fischer, 1987) when the relation was occasionally turned upside down during periods of so-called *stagflation*, where unemployment and inflation increased simultaneously. We have then a curve that, unlike the Engel curve,

Table 4.12 Proportion of expenditure spent on food

	Year 1	Year 2	Year 3	Year 4
Total expenditure	$80	$90	$100	$90
Food expenditure	$20 = 25%	$21 = 23%	$20 = 20%	$21 = 23%

Figure 4.8   Phillips curve (cost-push effect)

Year	0–1	1–2	2–3	3–4	4–5	5–6	6–7	7–8	8–9
Annual price rise (%)	+6	+5	+4	+3	+2	+1	0	−1	−2
Annual wage rise (%)	+9	+8	+7	+6	+5	+4	+3	+2	+1

Year	1	2	3	4	5	6	7	8	9
Unemployment rate (%)	1	1½	2	2½	3	4	5	6½	9

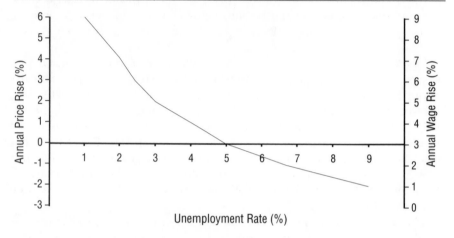

Unemployment Rate (%)

does not move along a smooth slope in the long run and therefore on its own has only limited validity as an indicator.

As a statistical indicator the Phillips curve has some unusual features. In discussion about inflation, changes in the wage rate, on the y-axis, are often equated to price changes by showing annual percentage price rises on the left side and corresponding wage rises on the right side in fixed proportions. Thus price rises of 1%, 2% and 3% were assumed to be equivalent to wage rises of, say, 4%, 5% and 6% respectively, the difference of 3 percentage points representing (non-inflationary) wage rises connected with productivity gains. The untenable proposition of long term stability in the wage–price relation is avoided in the more frequent diagrams that score only wage rises.

Wages and prices refer to annual flows that are different in nature from the ratio of unemployment to the labour force at a point of time on the x-axis. The x and y scales are independent; so the shape of the curve can be flattened or steepened simply by altering the steps on either axis. While at most the curve states that a certain rate of unemployment corresponds at a particular time to a certain rate of inflation, it does not explain the functional relation between them.

Much of the debate about the Phillips curve has been concerned with its usefulness in demonstrating cost-push inflation and a natural or permanent unemployment threshold at the intersection of price stability with the x-axis, and with aspects such as linearity, reversibility, simultaneity, short/long term effects and the role of expectations. However, its relevance for policy making remains in doubt.

The *Laffer curve* (Figure 4.9) provides an example of matching behavioural reactions with economic policy measures to the extent that expected results are lagged or even reversed, with a corresponding change in their indicative relevance.

We might expect that a rise in tax rates, with everything else unchanged, would increase tax revenue. We might further expect that such a rise would have a disincentive effect for whatever is being taxed (work, saving or spending) as well as make tax evasion more attractive. The fiscal question then is to what extent the increase in tax revenue will be offset by a reduction in tax payments, leaving aside further macroeconomic effects on income distribution.

There is no easy way to determine the variable effects of tax measures. We can only speculate on some likely reactions: people get conditioned to accept 'tax creep' into higher tax brackets due to inflation, at least for a short period before it becomes a political issue; or the effects of tax cuts are not symmetrical with those of tax rises as far as incentives (or political point scoring) are concerned, any more than the incentive effects of taxes are similar at different income levels. So it was regarded as a bold claim when Professor Laffer, and others promoting the so-called *supply-side economics* in the United States, argued in the 1980s that a cut in tax rates

Figure 4.9 Laffer curve

	Year 1	Year 2	Year 3	Year 4	Year 5	Year 6
Income ($)	10 000	11 000	12 000	12 000	6 750	0
Tax rate (%)	0	20	40	60	80	100
Tax revenue ($)	0	2 200	4 800	7 200	5 400	0

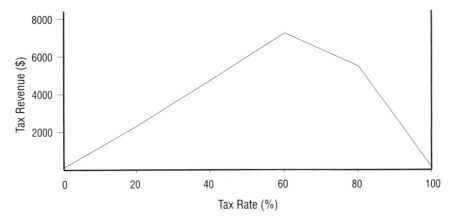

in the United States would increase tax revenue by promoting extra work time and better tax compliance (i.e. reduce evasion).

The theory can be demonstrated as a slowly rising and then more quickly decreasing tax-revenue curve, because the disincentive effect is likely to be progressive. However, the Laffer curve does not reflect actual budget experience, because many other factors operate on income. For example, opportunities to manipulate taxes vary at different income levels; broadly speaking, low and middle income earners have no great command over their work hours except in a few cases for overtime; and opportunities to vary earnings are greater in the private professions and for top earners, who, however, have less incentive to earn or spend more. A curve showing tax collections and changes in tax rates may be of general interest, but it has little indicative relevance.

Tobin's q factor refers to an article by Tobin (1969) in which he discusses the capital investment decision, both micro and macro, in terms of the ratio of the current market value of assets to their replacement cost. This ratio has become known as *Tobin's q*, and might be expected to relate positively or negatively to the rate of investment. A high ratio signifies incentives to invest in new capital, rather than taking over existing firms, and the reverse applies if $q < 1$. However, this simple relationship does not yield an unambiguous indicator because other factors also come into play (e.g. lags, adjustment costs, uncertainties, irreversibility of investment). Also, there are statistical difficulties in measuring investment and its returns.

Using statistics of capital stock at constant prices, and scaled-up stock-exchange data for current market value, a research report by the Reserve Bank of Australia (Dews, 1986) has estimated Tobin's q in Australia over about 20 years. There is some broad, but not precise, correspondence between q and new investment, as percentage of GDP, when the latter series is lagged for a year, but the influence of other factors is evident in divergences of movements and amplitude. It also appears that the data are not sufficiently accurate to fix a theoretical equilibrium point at the value where $q = 1$. In Figure 4.10, based on Australian proxy statistics for market and replacement values of capital for 1977–88, the Tobin q ratio roughly corresponds to investment booms in years 4–6 and 8–9.

Tobin himself has said that his models of monetary analysis are illustrative only as general observations. The significance of Tobin's q seems to lie in theoretical analysis of an important part of the economic system, rather than as a practical indicator of current and future investment.

Misery index

A *misery index* is a device to compare human well-being, however defined, over a period or between countries. Different types have been constructed, at various levels of sophistication, and we will quote here only a few examples.

The Population Crisis Committee in Washington (1987) has published a *human suffering index*, which purports to measure, in a single figure,

Figure 4.10   Tobin's *q*

	Year 1	Year 2	Year 3	Year 4	Year 5	Year 6	Year 7	Year 8	Year 9	Year 10	Year 11
Annual % changes											
Private investment as % of GDP	-5	+10	0	+14	+5	-5	+4	+10	+20	-20	-10
Replacement cost per capital unit	-10	+8	0	+10	+3	+1	+5	-5	+15	-10	-3
Investment/replacement ratio											
Tobin's *q*	+0.5	+1.3	*	+1.4	+1.7	-5.0	+0.8	-2.0	+1.3	+2.0	+3.3

* *Indeterminate.*

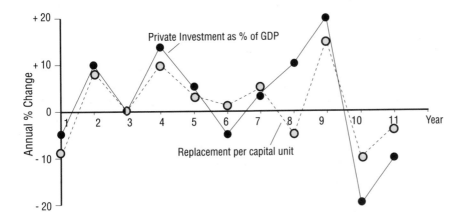

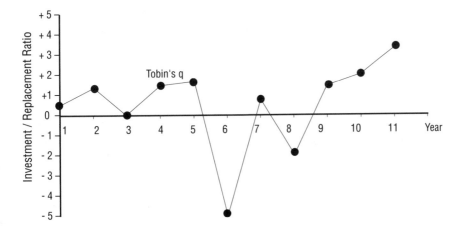

differences in living conditions between 130 countries. It is published as a coloured wallchart that ranks each country on a 0–100 scale, with Mozambique at 95 at the top and Switzerland at 4 at the bottom. This is juxtaposed by a chart of annual population increase for these countries, which presents to some extent, but not for all countries, a mirror image of the *sufferings chart*, with a correlation coefficient of 0.83. The latter is based on ratings from 1 to 10 for the following measures:

Income (GNP per capita)	Nutrition (calorie supply)
Inflation (GDP deflator)	(Access to) Clean drinking water
(Growth of) Labour force	(Efficient) Use of energy
Urban population growth	(Adult) Literacy rate
Infant mortality rate	Personal freedom

Rating for items on the 0–10 scale is done partly subjectively with varying intervals. For personal freedom a three-point rating, 0–5–10, used by Freedom House, was applied, which is a little different from the World Human Rights Guide quoted in section 5.5. The ratings are shown in detail on the sufferings chart, with their unweighted sums producing the human suffering index, which is superimposed on a colour-coded world map to contrast areas of extreme, high, moderate and minimal suffering.

This index, and its diagrammatic presentation, are impressive in carrying the message of the strong influence of excessive population growth on the welfare of African, Latin American and Asian countries. However, beyond this it may be considered too simplistic to relate human suffering in equal parts to demographic factors, income and a few aspects of daily living, particularly as, unlike some other indicators previously discussed, the index does not record change, except for the demographic components, but gives the situation at a given date.

In 1990 the Population Crisis Committee issued another colourful chart on *progress towards population stabilisation*. This lists and graphically illustrates estimated current and projected contraceptive use and its cost in a large number of countries, as well as population and other development assistance by major donor countries in 1987 and targets for the year 2000.

'Misery index' is also the name given to journalistic exercises that try to combine two or more unfavourable aspects of the economy (e.g. unemployment and inflation or interest rates, balance-of-payments deficit and exchange rates), and to these one can add other *negative welfare indicators* (e.g. bankruptcies, suicides, crime rates). The misery to which they allude can refer to personal, group or national situations. As indicators, their weakness lies in the attempt to use a few loosely connected features as proxies for a complex situation, without a firm base for estimating their relative strengths, direction and interdependence—all factors that can change over time and between countries. Furthermore, misery has different meanings for personal quality of life and for achievements of national goals of full employment or internal and external balance. In general it is therefore preferable to use single indicators to highlight the state of misery for a particular aspect, rather than to try to combine disparate indicators.

Finally, returning to an economic indication of 'misery', we may mention the quick measure of *economic recession* that is said to apply when GDP declines in two successive quarters—GDP being variously specified here as measured in constant prices and/or per capita. This measure falls in the category of simple indicators that are useful for a first approach, but should be put into a broader context of time and place for further analysis. A fall of, say, 1% in GDP over two successive quarters may well ring alarm bells and justify debate and even policy changes. However, further investigation could show that the drop follows GDP rises of 2% or more in previous quarters, due perhaps to a brief export boom, or that, while not favourable, it represents a deceleration of declines in earlier periods.

CHAPTER 5

SOCIAL APPLICATIONS OF INDICATORS

5.1 'Social indicators'

The term *'social indicators'* has long been used for statistics that are relevant for the analysis of the situation in a particular social field or for society as a whole, similarly as statistics for economic analysis are referred to as economic indicators. We need not enter here into the debate about a precise definition of 'social', beyond noting that in some ways it overlaps with 'economic' because social demands are subject to economic restraints and because economic processes are linked to their social and societal environment. At most we can say that some indicators belong mainly to the social sphere (e.g. school performance, sporting performance), while others (e.g. exchange rate, productivity) are mainly economic phenomena, or that economic indicators deal mainly with things and money while social indicators are more concerned with people.

Social indicators, in this general sense, go back thousands of years. The early enumerations of the population mentioned in the Bible, and ancient registers of land titles, had a social element of ascertaining the population structure and military preparedness connected with the economic purpose of establishing a tax base. The British poverty studies since the seventeenth century, and two centuries later the family budget studies of European statisticians (Brussels Congress, 1853), mark the beginning of *social reporting* and the application of indicative statistics. They set the pace for the government collections published in yearbooks that translate social phenomena into the neat numerical language so persuasively developed for economic analysis.

This led up to the contemporary specific meaning of social indicators, or the *social indicator movement*, whose beginning can be set in 1966 when

146

the American sociologist Bauer, and some of his colleagues, were commissioned by the American Space Agency (NASA) to investigate the social effects of its space exploration program. They discussed how to design a comprehensive system of social indicators that could serve as a yardstick by which to know whether things are getting better or worse. This enquiry came at a time when there was increasing interest in the description and measurement of social change by public authorities, welfare advocates, social scientists, and bodies like the Russell Sage Foundation, in its project for monitoring social change (1965), and the US Department of Health (*Toward a Social Report*, United States, 1969). However, it was Bauer's focus on a systematic review that initiated the social indicator movement during the 1970s. This branched out from US public reports into a more general methodology for such indicators in statistical frameworks applied to social reporting and policy planning.

The message spread from the United States to international organisations such as the Organisation for Economic Cooperation and Development (OECD), which carried out a social indicator program in 1970–82, and the Social and Economic Council of the United Nations, which contributed (through Professor Stone) a system of socio-demographic statistics as a follow-up to its system of national accounts. Many countries now publish statistical compendia under titles such as *Social Indicators*, which gather together relevant official data. Various monographs and some textbooks have been published in this field (e.g. De Neufville, 1975; Zapf, 1977; Rossi and Gilmartin, 1980; Hillhorst and Klatter, 1985) as well as journals such as the quarterly *Social Indicators Research* and the *Social Indicators Newsletter (SINET)*.

Applications have been extended from a narrowly defined area of social problems to urban planning, international development and the quality of life, and from the description and measurement of social conditions to comparisons over time and place and to policy planning. For example, a quantitative indicator such as hospital beds available might lead on to bed occupancy rates, particularised by reason for admission, to more qualitative indicators of the incidence of diseases and provision for their care in and outside hospitals, which combined with other indicators might help to develop general indicators of the nation's health. The general functions of social indicators can then be fitted into a systematic sequence from observation and assessment to prognosis, to policy planning and the monitoring of plan performance. The position of social indicators in such a sequence can be demonstrated as in Table 5.1.

The distinctive roles of social indicators are reflected in the definitions given by various authors:

> Social indicators . . . are statistics, statistical series, and all other forms of evidence that enable us to assess where we stand and are going with respect to our values and goals, and to evaluate specific programs and determine their impact. (Bauer, 1966)

Table 5.1   Social process functions of social indicators

Assessment	Cognition
Observation of trends	Analysis
Verification of societal interaction	Conceptualisation
Prognosis of present trend	Projection
Formulation of planning alternatives, including priority rating and trade-offs	Orientation, operationalisation, direction
Policy decision	Planification, targeting
Audit of planning progress	Monitoring
Review of plan performance	Retrospective analysis

Social indicators relate to some area of social concern . . . may serve the purposes of curiosity, understanding and action. (Stone, 1975)

A social indicator may be defined as a statistic of direct normative interest which facilitates concise, comprehensive and balanced judgments about the conditions of major aspects of a society. It is in all cases a direct measure of welfare . . . if it changes in the 'right' direction, while other things remain equal, things have gotten better or people are 'better off'. (United States Department of Health, 1969)

Social indicators are constructs, based on observation and usually quantitative, which tell us something about an aspect of life in which we are interested or about changes in it. Such information may be objective . . . to show the position or changes, or subjective to show how they are regarded by the community or constituent groups. (United Nations Statistical Office, F/18, 1975)

Social indicators are needed to find pathways through the maze of society's interconnections. (Rice, 1967)

A social indicator is . . . a measurement of social phenomena, which are trans-economic. It is normative and integrated in a self-consistent information system. (Cazes in Shonfield and Shaw, 1972)

Social indicators trace out the topography of the human landscape. (L'Inguiste, 1978)

Indicators are quantitative variables that somehow reflect the human condition in a social setting. (Galtung, 1973a)

Social indicators are facts about society in a quantitative form. They involve . . . interpretation of advance or retrogression against some norm. (Hauser, 1975)

A social indicator is the operational definition . . . of any of the concepts central to the generation of an information system descriptive of the social concepts . . . which may be categorized as systems components and goals, social problems, policy goals. (Carlisle in Shonfield and Shaw, 1972)

Social indicators are statistics which measure social conditions and changes therein over time for various segments of the population, both the external (social and physical) and the internal (subjective and perceptional) contexts of human existence in a society. (Land, 1975)

For preference a series should be termed a social indicator only if it belongs to a structure or system of series . . . if it is genuinely 'indicative' of something . . . part of some kind of model whether explanatory or predictive. (Moser, 1973)

For about 17 years, from the publication of Bauer's book in 1966 until the demise of the Social Science Research Council's (SSRC's) Centre for Research on Social Indicators in 1983, the social indicators movement developed as an allied but separate discipline within the social sciences. Rather than fading out it has since been integrated into those sciences (Ferris, 1988), whose indicative expression it has influenced.

Value load: Social statistics present objective-type information as value-free data, which take on a *normative* role as social indicators that make implicit or explicit assumptions about desirable directions. The same statistics can be used to indicate different goals; for example, the employment of married women can be applied to work opportunity and to delivery of child care.

In this connection we may mention the distinctions drawn by Professor Mukherjee (1975: ch. 5) between statistics that represent *constituent variables* (e.g. birth and death rates) and statistics that represent the *contingent variables* based on them (i.e. population change). They can become societal indicators when they are used to indicate changing supply/demand conditions in the market, and finally social indicators when they refer to differential human relationships (e.g. conflict arising from imbalances).

Dimensions of measurement (e.g. adequacy, quality) are usually graded in *ordinal* scales, ranging from insufficient to abundant or from bad to good. Assessment is based on perception or attitudinal surveys designed to measure subjective phenomena (Turner and Martin, 1984), rather than on objective-type *cardinal* series expressed in monetary terms. Social indicators make use of both ordinal and cardinal statistics. When appropriate, ordinal series can be cardinalised by giving value dimensions to certain ranges, or cardinal series ordinalised by imposing a number scale (e.g. from 1 to 10) on cardinal values.

Ordinal grading is important for the flexible disaggregation of individuals into kindred groups. Simple averaging glosses over group and individual differences, and objective distribution measures, based on probability patterns, are inadequate for needs determination. However, they can be applied for testing goodness of fit via chi-square, to bring out historical or regional discrepancies in cardinal series. It should be noted that subjective ordinalisation not only should be based on judgemental perceptions of needs and so on, but also must consider physiological and ethnocultural variability of needs. Particularly in the upper ranges of adequacy, political considerations can also play some part.

Scope: The field of social indicators goes beyond the traditional series typified in government statistical yearbooks. They look at a wider spectrum of human needs and at the interrelations between those needs beyond material factors in the personal, social and physical environment. They also include in the process of needs satisfaction an assessment of adequacy, quality, accessibility, choice, participation and dependency in the context of ethnosocial and cultural standards. The general orientation of social indicators has been characterised by Professor Bauer (1966) as 'assessment where we stand and are going'. They therefore bear on the direction and tempo of the desired social change, and their scope reaches beyond social reporting into policy planning for social change.

Structure: Social indicators are directed towards a wider and more integrated area of social concerns than traditional statistical compendia. They are often part of some system of such concerns or of development. This can mean a subtle shift in conceptualisation. Previously statistics were usually gathered under convenience headings such as health or education, with the borderlines drawn between them on administrative and budgetary lines, which vary substantially between countries (e.g. in the treatment of health, education or library provisions). For social indicators we may initially have only a vague division of areas which is directed more towards ends than towards means (e.g. skills rather than number of schools and teachers). The initial concept will then become gradually specified as measurement proceeds in an 'iterative learning process'. For health, for example, the sphere of the basic statistics of facilities, incidence of diseases, mortality and so on becomes widened towards indicators of the healthfulness of life, disability, access to services and so on. Information about one aspect leads on to quests for further indicators, in contrast to the lateral blindness of the traditional formulation of social concerns.

The most conspicuous outcome of the social indicator movement has been the regular publication of such collections by the statistical offices of many countries. The United Kingdom set the pace in 1970 with its annual *Social Trends*. By 1979 the United Nations (F/24) was listing 39 compendia of social statistics and indicators from developing or developed countries; and 30 other developing or socialist states were issuing social compendia that included social statistics. Since then more countries have followed this example. The titles themselves are indicative of their scope and variety. They include: *Social Indicators, Perspectives, Trends, Data* and *Panorama; Indicators* of *Social Life,* of *Social Development,* of *Living Levels* and of *Life Quality; Perspective* in Canada, *Society* in Israel and *Life* in the Netherlands.

There is fairly general agreement about the field covered, sometimes called the *domains* or *areas* of social concerns. Table 5.2 juxtaposes three examples of national and international lists. They share the elements usually regarded as pre-eminent for our personal and societal situation, with only passing reference to economic factors.

Table 5.2   Major domains of social indicators

OECD list of social indicators, 1982	Major social time series, Canada 1974	SPES Indikatoren Tableau, Germany 1988
Length of life (health indicator)	Population growth, distribution, family formation, composition	Population, households, families, migration
Healthfulness of life	Health	Health
Education and learning	Education	Education
Employment, quality	Work	Labour market, employment
Time/leisure, time use	Allocation of time	(Time use included in labour market)
Command over goods and services, income, wealth	Income, consumption	Income: distribution, use
Physical environment: housing, services, nuisances	Quality of environment	Housing
Social environment	Cultural diversity, bilingualism, natives	Social status, mobility
Personal safety	Criminal justice	Transportation

The lists try to go beyond means and material conditions into aspects of satisfaction and life quality. However, lack of existing data from collections and surveys means a neglect of the dimensions of access, participation or self-reliance and of the domains of family life, culture, sport and other leisure-time activities. Very little reference is made to human rights or social networks, and even less to the spiritual and aesthetic values that are supposed to underpin our society.

There is also a general restriction inherent in government-sponsored publications that has been carried over from the traditional statistical yearbooks. Governments, of whatever political persuasion, are reluctant to acknowledge social change until it has become respectable. The compendia reflect the status quo of society as viewed by middle-aged officials. They suggest that divisions by sex and wealth are immutable and are silent about the part played by power groups (e.g. local and transnational businesses and trade unions, churches, lobby groups), although these may be prime factors in determining and changing social conditions. Developments in family structure and lifestyle are slow to be incorporated into codes, and the relevance of the natural environment to our lives is only perfunctorily expressed in statistics of land and water use, pollution and atmospheric change.

Various international agencies have published collective volumes of social statistics with an indicative direction, such as the pioneer effort by the

United Nations Statistical Office in 1954 (E/CN.179) and 1961 (E/CN.3/ 270), leading up to its *Compendium of Social Statistics* (K/4, 1977), or the publication *Social Indicators for the European Community* (Luxembourg, 1974). Perhaps the most interesting and influential project, however, has been the Social Indicator Development Program of the OECD, which began in 1970 and culminated in a list published in 1982, followed in 1986 by a compendium entitled *Living Conditions in OECD Countries*.

The program was carried out conjointly by the 24 OECD member countries, based on a 1970 ministerial declaration (see OECD, 1982: 7–8) that:

> Growth should be considered as an instrument of creating better conditions of life with increasing attention to its qualitative aspects and the formulation of policies with respect to social choices in the allocation of growing resources.

Its objectives were:

> . . . the identification of social demands, aspirations and problems [relevant to] the socio-economic planning process; measure and report changes in the relative importance of these concerns; better focus and [to] enlighten public discussion and government decision making.

The list of concerns (Table 5.3) does not look very different from others previously quoted, nor does the proposed collection of indicators go much beyond what has been published in most countries. The general criticism of such enumerations as being limited in scope and conservatively biased also applies to this version. However, it is a solid list with some tentative excursions into fresh fields (e.g. the environment), and it has encouraged some countries to develop their own schemes.

Moreover, during its 12 years of gestation the OECD program has generated more research into the measurement of well-being, and the conference reports reflect the vigorous debate about issues such as the relation between individual and societal well-being, the role of institutions, validation, the use of proxy indicators and the aggregation process. The program has also been an object lesson for the art of the possible in getting a group of countries that are at different levels of socioeconomic development to agree on areas of common concern, even if this meant that some indicators discussed in the early stages for the administration of justice and social inequality fell by the wayside.

More recently the World Bank has begun issuing annual publications under the titles of *World Development Report* (*WDR*, since 1978) and *Social Indicators of Development* (*WDI*, since 1990) to serve as economic gauges of development and for the formulation of development policies. *WDR* (1978) presents summary tables of gross national product (GNP), labour force in agriculture, infant mortality, calorie supply and primary school enrolment for a large number of developing countries for the 1965–85 period, with growth rates and percentage change in that period, as well as aggregation averages for low, middle and high income countries, for oil

Table 5.3   OECD list of social concerns and social indicators

Social concern	Indicators
Health	
Length of life	Life expectancy, perinatal mortality rate
Healthfulness of life	Short and long term disability
Education and learning	
Use of educational facilities	Regular and adult education experience
Employment and quality of working life	
Availability of employment	Unemployment (including part time, discouraged)
Quality of working life	Work hours, travel to work, atypical work, leave, earnings, injuries, environmental nuisances
Time and leisure	
Use of time	Free time, free time activities
Command of goods and services	
Income	Distribution, low income, deprivation
Wealth	Distribution
Physical environment	
Housing conditions	Indoor and access to outdoor space, amenities
Services accessibility	Proximity of selected services
Environmental nuisance	Exposure to air pollution and noise
Social environment	Social attachment, suicide rate
Personal safety	
Exposure to risk	Fatal and serious injuries
Perceived threat	Fear for personal safety

Source: Adapted from OECD (1982: 13).

and manufactures exporters, for highly indebted countries (which rank relatively high in income, nutrition and schooling) and for four major geographical regions. This is supplemented by data sheets for individual countries, which give more detail for these headings of social concern and comparisons with the averages of some development reference groups at higher income levels.

The major directions of the social indicator movement towards development, quality of life and so on are also reflected in the various other systems mentioned. These range from the simple German SPES tableaux with binary ordinal marks to the complex structures suggested by the United Nations Research Institute for Social Development (UNRISD), United Nations Develoment Program, Land and Fox, and cover a wide range of types of social concerns and of modes of satisfaction.

In sections 3.2, 3.3 and 3.4 reference has been made to attempts at combining social and other indicators or subsystems into single comprehensive welfare measures, such as the extension of gross domestic product (GDP) or summary indexes derived from the Drewnowski or Zapf tableaux. It remains doubtful whether the OECD approach is any more suited to aggregation of the disparate notions involved. The indicative relevance of social indicators lies rather in the specific features they present for building up a picture of a particular concern and for analysing correlative connections between domains or parts of domains.

The media (newspapers, magazines, radio and television) present a continuous, albeit unsystematic, reportage of social conditions for our entertainment and instruction, and they occasionally juxtapose them for an impressionistic picture of the human condition. An example of a collection of odds and ends whose social relevance, mixed with triviality and frivolity, has long attracted readers is *Harper's Index*, published monthly by the New York magazine *Harper's* in the format of a list of some 40 items with the source stated for each. Here are just a few samples from the issue of December 1990:

- number of new businesses started in Poland this year: 175 000; number folded: 147 000;
- price of a gold-plated refrigerator from the Mitsukoshi department store in Tokyo: $6181;
- members of the Christian Motorcyclists Association: 33 805;
- average amount of time that a black American waits for a kidney transplant: 13.9 months; same for a white American: 7.6 months;
- market value of three French hens: $15; of seven swans a-swimming: $7000;
- average score that Americans give themselves on a 1–10 scale of looks: 6.5;
- percentage of Americans who do not know that the United States supplied arms to Iraq during its war with Iran: 73%.

5.2 Health

Health has been described as a broad social concern with ill-defined boundaries. It is therefore not surprising to find much debate about the concept itself and its measurement. We will here refer only to some aspects relevant to the formulation of indicators.

According to its constitution the World Health Organization (WHO) maintains that health is a state of complete physical, mental and social well-being and not merely the absence of disease or infirmity. This stresses the positive sides of health, rather than the negative of ill health, and passes the burden of description on to the subjective notion of well-being, without specifying the complementary relations of the physical, mental and social elements.

This positive approach is also reflected in the following statement of WHO policy: attain the goal of a level of health for all the people of the world by the year 2000 that will permit them to lead a socially and ecnomically productive life (WHO, 1981: 9).

In pursuing this goal WHO recommended in 1981 a general list of indicators, not claimed to be comprehensive, to assess progress towards health for all:

- *Health indicators:* political commitment in declared policies and their implementation; resource allocation for primary and other health care, as percentage of GDP and so on; equity of resource distribution by areas, socioeconomic groups and so on; community involvement in health decision making; its decentralisation; organisational frame and managerial process; communication channels.
- *Social/economic indicators* related to health: population growth; GDP; income distribution; work conditions; literacy rate; housing; food availability.
- *Provision of health care* in terms of: physical, economic and cultural accessibility; utilisation by those in need of service; quality of care; coverage by primary health care through promotion, maternal/child care, immunisation control of endemic diseases, drug services and health workers; income distribution; work conditions; literacy rate; housing; food supply.
- *Health status indicators:* nutrition; height/weight; disease-specific child/ maternal mortality; life expectation; morbidity; disability; social/mental quality of life (adapted from WHO, 1981: 18).

WHO is sceptical about aggregation, such as the simplistic physical Q/L indicator of the Oversea Development Council (see section 3.9), and for global indication the World Health Assembly suggested in 1981 a list of twelve criteria for reasonable standards reached by various countries:

- government commitment to, and organisation of policy of, health for all;
- decentralised and participatory strategy forming and implementation;
- at least 5% of GNP spent on health;
- portion of national health spending devoted to local health care;
- primary health care distributed between regions and groups;
- developing countries with above policies, supported by others;
- primary health care available to all; also water, sanitation, immunisation, drugs, trained personnel for pregnancy and baby care;
- standard weights (e.g. 90% of new-born weighing 2500+ g);
- infant mortality below 50 per 1000 live births;
- life expectancy at birth over 60 years;
- adult literacy rate for men and women in excess of 70%;
- GDP per capita in excess of $US500 (adapted from WHO, 1981: 124–5).

This is a 'wish list' made up largely from objective-type statistics with some elements of a subjective setting of targets and attainment. The targets set for statistical collection are high; but even by 1989, when WHO issued a document on *Global Strategy for Health for All—Detailed Analysis of Global Indicators*, it could assemble only a limited collection of such statistics for countries and regions. It seems to have refrained, wisely so, from any attempt to aggregate the disparate target data and even from trying to rank-order countries on the basis of such a mixture of cardinal and ordinal lists. The catalogue seems to emphasise certain aspects: new-borns and infants, facilities for primary health care and living conditions, and cost of health services. It does not go into detail on morbidity, on provisions for the aged and for invalidity in general, nor on structure of health personnel, and it eschews any subjective indicators of perceptions about personal health, effects of ill health or adequacy of services that could be derived from surveys.

As their contribution to the target of 'health for all by the year 2000' (WHO, 1981) the 33 countries of the European region of WHO set 38 regional targets in 1985, many of which had been initiated or even implemented by a number of members 18 months later in 1986, when the second edition of WHO's program was issued. This included an extensive list of indicators to monitor progress towards health for all, 38 altogether, in addition to the twelve global indicators agreed on by the World Health Assembly, listed above. The emphasis is on health promotion and disease prevention policies, environmental factors and quality of services, apart from the usual mortality, morbidity, life expectancy, accident and disablement indicators. There is advice on how to collect such information from existing sources, reports and surveys, without attempting to formulate a definite framework of indicators or possible aggregations.

In a follow-up survey, *Monitoring of the Strategy for Health for All by the Year 2000 Part I, European Region 1987/88* (WHO, 1989), a variety of indicative presentations were used to demonstrate progress in the various fields. They included non-parametric counts of declining/increasing/reversed or improved/worsening trends (e.g. in mortality from specified diseases) and progress in stated periods in terms of good/moderate/little or none/negative—also regression of growth for standard mortality rates for various countries separately and with population-weighted averages.

The OECD seems to take a somewhat broader view of health but also is hamstrung by the paucity of existing data. It divides the health domain into length and healthfulness of life, with the following indicators:

• *Length of life*: life expectancy; estimate of years remaining at stated ages; perinatal mortality rate; still-born and early neonatal deaths.
• *Healthfulness of life*: *short term disability*: average number of disability days per year per person, by level of restriction in terms of temporary deviations from usual level of functioning; *long term disability*: percentage of population at different levels of long term disability.

As with other parts of the OECD list, this reflects the problem of obtaining agreed data from a large number of countries. Originally the OECD had suggested taking the *probability of a healthy life through all stages of the lifecycle*, which would be preferable to taking survival rates at whatever level of health, but is not easily measured.

Perinatal mortality, a refined version of counting stillbirths, must be regarded as a function of nutrition and of the provision of maternal care rather than as an indicator of the healthfulness of subsequent life. It can be disaggregated by age or marital status of mother (where it is usually higher for unmarried than for married mothers). Healthfulness is then reflected only at the functional level of restricting disability, in terms of time of disability in short term incidence or of types for long term disability. The data can be collected through sample surveys graded in socioeconomic categories and types of difficulties suffered by the disabled. More generally, the series published by the OECD (1986) are useful for the comparison of major features between countries, but they do not give information about the distinction between acute and chronic unhealth or its manifestations and severity, nor do they show the extent of institutionalisation or other provisions for health care.

Health perception is a more direct approach to healthfulness. It is ascertained from quality-of-life surveys with questions about situations and attitudes that can be combined into a single index within the limitations mentioned in section 3.8. A more specific health indicator of this type has been developed by the German Zentrum für Umfragen, Methoden and Analysen (S. Weick in *Informationsdienst Soziale Indikatoren*, January 1989: 5-7). This is based on a regular survey of a sample of 2000 persons since 1950, who describe their overall state of health in five categories: very good, rather good, all right ('es geht'), rather poor, very poor. One notable conclusion is the decline from those in the two lowest categories, rather poor and very poor, from 12% in the late 1950s to a steady 6% in the 1970s and early 1980s. Similar surveys have been done in Germany by teams from the Goethe Universität—Frankfurt and Mannheim (Institut für Angewandte Sozialwissenschaft). They grade socioeconomic characteristics on a 0-10 scale, where 0-4 signifies dissatisfaction and 6-10 rather satisfied in different degrees and 5 neither-nor. Health dissatisfaction averaged 2.4 on the 0-10 scale overall in 1988. It rose from 10% at age 50 to 30% for those aged 70+. Dissatisfaction was somewhat greater for women than for men; for those living alone than for couples; for those not employed than for employees; and for the less educated than for those with the higher school certificate. Further questions link dissatisfaction with the respondent's state of health as given by frequency of consultation with doctor. There was no significant change in these relations over the four surveys since 1978.

Questions of health perception also sometimes creep into major surveys by government or research agencies. For example, the Australian Health Survey in 1977-78 asked persons about the degree of concern or pain associated with a recent illness; 20% replied 'a lot', 50% 'somewhat' and

30% 'not at all' (Australian Bureau of Statistics, 1979, 1983). The American Health Insurance Study (HIS, Brook et al., 1979) asked respondents to self-evaluate their own perceptions of their general health in terms of excellent, good, fair or poor. A household survey of 1350 dwellings (about a 2% sample) in the northwestern region of Melbourne (Krupinski and Mackenzie) in 1979 asked about perceived health status. Most (90%) of those aged 0–24 years described their health as 'good', declining to 72% of those aged 65+ years; a further 20% of males (17% of females) said that their health was 'fair', only 8% (6%) said 'poor'. This survey also probed public attitudes to health care.

'Health' and 'ill health' are customarily used as mutually exclusive antonyms. Etymologically, health relates to *wholeness* in English (as do the corresponding terms in Greek, Latin, French, German and Hebrew) and is not related to sickness (Kass, 1981). The WHO definition previously quoted suggests that health is a positive notion, while others describe it in negative terms as the absence of illness. In practical terms the latter view is usually preferred.

Indicators of positive well-being are more general, and some have been mentioned above in connection with quality of life. They reflect individual health perceptions, which are obviously age-dependent and probably also status and culture bound. Health perception is important in the context of quality of life, but not so much for other indicative purposes (e.g. provision of health care). There are a few other indicators (e.g. fitness statistics from the army, schools and sports institutes) that can provide interesting sidelights on health without covering the major aspects usually represented in aggregate health indicators.

With the measurement of ill health symptoms, the emphasis is put firstly on the cause (i.e. the disease or affliction), secondly on its effect on the patient and thirdly on the required service. However, one of the more frequently used indicators looks at *outcome* rather than *cause*, namely the various mortality statistics (e.g. infant deaths, average age at death, age-moderated survival prospects). Such rates have the practical advantage of being available for many countries over long periods, but their indicative relevance for good health is limited (see Fuchs in Caplan et al. (eds), 1981: 86). Bad health can lead, but need not lead, to premature death; nor does good health prevent premature death from war and accidents. There is, however, some evidence for a frequent correlation between survival rates and the general state of health of the population, measured by incidence of disease (Fuchs, op. cit.: 87). The two main types, life expectancy at birth and infant mortality, are particularly useful for comparing health situations between ethnic and other population groups and between regions both within and between countries.

Looking at health in the context of its absence requires a *taxonomy*, such as the four-digit codes in the *Manual of the International Statistical Classification of Diseases, Injuries, and Causes of Death,* issued in several volumes by WHO (1977 et ante); or a grouping as used by the *Cornell*

Medical Index (Abramson, 1966) under such headings as eyes and ears, respiratory and so on; or a few broad groupings such as physical, mental and emotional diseases. In practical terms such statistics are available in detail only for notifiable diseases or for particular locations (e.g. hospitals). They are useful for finding trends in particular diseases or groups of related diseases, but less so for aggregation. As health indicators for a population they lack the dimension of severity, which can vary widely for most diseases between light and heavy attacks. Minor classification problems also arise when one patient suffers from several diseases, which by itself often increases the severity compared with single sufferings, also regarding the treatment of disease as inherited or acquired, and also regarding handicaps, some but not all of which require formal treatment.

Health service organisation is a further area for the application of indicators. While some people are interested in the measurement of health as a medical or social phenomenon, others want to know more pragmatically about the allocation of resources involved and about the costs of health to both persons and the business and public sectors of the economy. Some of the information gathered under the headings of health perception and symptoms can be used for this as ancillary information, but a different approach is required for economic evaluation. This is again a field of considerable debate between health economists and administrators (see, for instance, Culyer and Wright, 1978), and we can mention here only some of the issues relevant for indication.

The public sector in most countries is a major, or even predominant, supplier of health services, because health is regarded as a *public good* that should be accessible to all and that, if neglected, would put others at risk. A free market works well when users do not receive unbiased information about alternatives. *Demand* is largely, but not wholly, identified with health needs: to prevent and cure a reduction in health status, with some uncertainty about the place of palliative care and cosmetic treatment. For the individual, demand for health care varies not only with severity of affliction but also according to location and availability of support services. Methods for rank ordering a patient's degree of dependence for multiple needs include the application of Guttman scales (Culyer, 1978: 13) or factor analysis to separate out like clusters. Various weighting systems have been devised for program priorities based on combined indexes for mortality, hospital days and so on, or on ordinal severity ratings.

Index numbers for the state of health can be derived in various ways (Culyer, 1978: 23). In the 'category and magnitude' method equal improvements or deteriorations in health status are assigned equal interval or equal ratio numbers; in the 'equivalence' method the ratings are based on distance from perfect health; and in the 'standard gamble' method changes in health are calculated with the aid of utility-based probability.

Output measurement of health care for particular groups (e.g. the elderly) has been attempted by ranking mobility, capacity for self-care and mental state in four divisions: high, medium, slight, low (Culyer, 1978), and the relation between costs and needs for the disabled is discussed by R. Horn (1981).

Traditionally, health statistics gather information on the number of health providers, hospital beds and occupancy, notifiable diseases, health insurance and so on, as well as the cost of these services. A quick measure of an individual's body fat ratio is sometimes used in the form of a *body mass index*, which relates weight to height on the formula

$$BMI = w/h^2$$

and grades persons according to a predetermined healthy weight range. If that is set, for example at 20 to 25 for adult males of an average height of 1.75 m, their 'healthy' weight should be between 60 and 76 kg. This can be depicted by a graph with height and weight on the x- and y-axes and healthy weight as an upward-sloping band.

Another aspect of physical well-being is the effect of stress, which can be demonstrated by plotting indicators of personal efficiency against stress. The resulting bell-shaped curve, known as *Yerke's curve*, suggests that at first efficiency rises with increased demand on personal resources, with performance rising at a decreasing rate past an optimum to a maximum, but from then on further stress reduces efficiency to the point of breakdown and burnout. The measurement of both efficiency and stress would rely on physical tests.

There are obvious limitations to the validity of such indicators (Wilson, 1984), but they throw at least some light on the state of healthfulness.

5.3 Education

Education, like health, can be described as a broad social concern with ill-defined boundaries. Learning is the basis for human development, leading to the cultural evolution that has given humankind dominion over all creation. More formally, the objectives and means of education have been debated since ancient times among philosophers, statesmen and religious leaders. Modern scientists like Ornstein and Ehrlich (1989) believe that it can produce the new mentality of environmental constraint that will confer on us the role of global custodians rather than global despoilers.

Like health, education has in recent years drawn the interest of international organisations. Both have initiated considerable research into measurement, of which we can here mention only some applications. In both instances we have a large formal sector marked by government accreditation of practitioners and institutions, which generate their own statistics that lead on to the construction of indicators. However, we must not forget that education as personal development is only one side, just as 'public health' is not the sole factor in the wider notion of health as healthfulness, for both education and health have also large informal sectors of care and propagation integrated into the domestic and community life. They contribute to lifestyle in learning by doing, for which few statistical records are kept. They may be in competition with the formal sector (e.g. naturopaths or coaches). More often the formal and informal sectors interact, and both are at times included in official surveys (e.g. the role of home study in school curricula). However, the likeness of education to the health concern should not be taken too far, for there are also major differences, which influence the approach to education indicators.

Health at the personal level, in contagion and in the provision of care, affects others beyond the individual. Death, as the antithesis of life, becomes the signpost for scaling survival rates. Education is not quite so pervasive. In its formal frame it is nowadays widely spread through most countries, by means of a hierarchy of look-alike institutions. It has become depersonalised into skills that can be evaluated in money terms by earnings or through corresponding opportunity costs of earnings forgone. This is sometimes attempted with health also (e.g. in the evaluation of disability days) but is not a reliable measure for minor sickness. With education the concept itself becomes identified with its skill measure, and an important sequence of indicators is scaled according to length and depth of training. With health we look for the presence/absence of disease (i.e. a negative factor). With education we are more concerned with the positive characteristic of acquisition of knowledge and skills. However, unlike health, which has death at the negative extreme of survival, there is no firm boundary for an upper limit to education.

With health we can draw a useful distinction between subjective indicators, based on patients' perceptions, and objective indicators, based on doctors' surveys, hospital records and so on. For education the depersonalised systems of skills and large formal organisations strengthen the objective basis of indicators, perhaps even more so because educators generally have been better trained formally for assessment than medical personnel. There are also some occasional census-type surveys where individuals state their educational achievement in terms of years or degrees, but it is difficult to determine, by interview or self-assessment, how knowledgeable a person is in cognitive skills or how far individuals have realised their economic or social potential.

It would be similarly difficult to determine to what extent personal capabilities correspond to formal training. To a limited extent Binet- or Cattell-type intelligence tests are used to rank intelligence, but their relation to education remains subject to a debate that has raged for 100 years or more among social scientists. To see another, less debated, illustration of such a puzzle, we only have to look at statistics that say that 99% of young adults have gone through the school system, and another set that tells us that 10% are illiterate (however defined). Alternatively, we might take the common view that (formal) education is the key to advancement in life, and find it backed by a fairly high correlation between education and worldly success. Yet we also find a number of political, business and other leaders who boast that they have studied only at 'the university of hard knocks'.

Economists take a simple approach to the assessment of education. They regard it as an *investment*, whose value is measured in terms of money outlay with subsequent earnings as the *private rate of return*. As education does not only give pecuniary benefits to the individual but also has national development advantages, they add those as *social returns* to education. This leaves the problem of non-pecuniary rewards in personal and social life, which are more difficult to determine. The indication of the value of education by actual and proxy rates of return has great advantages for the evaluation of skills, work time, labour supply and so on, but it has considerable limitations in its linear assumptions about available options, future returns and cost incidence. It can lead to major distortions, for instance when a simplistic reading of this labour market theory is applied to prove that it does not pay to educate women or handicapped persons because they yield lower returns than money spent on the education of men.

We now turn to more analytical and instrumental approaches to indicators of education. The United Nations Educational, Scientific and Cultural Organisation (UNESCO), whose stated purpose is to contribute to peace by promoting cooperation within the fields of education, science and culture, does not seem to have specified a single underlying notion of education on which it bases various programs for the advancement of knowledge, promotion of teaching and so on. Indicator systems are developed for each project as required (see section 5.7 for culture).

The OECD included the following classification of *individual development through learning* in the 1974 version of its Social Indicator Programme:

B-1 The acquisition by children of the basic knowledge, skills and value necessary for their individual development and their successful functioning as citizens in their society.
Subconcerns about the extent to which economically and socially disadvantaged families and handicapped persons reach appropriate standards.

B-2 The availability of opportunities for continuing self-development and the propensity of individuals to use them.

B-3 The maintenance and development by individuals of the knowledge, skills and flexibility required to fulfill their economic potential, to enable them to integrate themselves in the economic process if they wish.

B-4 The individual's satisfaction with the process of individual development through learning, while in the process.

B-5 The maintenance and development of the cultural heritage relative to its positive contribution to the well-being of various groups.

When attempts were subsequently made to attach specific indicators to the various domains, B-2 and B-3 were combined, and the following list of indicators was suggested in 1976:

B-1 Percentage of individuals, at stated ages, with educational qualifications.

B-2 (and 3) Average years of regular education.
Percentage of population participating in organised non-regular learning in past year.
Physical access: percentage of population within reasonable distance from opportunities.
Economic access: grants for the full cost of postcompulsory education; net expenditure by households on postcompulsory education.

In the final version (OECD, 1982) the phrase 'self-development' was dropped, as was the relation of education to personal satisfaction, good citizenship, economic potential or cultural heritage. In the pragmatic spirit that finally prevailed in the OECD program, the domains were reformulated as follows:

• *Use of educational experience*: Number of years of regular education (including tertiary) experience completed, disaggregated by most advanced level reached, household type, socioeconomic status and so on.
• *Adult education*: Indicated by percentage of population who in previous year participated in adult education, organised for people outside regular school/college, disaggregated by type, number of hours, institution, demographics and so on.
• *Literacy rate:* Indicated by percentage of population with adequate level of functional literacy for activities in which literacy is required for effective functioning (based on testing rather than self-assessment), disaggregated by most advanced level of education and demographics (adapted from OECD, 1982: 26-7).

In the compendium based on the list (*Living Conditions in OECD Countries*, OECD, 1986) the education experience series are ordered by reference to the International Standard Classification of Education (ISCED) for levels attained, and are disaggregated by age, socioeconomic status and community size. The statistics cover the period 1950–80 for some OECD countries, and it is interesting to quote some of the comment provided with the tables (1986: 48):

Whatever form of measurement of the educational level the various countries use and whether they compare over time or between age groups two conclusions emerge for all countries: first, the population's educational level is rising, often very sharply, and second, rise is usually relatively greater for women of the new generation than for men, although not yet closing the gap accumulated over past generations.
   The population's average number of years of education has increased continuously and even at an accelerating pace in the OECD area since 1950 . . . 10 years in most countries, usually less for older women than men but same for younger men and women. Proportion of population who have at least started higher education is rising but mostly still below 10%.

Only partial data are available for adult education in OECD and other countries, and comprehensive data are even rarer for literacy rate. In 1987 the OECD, at the suggestion of the US government, initiated an international study in the form of an International Indicators Project through the Centre for Educational Reform and Innovation (CERI) (see Ruby in Wyatt and Ruby, 1988; also CERI–OECD conference papers since 1987). The topics discussed at the CERI conferences, held in Washington and Poitiers, have included performance indicators, quality of education and systems evaluation. Country networks have been established for the first phase, which will explore enrolments and career paths, student outcomes, costs and resources, and the ecology of schools. Work is also proceeding on a coordinated scheme of education indicators for the Scandinavian countries (Gouiedo, 1990) which will include secondary and tertiary enrolments and graduations.

Among alternative divisions of education indicators, the one often used in the past distinguishes between:

- *inputs*, referring to educational resources;
- *outputs*, referring to skills or other outcome characteristics; and
- *processes*, referring to systems that turn inputs into outputs.

Somehow cutting across these divisions is the currently popular term *'performance indicators'*, in the economic sense of efficiency of resource allocation.

Such systematic classifications are useful in clarifying aspects of measurement, but to be practical must distinguish between structures (e.g. private and government schools) and types (e.g. skills by years of schooling). The standard series of educational statistics published by international agencies, as quoted above, and by national and regional statistical bureaux and education authorities, refer to details of both educational resources and outcome, as well as to the structure of the educational system and its institutions. Separate attention to education is given in the analysis of other social fields, such as the role of skills in employment and income generation or in quality of life, science output or the overall allocation of public resources.

The types, techniques and presentation of such indicators correspond to our earlier general exposition and have been examined in detail by Johnstone (1981). Here we will mention just one aspect that has become topical in recent years in several countries, namely performance indicators for universities and colleges.

A good example of this discussion is the report by a joint working party of the Australian Vice-Chancellors' Committee (AVCC) with Australian Committee of Directors and Principals in Advanced Education Ltd (ACDP), issued in December 1988 (AVCC, 1988). It refers to the performance of *institutions* rather than individual staff members, and does not cover separate aspects such as financial management (which its UK counterpart did) or health. The committee's main concerns were:

- review of academic performance within a single discipline;
- periodic evaluation of academic performance of schools, faculties and so on; and

• priorities for staffing and the disposition of resources.

One of the simplistic views of performance indicators is that they can be used as such to back funding claims, but the committee held that they are only part of the necessary raw material for evaluation and assessment in relation to stated objectives and should therefore not be mechanically applied to formula funding. Most of the indicators the committee proposed are based on objective-type statistics, but they stressed the importance of informed judgement by knowledgeable people in using these statistics— that is, evaluation of whether the institution or faculty is in a healthy condition within an acceptable 'normal' range.

A distinction is drawn between context measures, which refer to *operations*, and performance indicators, which refer to *functions*.

Institutional context measures:
• *Staff*: Number by full/part time; permanent/casual; teaching/research; gender.
• *Student demand:*
  Commencing students: first preferences (accepted) and number of offers as ratios of (actual) enrolments.
  Retention ratios in second year in same subject and in major subject sequences.
  Postgraduate ratio of applications to commencements.
• *Quality of intake*: Average, median-based, entrance score.
• *Types of entrants*: From school, mature age and so on.
• *Numbers*: First/all by course, age, gender, full/part time, no fee paying.
• *Resource management*: Income and expenditure; student/staff ratios.

These context measures are intended to facilitate the normalisation (standardisation) of performance indicators for intra- and interinstitutional comparisons, and also have a subsidiary function to monitor specific goals (e.g. equal opportunity). They therefore play a lesser role than the constituent variables that lead to the contingent variables of indicators, as discussed in section 5.1.

Performance indicators:
• *Teaching and curriculum:* Student evaluation for defined aspects of perceived quality and relevance.
• *Student progress*: Proportions who complete study eventually and in minimum time for undergraduates and postgraduates; regression of completion rates against indicators of quality of intake, employability, satisfaction and course relevance for graduates.
• *Research:* Type, value and number of grants; publications by type (books, refereed and other articles, creative works); citation indices for impact of pure research; patents where applicable.
• *Research degrees:* PhDs and research Masters completed.
• *Professional services:* Details of consultancies and of contributions to professional bodies, journals, education, media.

The report does not recommend general aggregation of the series, except for subseries such as professional services.

This attempt to capture something of the quality of education is an advance on older projects concerned only with its credentials, such as the proposal for a 'higher education production index' based on five types of degree with weights ranging from 1 for a bachelor degree to 3.2 for a PhD (Ferris, 1969; Johnstone, 1981).

As a further example of the current, more subtle approach to the assessment of teaching performance, we may mention the indicators used by the Vice-Chancellor of the University of New South Wales, for the Awards of Teaching Excellence, which were first instituted in 1989 with a cash prize of $A3000 each for up to six winners (in the event only three were awarded in 1989/90) 'to encourage and reward excellence in teaching by individuals and teams [of staff members of that university]'. In judging excellence some or all of the following criteria were considered:

- interest in teaching and promoting student learning;
- command over subject matter and recent developments in subject;
- keen and sympathetic guiding of students, understanding their needs;
- responsiveness to colleague and student feedback in teaching;
- ability to organise course material and present it cogently and imaginatively;
- ability to assess student learning and to provide them with feedback;
- ability to stimulate curiosity and independent learning in all students and creative work in advanced students;
- evidence of innovation in course design and delivery;
- evidence of successful supervision of postgraduate students.

Applicants were required to submit evidence and affidavits on their courses, student evaluation surveys, supervision, authorship and research, as well as names of referees for peer evaluation.

This form of assessment, even more so than the previous general example, carries a considerable judgemental element, but looks sufficiently varied to balance out bias for any but the most hostile committee. It is certainly an advancement on previous, and still surviving, practices to base appointments and advancement mainly on partial indicators such as non-specific reports by distant referees and publications lists. This will be further discussed in section 5.11.

5.4 Intelligence tests

Experts disagree about the notion of intelligence, and tests are not based on sound scientific principles, but intelligence testing has been very successful for practical applications (Eysenck, 1962: 8). Indicators of the level of intelligence are usually cast in the form of an *intelligence quotient* (*IQ*), based on the psychological testing of intellectual, mechanical, combinatory, analytical and similar aptitudes. Used in the last century for the identification of mentally retarded persons, they were later applied to the grading of school children to fit them to a type of education suited to their abilities and needs, and for the attendant task of counselling. More recently testing has also been widely employed for the selection, training and promotion of commercial and industrial personnel in both the private and public sectors of the economy. Research into the action and interaction of factors used for testing gives an analytical function to the indicators themselves.

An example of a test for the assessment of personality dispositions and preferences, based on Jung's theory of types, is in the *Myer–Briggs type indicator*, which reflects relative preferences in the areas of extroversion–introversion, sensing–intuition, thinking–feeling and judging–perception. The respective scales are ordered as a matrix that reflects sixteen personality types.

The history of intelligence scaling runs from skull and other physical measurements in the nineteenth century to the development of mental tests by Alfred Binet in France and Lewis Terman, David Wechsler and James Cattell in the United States, to name only some of the pioneers whose names remain associated with well-known IQ tests in this century.

The tests use a series of questions in verbal, quantitative and abstract/visual reasoning and short term memory for the *Standard–Binet test* (fourth edition), or a verbal scale that includes information, digit span, vocabulary, arithmetic, comprehension and similarities, as well as a performance scale for picture arrangement, block designs, object assembly and digit symbols in the *Wechsler adult intelligence scale*. The results are added on right–wrong or interval scales. Preliminary and subsequent manipulation allows scores to be standardised and normalised for age, model sample, standard deviations and other factors, and they are sometimes subjected to factor analysis to enhance presentation. In their final form there is frequently reference to *mental age*, expressed by the ratio of mental to chronological age ($100 \times MA/CA$), where 100 represents normal or average performance. A recent reformulation of the Standford–Binet–Wechsler test makes adjustment for standard deviation between ages for a so-called *deviation IQ* that is not based on the MA/CA formula.

On the statistical side the methods for indicator construction have been well developed and applied to such features as comparison between tests and validation of national profiles. They have been particularly useful as a tool for grading large populations of school children, students or job and training applicants by their level of intelligence as defined *ad hoc*. However, prior to such eminently practical applications IQ testing had a dark past, and shadows of social and racial bias still dog present interpretations. The biologist Gould (1983) claims that intelligence testing, like its predecessor skull measurement (i.e. craniology), rests on the premises of 'biological determinism'—that is, a belief in inherent inborn characteristics that justifies their acceptance by society. This means accepting present economic and social divisions as the natural order, including the dominance of white races over others, of the powerful over the weak, of men over women. For this purpose the scientists concerned, using their academic authority, have rendered down the complex set of human capabilities into a single artificial concept called *intelligence*, which can be quantified in seemingly objective numbers to rank the status of individuals. Gould has also criticised the calculation of IQ by means of factor or principal components analysis, because it uses a correlation matrix that presumes, rather than proves, the existence of a concept of intelligence and uses arbitrary restraints on parameters; or to put it more simply, the mathematical elegance of the process cannot hide its speciousness.

Strictures of bias, hypocrisy and indeterminacy in intelligence testing, as voiced by Gould, may be exaggerated, and he seems to overstate his case when he forswears altogether the notion of intelligence. However, the partisanship for deterministic causes and for eugenics of many of the US and UK pioneers in this area is well documented. It can be said that IQ testing became respectable only when it left behind its early use for advocacy of social engineering, and its selective cavalier treatment of the data, and concentrated on the streaming of particularised populations.

We have referred earlier (end of section 1.2) to the process of 'reification' by compounding various seemingly related features into a new concept. Many of the headings used in this book fall into this category; health, education and quality of life, for instance, are notions that only come to life through considering their component indicators. In such cases the quetions arise of what to include or exclude in the aggregate and of how to combine partial indicators constructed on different bases. Nor is intelligence the only such collective term that can be influenced by political bias. This can be partly avoided by adding appropriate sub-indexes.

5.5 Science

Section 1.3 discussed the general role of indicators in scientific enquiry, with reference to the role of deduction and to techniques relevant to all sciences. The discussion of *applications*, however, has generally been restricted to the social, or economic and social, sciences, because a coverage of the role of indicators in the natural sciences would open up debates about methodology that are specific to a host of fields, from astronomy to zoology, and well beyond our present scope.

However, beyond the cognitive aspects, substantiated by its analysis of expert knowledge, science can also be viewed as a social process that reflects the attitudes and norms of individual scientists and the communications system between them. This is reflected in what have become known as *science indicators*—a term that, like 'social indicators', has received the blessing of the US government in the publication of *Science Indicators 1972* and is now in common use among social metrologists. Science indicators are concerned not with hypothesising or the experimental testing of, say, the constellation of the stars or DNA, but with the material and mental effort that has gone into such endeavours—that is, with science as an intellectual activity by itself over time and in relation to other activities.

Much attention in reference to non-cognitive indicators in this area has been given to the development of *citation indexes*, which measure the quantity and quality of scientific activities (Elkana et al., 1978; Garfield, 1979; Cronin, 1984). This methodology can be regarded as an extension of education assessment, described in section 5.3, which mentioned citation as a performance indicator for tertiary education. However, citation, and citation indexing derived from it, are of interest also for the development of indicators generally.

Citation in this context usually refers to documents and similar source material quoted in scientific journals and like periodical publications, and can be extended to books. A citation index is:

> . . . an ordered list of cited articles, each accompanied by a list of citing articles. The citing article is identified as a source, the cited article as a reference. (Cronin, 1984: 6, fn.)

This seemingly simple method of judging the worth of an author's contribution to his/her field of study has long been applied superficially by rough counts of the author's work as quoted in bibliographies. Implicit or explicit reservations can be raised about aggregating something that depends at least partly on type of science, authors' habits, editors' requirements and other such extraneous factors. However, it is claimed that such objections can be either overcome or ignored as insignificant overall; so source lists have been elevated to the status of a useful research tool.

Garfield (1979), a pioneer of citation analysis, regards the listing of legal precedents in *Shepard's Citations*, issued in the United States since 1873, as a forerunner. The more recent progress in library science and structural linguistics has lent impetus to his own work since the 1950s. Others (e.g. Merton in Garfield, 1979; Cronin, 1984) have pointed to the concurrent rise of the *sociology of science* and of the Institute of Scientific Information at that time, as well as to progress in commercial citation indexing made possible by the computerisation of data.

As a result of these developments we now have:

- a debate about the nature and structure of scientific research based on citation;
- applications of quantitative measures to:

> . . . the estimation of the quality, impact, originality, penetration or visibility of performance within and between disciplines . . . frozen footprints on the landscape of scholarly achievement to deduce direction . . . a picture of those who have passed by . . . clues whether the advance was orderly and purposive [and] the process of innovation (Cronin, 1984: 25–6)

- a set for comparison with other performance measures.

Considerable work and ingenuity have gone into the development of citation analysis for search, ordering, grading and related purposes. This has been extended into *co-citation*, which refers to the citation of two or more documents in the one paper as a measure of cohesiveness through matrix analysis. It can be demonstrated in the form of a *co-citation map* (e.g. for social indicators; White, 1983). Citation indexing has been validated to some extent by comparison with other quality measures, and it is increasingly applied to structural and cross-disciplinary studies.

Apart from citation, other indicators for the circumstantial performance of science by individuals or faculty groups include: lists of research grants, prizes and awards; number of reviewed and other publications; memberships and fellowships of learned societies; honorary degrees; and other such expressions of collegial encomium. Most of them rely on peer review, which in theory, though not always in practice, should minimise establishment bias.

The *Nobel Prize* is in a special category here, not because the selection process is always entirely beyond doubt on political and professional grounds, but because it carries the popular mystique of the acme of scientific achievement. This has made the award also the top reference point for scaling performance indicators in various fields. It is positively correlated with high citation counts, not only after the award but also for future prize winners.

Peer review is often used in a minor way to indicate relative worth in science (e.g. for grants, appointments or awards). As an example of a more structured application we can quote a comparative study of five large-scale ocean research projects by a large group of scientists, which established a group of factors that divided the more from the less successful projects. It included differences in origin or research problem, quality and interest of participants, presence of a core of leaders and degree of independence from the funding agency; formal organisation, extent of social friction and communication problems made little difference (Mazur and Boyko, 1981).

Finally, it should be noted that the measurement of science inputs and outputs corresponds to health or education in the sense that those also require personnel and materiel. Expenditure on science is likely to lead to a more than proportional effect on personnel engaged in research and development (R&D). On these lines the OECD has proposed a *science productivity indicator* that relates national expenditure on R&D to R&D personnel (Price in Elkana et al., 1978: 92):

$$\frac{\text{Gross national expenditure on science}}{\text{Total GNP}} = k \frac{\text{R\&D manpower}}{\text{Total population}}$$

It has been found that the multiplier k has been fairly steady around 4.3 in developed countries. This means that an extra 1% of GDP spent on science would correspond to the extra deployment of about 23 R&D workers out of a population of 10 000.

5.6 Environment

The environment is all around: soil, water, the earth, flora and fauna, the biosphere. It surrounds us and permeates our existence as individuals and part of society. It links the animate world with the inanimate or no longer animate, in regular cycles, elemental outbursts and gradual change over millennia. It is often identified with nature and the everchanging forcefield of the world.

We speak of *ecology* as the study of organisms within and in relation to the environment. The manifestations of the environment in its internal and external interactions are governed by rules, some of which we do not yet understand and others of great complexity, which make the task of constructing indicators of ecological change very hazardous. In some cases certain features of change can be described by physical measures such as temperature and speed. However, this gives us only a partial picture of environmental change and effects; if we measure water flow at one point, this has to be seen in the context of water flow at other points in the area and of weather and other environmental conditions.

The United Nations Statistical Office (M/75, M/78, 1983) has listed a number of *environmental subject areas*, including:

- atmosphere (temperature, humidity, rainfall, pressure, windspeed);
- marine environment (desalination, fishing areas, fish catch, coastline);
- inland waters (area of lakes and wetlands; river length and discharge; water supply, quality and treatment; fisheries);
- lithosphere (land area use, mountains, soil loss, degradation, conservation);
- terrestrial biota (land by vegetation, national parks, wildlife);
- bioproductive systems (land use, irrigation, livestock, fertiliser);
- energy (reserves, production, use);
- pollution (emission, contamination, waste discharge, monitoring, standards);
- natural disasters (earthquakes, storms, floods, fires);
- environment (quality, perception, spending, technology).

This collection, which also includes population, human settlement, minerals, transport and recreation, comprises three groups of indicators:

- fixed, or rather slowly changing, features (e.g. coastlines, mountain heights), and
- other recurring phenomena (e.g. rainfall, energy use),

both of which can be described and applied as statistical indicators, mainly in physical units, and, partly overlapping these two,

- parameters now of great general concern (e.g. pollution, soil degradation, climatic change).

We could also distinguish in such a listing between descriptive, instrumental and outcome indicators.

Viewed from whatever angle, the construction and analysis of most of these indicators fall within the scope of the natural sciences (e.g. meteorology, geography) and do not concern us here as such. However, these indicators are related to the state and functioning of society and to that extent are subject to socioeconomic analysis.

The best-known scenario has been developed under the telling title *The Limits to Growth* by a group of scientists who formed the Club of Rome (Meadows et al., 1972). Looking at the predicament of mankind, they concluded that:

1. If present growth trends in world population, industrialisation, pollution, food production and resource depletion continue unchanged, the limits to growth on this planet will be reached sometime within the next 100 years. The most probable result will be a rather sudden and uncontrollable decline in both population and industrial capacity.

2. It is possible to alter these growth trends and to establish a condition of ecological and economic stability that is sustainable far into the future. The state of global equilibrium could be designed so that the basic material needs of each person on earth are satisfied and with an equal opportunity to realize his individual human potential.

3. If the world's people decide to strive for this second outcome rather than the first, the sooner they begin working to attain it, the greater will be their chances of success.

While their illustrious forerunner Malthus 183 years earlier saw the threat of disaster in the tendency for population to rise by geometric progression while food supplies rose by arithmetic progression, Meadows et al. added to that the threats of the uncontrolled exponential growth of industrialisation and consumption of non-renewable resources and the effects of pollution. Their conclusions were based on an MIT model of *system dynamics* that demonstrated different circular or time-delayed or interlocking relations of the structure through feedback loops and graphically described the results of different vector assumptions over time. Formally, this provided an impressive indicative statement for a bleak future unless several of the elements were brought under control, and from this need the notion of *sustainable development* has since been evolved.

Discussion in recent years has centred on so-called *economic environmental problems*, with some interesting applications of analytical techniques such as cost–benefit analysis, matrix analysis, input–output models and linear programming, as well as alternative indicative approaches of a more partial type than the Club of Rome's world model.

One major aspect has already been mentioned, namely the scarcity of resources that lies at the heart of economics, pumping valuation and allocation signals through the system. Reference has been made to the realisation that the supply of resources is limited not only for the individual user but also in the world overall, and to the emerging discussion of *limits to growth* and *de-development*. In this connection attempts have been made to *internalise the externalities*, meaning that, whereas previously some effects of economic activity have been ignored because their costs, or benefits, are *free* in the sense that they do not affect the market prices of products, a charge is now imposed on firms for the costs (e.g. use of the sea or public roads) or by firms on *free riders* (e.g. viewers of commercial television). For the environment in the wider sense, industrial, commercial or individual resource users do not often create external benefits, though tree planting may be taken as an example. More often they do cause some sort of environmental despoliation, the costs of which, in the form of immediate disamenities or long term damage to the environment, fall on the community and beyond. Scientists may argue about whether there are any *renewable* resources at all (i.e. resources that can be restored after use); for example, pine trees felled and replanted renew timber supplies, but the store of soil nutrients is less for the next generation. Or it can be speculated that nature is not a static system but moves in a cosmic swing from its beginning to its end and perhaps rebirth, and that our use of its energy and substance cannot be called *unnatural*.

Economists sometimes confuse the terms 'growth', defined by Daly (1987: 323) as *quantitative* increase in physical dimensions, and 'development', if this is defined as *qualitative* improvement in non-physical characteristics. Few will admit that we may be approaching the limits of growth in the sense of a loss in natural ecosystem service that, as Daly points out, may easily exceed gains in economic welfare, even assuming that we have not yet reached the limits of development.

Lowering our sights to the more immediate problem of indicators, the major questions of concern are the assessment of the economic cost of externalities in the form of resource use and pollution. Even at this stage it can be, and has been, said that, if there is any such cost, no amount of money can compensate for it; therefore a total ban on such resource use is the obvious answer. For example, if a factory emits smoke, that smoke may be harmless, say no more harmful than the carbon dioxide-laden air we breathe out, and therefore not subject to a charge; or it may be harmful to others, directly or indirectly, and therefore the factory should either reorganise its production to avoid causing emissions or change to producing something else less noisome—a substitute product; but if there is none, we just have to do without. Some environmental economists, however, take a more optimistic view (e.g. Baumol and Oates, 1988). They assume that externalities are undepletable, or even if depletable can be assessed the same way.

This rather narrow economic approach is based largely on two strands of thought: Pigovian welfare theory and its application to public finance theory. Whatever the theoretical merit of such an approach, and that is debatable, the underlying utility and behavioural functions are vague, and application to the formulation of indicators is hazardous. However, it is worth looking at some of the proposed schemes, however partial their validity, because of the current importance of environmental impact statements, the controversy between environmentalists and economic rationalists, pollution and waste control, and related problems.

Welfare economics, whose main protagonist was the British economist Pigou (1877–1959), is concerned with efficiency in the allocation of resources and the maximisation of human welfare, also with social costs and gains of labour and requisite government action. Welfare measurement had earlier been proposed by Pareto (1848–1923) in terms of utility and indifference curves. The links with *public finance theory* lie in the notion of the environment as a public (or social) *good* that is available to all (i.e. non-exclusive), like a beach, and undepletable (to use Baumol's alternative term for joint supply), so that consumption by one user does not diminish supply to others.

In this connection there is a further link through the application of taxation or fees to regulate the supply of such goods and thus to affect the price and demand situation (e.g. by means of entry fees). There is further the free rider question inasmuch as any public provision for the benefit of one user will increase supply not only to that user but also to others without charge. Related to this are spillover effects, which refer to costs and benefits from production that go beyond the making of the product itself. The situation of the environment is similar to that of public goods when the latter represent an environmental asset such as a park, though not quite the same in the case of amenities such as street lighting.

However, even then the assessment of effects rests basically on a cost–benefit analysis. For the environment, or rather for proposals that may affect the environment, this is mostly expressed by way of an *impact statement.* The following sample demonstrates that such assessments are based on a mixture of facts and general and specific assumptions rather than on definite indicators for the various aspects. The outline can apply to any government or private development proposal that requires an impact study in the planning stage before decisions are made about implementation.

The task begins with the collection and analysis of data leading to a description of the quantitative and qualitative characteristics of the present situation, with particular attention to unique or outstanding features, including the social and biological environment. Interaction can be demonstrated by a detailed matrix.

Table 5.4   Proposed actions that may cause environmental impact

Characteristic	Modification of region	Land transformation
Physiological Biological Cultural	Drainage	Canal, airport

The impact statement requires verbal comments about short and long term effects, recurring and single effects, irreversible and retrievable commitments of resources, avoidable and unavoidable side effects and similar aspects. In some cases such historical, scientific and derived data may be convertible into one or several indicators, but the quality of the latter cannot be better than the quality of the underlying estimates, and there is a risk that the error of mistaken concreteness may overstretch their validity.

Various attempts have been made to measure pollution by expressing it as a single or combined index, both by analysts of public finance (e.g. R. Musgrave) and by the growing band of environmentalists. Until recently pollution was generally regarded as a nuisance, an economic *bad*, but it was assumed that at a cost we could live with it. The cost imposed on the polluter in the form of a tax and on the public in terms of reduced quality of life stood at the centre of this discussion. Since then the debate has been extended from manageable externalities to the greater issue of global effects (e.g. the greenhouse effect) that put our very survival at risk and call for the minimisation or avoidance altogether of pollution. This bigger concern puts assessment into a different light, concentrating on the aggregate damage in relation to the use tolerance of our environment (e.g. what level of carbon dioxide emission can be absorbed without a critical greenhouse effect).

As previously stated, such discussion is beyond the scope of this book, but the earlier micro-debate about pollution deserves at least mention, although its outcome has yielded few tangible results. The reason for this can be attributed to its connection with a welfare theory that is open to general criticism because of its reliance on theoretical utility functions— or more practically, because of the general problem of finding a common value standard for disparate types of measurement. Comprehensive pollution measurement requires a translation of different physical *damage functions* (James et al., 1978: 19) into a monetary damage function, whether the chosen methodology is neoclassical, welfare, input–output or systems theory. We are on safer ground with survey assessment of aspects of environmental change and management.

Pearce, Markandya and Barbier (1989: 82), following a table prepared by D. Miltz for the OECD (October 1988), list in detail problems with the mathematical-statistical treatment of environmental data and underlying economic assumptions. They illustrate their *Blueprint for a Green Economy* with a number of partial, and perhaps less controversial, instrumental series, such as:

- gases and greenhouse effect, scenarios for climatic change;
- factors in choice of environmental policy (e.g. time preferences);
- cost of environmental policy, GDP with/without environmental policies;
- public perception of trade-off between growth and environment;
- correlation of willingness to act on environmental policy and GDP;
- pollution cost by type (e.g. health) and benefits in dollar terms;

- effects on property values of air and noise pollution;
- effect of change in lake water quality on tourist industry;
- membership of conservation and related bodies;
- land use accounts by stage of development;
- emission accounts by type and cost;
- water accounts by source, aquifers, snow and destination;
- national expenditure on resource management.

To this list can be added waste disposal statistics at dumps and recycling depots, and litter indexes for collection at designated bins. This type of partial indicator can be useful for conservation and waste management, even if the series cannot be meaningfully combined into a single or group index.

When discussing extensions of the GNP concept in section 3.2, the recent interest in *national resource accounting* in the United States, Canada, Europe and Japan was mentioned, with the suggestion that it can lead to a separate system and with that to a different type of aggregate. For example, the French Institut National de la Statistique et des Etudes Economiques is constructing accounts of *le patrimoine naturel* (the natural heritage) (P. Cornière, 1986), as did K.H. Alfsen et al. (1987) of the Central Bureau of Statistics of Norway for their country (see Pearce, Markandya and Barbier, 1989: ch. 4 for both). The debate about the connection of physical accounting with monetary values continues. Physical accounts by themselves may be useful for specific resource strategies for forestry, mineral or fishing supplies, but they do not lend themselves to aggregation by types or species, which may have quite different significance. Valuation has the obvious advantage of a uniform standard, but often rests on an ambiguous value basis for, say, water resources or land use potential. Similar problems about the assessment of pollution and other disamenities have previously been discussed.

Nevertheless, some bold attempts to bridge the gap between physical and economical accounting are now under way. Repetto and his colleagues at the World Resources Institute, Washington, have issued a report on *Wasting Assets: Natural Resources in the National Income Accounts* (1989). They rely on the concept of economic rent for the valuation of national resources, going back to Malthus's notion of scarcity. They have applied this to the estimation of Indonesian timber, petroleum and soil resources. Although interesting on a microscale, their apparent ambition to integrate their resource use estimates into the GNP remains subject to the general objections to an imputation–amputation adjustment that leads to a mixed ill-defined aggregate.

U.E. Simonis and his colleagues from the Wissenschaftszentrum Berlin für Sozialforschung (e.g. Simonis, 1990) are concerned with *sustainable development* or, as they call it, the ecological modernisation of industrial society, in particular damage to and protection of the environment. However, rather than advocating incorporation into the national accounts, they seek a complementary assessment. They have compiled statistics for Germany for investment in environmental protection by government and industry, in the form of the costs of waste disposal, water and air pollution control, and noise abatement. An approximate estimate of some major categories of water, air and noise pollution and of soil contamination, in terms of material and health hazards, the degradation of vegetation and amenities and similar impacts, put the ascertained damage at over DM100 billion per year at a time when the (then West German) GDP was in the region of DM200 billion. The cost estimates included DM48 billion for air pollution, DM33 billion for noise pollution, DM18 billion for water pollution and several DM billion for soil contamination. The authors are at pains to point out that assessment will not stop the degradation of the environment and that curative policies should be pursued.

The general question of constructing separate environmental indicators from satellite accounts, rather than trying to build them into GDP, has been discussed in section 3.3.

5.7 Culture

The word 'culture' is associated with a wide range of activities and situations that become specified through the indicators attached to them (see section 1.2 for instrumentalism). Leaving aside culture in the sense of cultivating organisms, we are left with a variety of culture notions centred on civilisation, customs, tradition, refinement and so on. UNESCO, the international organisation charged with the promotion of culture (and science and education), admits that the term eludes definition and that there is no universally accepted description of its content (UNESCO, 1979). However, we may try an indicative approach.

There is a large literature dealing with the concept and with the history and impact of culture, which is usually focused on a particular manifestation (e.g. the visual arts) or on the penetration of culture into the social environment. This can lead to thoughtful, albeit imprecise, anecdotal listings. For example, writer Shirley Hazzard (1980), in her reflections on life in Australia in the 1930s and 1940s, has commented on the following cultural features:

- cumulative transmitted knowledge of the past;
- art being widely and freely and intuitively valued and given universal meaning;
- knowledge being esteemed;
- development of basic cultural amenities as signals of the prevailing state of mind, including the quality of works in public galleries;
- absence of oppressive laws of literary and artistic censorship;
- thoughts and discussion about ideas and art, acknowledging intellectual and spiritual values of culture rather than regarding it as an insincere affectation.

It would be a daunting task trying to derive a set of statistical indicators at that level of refinement. Indeed we could retreat to the position that culture is impossible to define, as was claimed by the German philosopher Schelling and his followers in the romanticist period of the nineteenth century:

> . . . understanding men or ideas or movements, or the outlooks of individuals or groups, is not reducible to a sociological classification into types of behaviour with predictions based on scientific experiment and carefully tabulated statistics of observations. There is no substitute for sympathy, understanding, insight, wisdom. (Berlin, 1988: 138)

Following a more pragmatic approach we find that culture, however defined, has always depended on direction and promotion by governmental authority, be it prince or parliament. It is thus involved with the allocation of national resources, and an attempt should be made to assess it from this point of view, even if available indicators give only a superficial description.

Some of the general and social indicator yearbooks issued by national statistical agencies in recent years carry a few uncoordinated series of cultural statistics. A more comprehensive effort has been made by UNESCO, which set up an intercountry group, under the Helsinki Agreements, in 1979, when the present author was a member of that Committee (R. Horn, 1983). It seeks to complement an *a priori* pattern of cultural features with empirical observations, leading to a *framework for cultural statistics (FCS)* that can be circumscribed by available or collectable indicators. The following scheme is largely based on the UNESCO work; it distinguishes between ten cultural spheres:

- *cultural heritage*: museums, sites, archives;
- *printed material and literature*: books and other publications;
- *music*: composition, performance, equipment;
- *performing arts*: theatre, dance, circus;
- *pictorial/plastic arts*: painting, sculpture, handicrafts;
- *cinema and photography*: films, still images;
- *broadcasting*: radio, television;
- *sociocultural*: social and religious activity, festivals;
- *sports and games*: active and passive participation;
- *nature and environment*: open air recreation, nature parks.

This is a pragmatic scheme. We could argue about omissions or about some of the more spiritual or intellectual issues raised, or about overlaps with educational and environmental spheres, but it does give a lead for tying cultural issues to statistical norms, as applied, for example, by the Australian Bureau of Statistics in its National Culture-Leisure Scheme or in a *statistical model of cultural identity* (S. Horn and Carrington, 1990).

Beyond a horizontal delineation, spheres can be divided up vertically into different aspects of activity. For example, a Canadian scheme (Ferland, in UNESCO, 1976) suggests five different viewpoints:

* *creators* and their activities (e.g. authors);
* establishments that *prepare* (e.g. publishers);
* establishments that *present* (e.g. bookshops);
* establishments that *preserve* (e.g. libraries);
* *utilisation* (e.g. readers);

each of which has subheadings of persons and costs.

There is also the alternative typology for indicators presented by Midzuno (1976):

* *cultural activity*: realised (e.g. concert attendance, hall seats);
* *cultural product*: realised (e.g. audience ratings, radio licences);
* *cultural facilities*: concert halls, musical instruments;
* *cultural finance*: income/expenditure, private and public sectors;
* *cultural personnel* engaged in production and distribution;
* *cultural time* spent actively and passively on cultural activities.

Finally, the FCS can more definitely be expressed in indicators for the various domains of culture (R. Horn, 1983):

* *annual flow*: production of material goods (plays) and services (performance), subdivided by government agencies, private/professional/ amateur;
* *stocks*: public/private halls, libraries, sites and so on;
* *expenditure*: public/private in money and as a proportion of public/ private budgets;
* *time allocation*: production/use; active/passive participation as a proportion of time;
* *personnel*: public/private production/distribution as a proportion of the paid/unpaid workforce;
* *source/use:* own country traditional heritage/modern, imports/exports;
* *additional indicators*:
  distribution: Gini indexes for various types;
  quality: survey ratings, index of alternatives;
  access: regional spread, user cost;
  participation: producers, active/passive users.

Indicators of cultural activity or performance can be built up to a certain extent from the basic level of specific domains for aspects that use the same unit (e.g. allocation of expenditure, attendance at events). They may also be combined for growth rates, either proportional or non-parametric (with plus/minus signs). This could show change in the strengths of, say, musical or literary activities and the relative development of such domains without ranking them by relative importance. The combination of domain features into a single index would have to rest on idiosyncratic choices.

Different people will have different views on whether the number of books published is 'more important' than money spent on public libraries, for instance. The weighting question would only be glossed over by combining growth or change rates, particularly if these vary much between elements.

5.8 Human rights

The interpretation of human rights varies between individuals, political schools and regimes. However, unlike with other social issues, international conventions, signed by most countries, provide a solid base for their definition and measurement to describe the human rights situation both within and between countries.

The *Universal Declaration of Human Rights* was adopted unanimously by the United Nations General Assembly in December 1948, and its principles have since been confirmed as treaty provisions by many countries in the International Covenants on Economic, Social and Cultural Rights, and on Civil and Political Rights, and in others concerned with the rights of the child, the disabled and mentally retarded persons, as well as with the elimination of discrimination in employment on grounds of sex or race. Some of the relevant provisions are set out in abbreviated form in Table 5.5.

The wide perspective of these rights can be further extended politically to reflect views, as held by the US Department of State, that:

> . . . the right of self-government is a basic political right, that government is legitimate only when grounded on the consent of the governed, and that government thus grounded should not be used to deny life, liberty and the pursuit of happiness. Individuals in a society have the inalienable right to be free from government violations of the integrity of the person; to enjoy civil liberties such as freedom of expression, assembly, religion, and movement, without discrimination based on race, ancestry or sex; and to change the government by peaceful means.

The very variety of human rights makes it difficult to fit them into a single structure for balanced measurement; nor are we interested so much in what is being done or should be done, as in violations that *should not be done*. This means that a taxonomy of human rights is only an intermediate step to classifying human rights violations, which may, and usually do, cover several aspects in a single case (e.g. unjustified arrest, torture, unfair trial and capital punishment).

The nature of human rights has been discussed throughout history in general qualitative terms in the form of descriptive country reports, such as the annual reports by the US Department of State to the Committees on Foreign Relations of the US Senate and on Foreign Affairs in accordance with the Foreign Assistance Act (February 1989, pp. 1560), or the annual reports of organisations such as Amnesty International. However, systematic

Table 5.5   Universal Declaration of Human Rights

(1)	U 13/1	Right to freedom of movement and residence within the state
(2)	U 13/2	Right to leave any country and to return
(3)	I 21	Right to peaceful assembly; unrestricted beyond public order
(4, 5)	U, I 19	Right to hold opinions and freedom of expression
(6)	I 27	Right to minorities' language, culture and religion
*(7)	ICESCR 10	Right to protection from economic/social exploitation of children
*(8)	I 6	Right to life; not to be arbitrarily deprived of life
*(9)	U 5	No torture or cruel, inhuman or degrading treatment
*(10)	U 23	Right to work, choice of job, protection from unemployment
*(11)	I 6	No delay in abolishing death penalty
*(12)	I 7	Antitorture; no scientific experimentation without consent
*(13)	I 9	Right to liberty/security of person; no arbitrary arrest
(14)	U 20	Right not to be compelled to belong to an association
(15)	U 18	Right to freedom of thought, conscience; to observe/teach religion
(18)	U 12	Right to privacy; protection against attacks on reputation
(19)	I 25	Right to participate, ballot secrecy, access to public service
(21)	U 2	No discrimination by race, colour, language, religion, status, origin
(22)	U 23	Right to equal pay for equal work
(27)	U 10	Right to fair, public hearing by impartial tribunal for rights
(28)	I 8	Right to form and join trade unions
(29)	U 15	Right to a nationality; to keep it and change it
(30)	U 11	Right to presumption of innocence until proved guilty
(31)	I 31	Right to minimum guarantees in trials on criminal charges
(33)	I 9	Right to prompt hearing/trial on arrest on criminal charge
(35)	I 17	Right to own property; not to be arbitrarily deprived of it
(36)	U 16	Right to marry and found a family, without limits of religion, race, nationality; equal rights in marriage and its dissolution
(39)	I 15	Right to enjoy benefits of scientific progress

* Given triple weight by Humana.
Source: Condensed from the International Covenant on Civil and Political Rights, with numbering as in Humana (1983).

quantification was not seriously tackled until the 1970s, when the American Statistical Association, the American Association for the Advancement of Science, various bodies like Freedom House in the United States and others elsewhere took an interest in such statistics, and human rights organisations attempted a more precise assessment of their work.

The direction of this work is discussed in *Human Rights Quarterly* (November 1986), which took the form of a Symposium on Statistical Issues in the Field of Human Rights. We will refer here to only some of the attempts to provide working indicators for listing and recording violations of human rights on a country-comparable basis. Whatever the theoretical difficulties, it must be kept in mind that such indicators are needed for public attention and as a guide for practical political purposes in intercountry relations.

The *Comparative Survey of Freedom* by Gastil (1978) calculates comparative measures of freedom for each of about 150 independent nations and about 65 related territories. *Freedom* is defined primarily in terms of equality to influence the political process, and this is reflected in the choice of two major and two minor categories:

- *political rights*—on a seven-point scale from free to partly free and not free, largely based on electoral rights;
- *civil liberties*—on a seven-point scale, based on freedom of the press and expression of opinion, the rule of law and fair trial;
- *status of freedom*—on a three-point scale of free, partly free and not free, derived from a cumulation of the two previous scores with some minor adjustments, so that a joint score of up to 5 is designated usually free, 6–10 partly free and 11+ not free;
- *outlook for freedom*—on a three-point rating of minus, zero change and plus (in the 1977 table only about 10% of listed countries scored a plus, and only Jamaica and Canal Zone scored a minus).

The gradings are based on a large number of surveys, reports and expert opinions and heavily rely on comparisons betwen countries.

Gastil does not sum his lists nor make comparisons between the two major variables. However, a closer look indicates that the status of freedom is expectedly highest among independent nations in Western Europe, North America and Australasia, rivalled by a few in Latin America or elsewhere; that British territories show up better than French or US ones, that Monaco, Andorra and Liechtenstein (described as Franco-Spanish-Swiss territories) rank low on political rights, probably because they have no competitive party systems; also that overall the rating for civil liberties, with a median of 3 out of 7, is a little more favourable than the rating for political rights with a median of 3¾. However, the significance of the distinction between the liberties and freedom indicators has been queried because of their close association (Banks, 1985: 65). Their most interesting application is perhaps in time series comparisons for various countries or groups of countries.

In 1983 Humana published a *World Human Rights Guide*, which was updated and republished in 1987. Similarly to Gastil's book it covers separately about 120 major countries with a population of more than 1 million. He gives them a comparative rating, using a 40 questions assessment that covers most of the United Nations list. This means that, beyond the political rights and civil liberties scrutinised by Gastil, Humana includes other indicators such as social and economic equality for women and for ethnic minorities. The questions are closely based on the major provisions of the Universal Declaration of Human Rights and the relevant international covenants shown in Table 5.5. The results are expressed positively in terms of observance, whereas Gastil's ratings are negative in terms of violations. The answers are rated as follows:

Yes	Unqualified respect for freedoms and rights	3 points
Yes	Occasional breaches, otherwise satisfactory	2 points
No	Frequent violations	1 point
No	Constant pattern of violations	0 points

Questions 7–13, of Table 5.5, are weighted by a factor of 3 because they represent intimidation or direct attacks rather than only a denial of political and social rights (Humana, 1983/1987: 4). The maximum rating is

$$(33 \times 3) + (7 \times 3 \times 3) = 162 = 100\%$$

The 89 major countries had a median index value of 59; 42% were rated as fair, 34% as poor and 24% as very poor. The other, smaller and less developed, countries were mostly rated as poor or very poor from such information as was available. Countries in North America, Western Europe and Australasia scored over 90% with a top performance of 98% for Sweden. The United States at 90% did not do quite as well because of the continued institution of the death penalty in some states and occasional discrimination against women and ethnic minorities and restrictions in court appointment of counsel for free legal aid. The poorer African countries scored least, 17–36%, with positive ratings from occasional gestures towards legal, social and marital equality for women. The larger Asian and African countries mostly scored around 50%, and recent democratic reforms have lifted some South American countries up to 90%.

Most of the 40 listed *rights* can be identified as rights respected or denied by relevant legislation. In other cases proxy indicators were applied, such as the proportion of women in parliament or top positions for their equal status, or incidence statistics for the tolerance of torture and extrajudicial killings, or (drawing a long bow) the legality of contraceptive devices for the right to enjoy the benefits of scientific progress and its applications (Article 15-1b-ICESCR).

Humana's indicators are presented in handy almanac style, with answers and comments on each question for every country and some demographic and economic data. Drawing on the expertise of many people and organisations, he, like Gastil in his way, takes a simple practical approach to avoid questions of intercountry differences by closely following United Nations precepts, to which most countries adhere at least formally. However, rather than putting human rights on a common denominator for the resulting indicators, the scoring pattern quoted above suggests that socialist (pre-*Glasnost*) and less developed countries do not accept the idealised Western view of human rights and allot them a lesser role in their systems, as compared perhaps with religious or political goals. This seems to support an *ethnocentric* view of human rights, rather than the assumption of a universally valid standard.

On similar lines, Banks (1985) has used cluster analysis to identify six groups that show the close association of human rights ratings with political and economic status.

Some organisations concentrate on particular abuses of human rights (e.g. slavery, torture, capital punishment, religious suppression). They want to collect, or obtain from others, statistics of incidence and geographical distribution as well as of the impact of their efforts in reducing such abuses. This then is a more realistic task than the construction of aggregates that try to balance disparate factors from direct or indirect statistical evidence. It shifts the emphasis from what may happen if there is no legal protection, to what has actually happened.

We will take as an example *Amnesty International (AI)*, an organisation, founded in 1961, that has been successful in terms of public response. The AI movement is mainly concerned with political prisoners—that is, persons who have been gaoled because they hold and express, without using violence, convictions to which they are entitled under the Universal Declaration of Human Rights. It is also opposed to the infliction of capital punishment or torture on any prisoner, and it has ancillary concerns about prison conditions, the treatment of refugees and so on. It therefore covers most of the field of human rights previously enumerated, with the major limitation that its primary concern is for those who have become victims rather than for those who might become victims. The indicators involved therefore refer to actual persons rather than to guesses of potential victims, and the counting unit is simplified to the number of persons detained for whatever reason, instead of the relative severity of different sorts of violations.

If we knew the number of prisoners, and how many were detained in normal prison conditions or subject to cruel treatment or death threats, with information also about trial conduct, we could perhaps construct fairly reliable indicators of the human rights situation over time and between countries. However, countries either do not willingly divulge the number of political prisoners they hold, or do not distinguish them from ordinary criminals. Although AI now has about 700 000 members spread over 150 countries, its resources are limited. Its annual adoptions and actions cover no more than about 2% of the estimated half-million political prisoners held in over 100 countries for offences ranging from political campaigning to membership of trade unions and other bodies declared illegal, and to conscientious objectors to military service.

The descriptive reports about the situations in various countries, and AI's actions there, in the AI annual reports provide material for the estimation of *incidence* indicators. The annual reports also provide *organisational* indicators in the form of statistics of membership, adoption and release of prisoners, various other action targets and finance. A third type of indicators concerns membership *involvement* and *achievements*. Similar information is of interest to many other community organisations also; and as they do not seem much developed, we will elaborate a little on a model for AI that has applications to other organisations.

In this model the incidence indicators can specify the type of human rights violations that particularly concern the organisation. They are shown in Table 5.6(a) by country or region and estimated number of persons affected, using the international classification of the Universal Declaration of Human Rights and covenants. Very approximate figures will be sufficient, or perhaps only a simple coding into many, some, few or none. Changes in the situation can be indicated by showing estimates of new cases during a year and of total cases. AI in its annual reports publishes some details of the situation in major countries with at least some explanatory figures about new arrests and so on.

General incidence leads to specific indicators of the activities of the organisation. They can be subjectively rated on a three-point scale signifying a minor, medium or major effort related to the average (standard) effort for all countries, as shown in Table 5.6(b). The division into activities is flexible and can be extended. A subjective assessment of significance is preferable to attempting numerical counts of campaigns, letters written and so on, but such unit counts can be done separately for internal purposes to assess the use of resources.

Table 5.6(a)   Model of human rights situation by numbers affected

Country or region	Threat of execution	Torture or maltreatment	Unjust detention		Disappear- ances
			Trial delay	Unfair trial	
A: Total					
New cases					
B: Total					
New cases					

Note: This and following tables are based on a personal submission by R. Horn to Amnesty International; they do not necessarily represent AI's views.

Table 5.6(b)   Model of organisational activities

Country or region	Campaigns (1)	Special actions (2)	Group actions (3)	Other (4)
A				
B				

Code: * minor, ** medium, *** major effort.
(1) Directed to particular country(ies), with worldwide participation.
(2) Country part of urgent, regional or other actions.
(3) Member or target group adoptions or investigations with letters to authorities concerned, enquiries, publicity and so on.
(4) Formal/informal high-level missions, trial observers, investigation.

The most desired statistic for such an organisation is its *success rate*, but this is also its most elusive one. Organisational efforts are directed to the reduction of transgressions against human rights, but when such alleviations occur, in the form of amnesties or improved treatment of prisoners, it is rare for a country to admit that the appeals of a particular person, organisation or country have made it see the light. In most cases several forces have been at work, and political and humanitarian pressures merge to seek conformance with internationally agreed standards.

Particular organisations involved, while welcoming improvements in the human rights situation, cannot and do not claim that they have made a specific contribution. Yet one of the most frequent questions they have to face from present and potential supporters is: what can you achieve in face of the worldwide suppression of human rights? One answer is that it is sufficient if we can help at least one unfortunate person—and this much can be proved with documentary evidence—but for most people it takes more than that to justify a large international organisation with a multimillion budget. *Anecdotal* evidence of known cases of appeals or other *démarches* having met with success is obviously important for reassurance and as publicity material for the organisation, but it provides only partial summaries, which can mislead by omitting less visible gains.

It is therefore suggested to take an indirect approach, trying to compare reported improvements in the situation with actions, on the understanding that the two events are not necessarily linked causally (i.e. that improvements may have occurred anyway). For Table 5.6(c) a three-point rating of none, some or many can be used to indicate magnitude of incidence and change. For the summary rating in the last column, the asterisk code can be combined as shown in the table or, if a severity weighting is attempted, by giving, say, double weight to the execution, torture and disappearances cases.

Table 5.6(c)   Model of change in human rights situation over the year

Country or region	Threat of execution	Torture or maltreatment	Unjust detention		Disappear- ances	Summary
			Trial delay	Unfair trial		
A: Known total						
Known change						
B: Known total						
Known change						

Code: * none, ** some, *** many.
Summary rating: 0-** = # few; *** = ## some; *** + = ### many. These can be weighted.

Table 5.6(d)   Model of estimated contribution to improvement of human rights situation in year

Contribution by organisation	Success
Halted threat of execution	
Halted torture or other maltreatment	
Halted extrajudicial killings	
Improved poor prison conditions	
Released from detention	
Released from other restriction of movement	
Located disappeared persons	
Obtained unduly delayed trial	
Obtained fair trial conditions	
Gained shortening of sentence	
Material and other support to prisoner	
Material and other support to prisoner's family	

Code: 0 nil, + a little, ++ some, +++ a lot. These can be weighted.

Proceeding from the overall situation, we can now attempt to assess subjectively the contribution made by the organisation on behalf of individuals and groups, using a four-point positive scale of success: nil, a little, some or a lot, as shown in Table 5.6(d). A severity rating would value assistance by some grading of violations (e.g. giving removal of threat of death sentence a weight of 2, as against 1 for other ways of assisting victims), and concern for individuals and groups of victims could also be distinguished. Such lists and coding have to be prepared for each country or group of countries.

Beyond indicators applied to the primary objectives, related supplementary activities can be similarly assessed with a simple impact rating, as shown in Table 5.6(e). Weighting could assign more importance to external effects than to internal ones. Such impact indicators can be constructed separately for different techniques (e.g. prisoner adoptions) or for general and special campaigns, as well as for countries or regions.

Evaluation can be carried further by taking particular actions and so on separately, as in Table 5.6(f), to which simple impact codes and weighting can be applied. One objective here is to stress that whatever impact the organisation makes in its campaign for human rights will depend on its structure and the efforts of individual members.

Table 5.6(e)   Model of supplementary impact indicators

Country or region	Impact	Response
Violating Country	Concern communicated to government Concern expressed to other organisations Press and other publicity Other impact of protest	
Other Countries	Effect on neighbouring countries Interest by United Nations, Non-Government Organisations, etc.[a] Contribution to world awareness	
Own country	Contribution to human rights education Enrolment of new members Increased involvement of members Enhanced standing in community Closer cooperation with own government	

Code: 0 none, + a little, ++ some, +++ a lot. These can be weighted.
[a] Non-government organisations (e.g. Red Cross, Oxfam).

Table 5.6(f)   Model of action indicators

Campaign X	Objectives:
	    direct (release etc.)
	       (4 point success score)
	    indirect (publicity etc.)
	
	Members involved:
	    specific (adoption) group
	       (4 point activity score)
	    indirect (other branch members)
	Non-members involved (petitions etc.)
	Letters and similar appeals
	Direct responses from governments
	Responses from victim or victim's family
	Other responses
	Direct campaign costs for branch

5.9 War and peace

The horrors of war, and its effect on people and countries, are juxtaposed to a state of peace. The consequences can be described by various types of statistics, such as:

- *direct impact:* victims of attack/defence, numbers of dead and wounded, number of military personnel, money cost;
- *indirect impact:* proportion of population in war region, non-participating victims, property destroyed, money cost.

The indicative use of such statistics is limited. Only when there are great differences in magnitude may they suggest that one war was 'better or worse' or 'bigger or smaller' than another war. The social, moral, political and economic impacts of such events vary immeasurably between warring parties and over time. Also, there is often public revulsion against counting lives lost or maimed in terms of cold figures, and to keep up morale leaders become cautious about publicly stating their calculus of military and civilian casualties or of using terms such as 'bodybags' for their losses. 'War destroys the quality of life and becomes an indicator of death. Victory carries the seed of its own defeat' (Quesera, 1990: 13).

Rather than considering the statistical determinants of war itself, we will look instead at some recent attempts to formulate indicators that will demonstrate the build-up or detente in international relations in connection with the risk of conflict that could lead to war.

In considering confidence building as a means of crisis stabilisation, Petersen (1989) looked at factors connected with *international tension* between superpowers, including its nexus with false alarms. He found at least three indicators that seem to have been highly correlated in the 1977–84 period: the annual sum of US accusations, by the President and others, as recorded in Department of State bulletins; the aggregates of Threat Evaluation Conferences about missiles and so on called by NORAD (the North American Air Defense System), as proxy for false alarms; and defence expenditure as a proportion of GDP. These indicators seem to reflect the psychopolitical dynamics of the period, much more so than the number of mutual accusations and consultations.

Riddell (1989) used the number of incidents in which the United States has used military power without military conflict as an indicator of power. He applied regression analysis to show that such power is positively related to the rate of business profits. The apparent relation between power and a stable international order has led J.K. Galbraith and others to claim that international tension supports military power and that one superpower's will to dominate the world serves the military designs of other superpowers. It remains to be seen whether the present subsidence of the cold war will call for a fresh approach to the assessment of international tension.

Various indicators have been used in attempts to gauge the role of *military spending* on the economy. Henry and Oliver (1987) have tried to show that increasing defence outlays in 1977–85 cushioned a reduction in other production jobs; but Melman (1988) has condemned military spending as being based on cost maximising and as tending to create excess capacity, to the detriment of efficient industries that depend on cost minimising.

A further problem is the use of *nuclear energy* for both weapons and general power. For military uses the potential effect of nuclear weapons can be measured by their kill rates or sometimes as multiples of Hiroshima and Nagasaki victims. It requires no elaborate analysis to verify the overkill potential of existing weapon stocks, nor any detailed accident and waste creation rates to show the byproduct risks of nuclear weapons.

Alex Michalos (1989), a leader in the contemporary discussion on social indicators and quality-of-life assessment, has put the case for and against the Canadian production and exports of military arms, both on moral grounds and on the statistical evidence of indicators. This approach leads to a general combination of moral or ethical standards with socioeconomic argument and could be applied to other countries.

Michalos refutes a number of arguments put forward in favour of producing and exporting arms (e.g. the rights claimed for a nation to produce and sell arms). Governments may be considered responsible for the protection of their country and bound by alliances such as the North Atlantic Treaty Organisation (NATO), but they tend to ignore the problems of minor participants, which suffer from a high debt burden aggravated by US deficits. The deficits in turn are due to high military spending, which drives up interest rates and reduces foreign aid. Imports reduce local initiative, while the local defence industry is often inefficient and wastes available resources. The balance-of-payments advantage, for a country such as Canada, is doubtful if the branches of foreign manufacturers rely heavily on imported machinery and their profits do not stay in the country. Foreign branches also can crowd out civilian industry and reduce its international competitiveness. Military industries create fewer jobs than equivalent investment in civilian ones, and it is significant that productivity growth in 1960–84 was inversely related to military expenditures and less than in other industrial countries. Furthermore, the concentration of military industries on the electronic and aerospace sectors can lead to lags in basic industries such as steel or transport.

Michalos does not extend this powerful indicative condemnation to a call for general disarmament for countries like Canada, but concedes a national and international subsidiary role for the military establishment in routine surveillance, disaster relief and peace-keeping efforts. He also demonstrates incidentally the multifarious roles that indicators can play in analysing the pros and cons of international relations.

5.10 Politics

Political indicators express *satisfaction and expectations* with respect to past, present and future actions by the government or individual politicians. They are drawn mostly from a sample rather than from the whole population, and as such are subject to survey error in defining the target population, specifying sample design, eliciting responses and interpreting results (see Lessler in Turner and Martin, 1984). It should also be considered that surveys reflect views at a given point of time and depend on factors such as the honesty of respondents and their volatility between survey and election dates. Some general features of subjective indicators, drawn from surveys, have been previously discussed in connection with scaling techniques, social indicators and quality-of-life assessment, and we will add here only some comments with reference to political indicators.

Attitude testing was first developed in the United States in the 1920s. It has been applied to public opinion polls by Gallup and others since 1935 and now has spread across the world for political and other testing and forecasting. The clear format in which results are presented, and their newsworthiness, promoted by the media, have made such polls the basis for one of the most popular type of indicators. Some academics and governmental statisticians remain sceptical about the scientific background of subjective indicators, and their nature is now being more critically reviewed (e.g. Turner and Martin, 1984).

Political polls by the Gallup and other organisations are now so regularly undertaken that the results not only provide information about the election of presidents and parliaments if the election were held *today*, but also become part of *time series* indicators of attitudes, so that their up and down movements bridge the gap between actual election dates. The significance of political polls now seems to be so firmly established that respondents regard a poll as part of the election process that allows them to have their say in the running of public affairs.

The significance of polls goes beyond the immediate purpose of sniffing out present and future winners and losers. They can be used, for example, to establish the popularity of party leaders or local members in relation to the ratings of their parties, or for the micro-analysis of subdistricts in relation to larger districts, or for the specific targeting of campaigns by mail-outs and door knocking. Combining poll results with socioeconomic indicators can build up area profiles for the analysis of supporters, neutrals and opponents.

Apart from socioeconomic data, poll results can be supplemented by objective-type political *background data*. For example, number of laws passed with voting and abstention details, number of parliamentary questions asked, number of committee meetings, number of reports, extent of media coverage, parliamentary attendance—all such instrumental indicators help to build up the picture of government activity.

The question of formulating questions to fit public perception categories has received some attention in the literature (e.g. Turner and Martin,1984: part 7), sometimes under the heading of *conceptual ambiguity*. This problem arises not so much in polls asking for preferences for named persons or parties, but rather in the formulation of less definite issue categories. For example, a series of questions might run:

For control of inflation:
(1) should the government make greater use of fiscal policy?
(2)   greater use of monetary policy?
(3)   greater use of economic regulation?

It may or may not be evident to respondents that the exercise of both monetary and fiscal policy involves a deal of economic regulation, but fiscal policy probably more so than monetary policy. Furthermore, unless definitely explained, it may not be clear to respondents that the measures are not mutually exclusive, it being arguable whether more of (1) and/or (2) implies less of (3). More generally, as with objective social indicators, the formulation of subjective ones may have the auxiliary function of clarifying the subject of the survey.

The number of seats held in parliament gives a ready indication of the relative situation of the political parties. This can be supplemented by calculating the swing required for them to win or lose seats. For example, if there are 100 voters and party A gains 60 votes, it has a majority of 20 votes or 20%. It would lose the seat at the next election if it scored 49 votes or less, that is with a swing of 11% of the electorate against it or a loss of 18% of its previous vote. Mackerras (1989) gives a visual expression of such changes in the form of an *electoral pendulum*, which indicates the required swing in the various electorates for a change in political incumbency.

5.11 Performance merit (see also section 4.9)

Most of the indicators discussed in this book can be said to rate *merit of performance* in some way: historically, cross-country or on a set internal scale. Grading people by specific characteristics goes back to the anthropological measurements used by Cesare Lombroso and Francis Galton, who tried to link physical features with inherited and acquired mental and social characteristics. Here we will consider separately what may be called specific merit indicators of top performances of human endeavour and of products.

The *Guinness Book of Records* (McWhirter and McWhirter, 1988), itself a record holder with some 60 million copies produced in 33 years since 1955, refers on its frontispiece to the following types of record: the 'largest/ smallest/fastest/heaviest/longest/highest/lowest/hottest/oldest/richest/ deepest/tallest/loudest/mostest/in, on and beyond the earth'. A record in these terms is of public interest, and so are the circumstances of time, place, history and so on. The description also points to the relative nature of superlatives, which makes the largest building not necessarily the longest and highest.

As an example of a 'useful' application of merit indicators to guiding *consumer choice*, various independent groups test goods and services by objective-type criteria (e.g. safety, technical efficiency, convenience) and rate them on a weighted or unweighted points scale to show the 'best product' or products of acceptable quality or, in combination with price, the 'best buy'. This service tells potential buyers not only what is best by the set standards but also which items excel on a particular feature that they are interested in. As quality and price are often not strongly correlated, it allows buyers to pick bargains where good quality is obtainable at reasonable relative prices. Beyond personal applications, the analysis of consumer tests can lead on to the investigation of *best buys* and price–quality relations generally, as well as the relative grading of home-produced goods and imports (R. Horn, 1971: 45–51).

The examples in Table 5.7 are all taken from the January 1991 issue of *Choice*, the monthly magazine of the Australian Consumer Association, an independent non-profit body associated with the International Organisation of Consumers' Unions. The tables and graphs list various makes, their prices, their country of origin and other features. The tests are usually done and judged by a panel of the organisation, or sometimes, as was here the case for running shoes, by an outside expert, with extensive comments for an evaluation of the results.

Table 5.7   Consumer tests

Running shoes: 12 brands (training models); 7 criteria, equal rated: comfort, moisture evaporation, shock absorption, stability, construction, terrain-riding ability, flexibility and springiness.
  Scores 96–82; price $A142–39, top scorer $A120.

Colour print film: 24 brands, 4 speed groups; 4 criteria, equal rated: sharpness, graininess, colour rendition, latitude.
  Scores 88–6; price (24 exposures) $A9.58–$A4; top scorer (standard) $A4.

Washing machines: 15 front loaders and 18 top loaders; 5 criteria: energy efficiency (30%), spin efficiency (25%), water efficiency (5%), gentleness (fray test) (20%), soil removal (20%).
  Scores 83–63; price $A2710–$A560; top scorer $A1850.

Juice extractors: 9 brands; 4 criteria: juice extraction and juice quality (20%), ease of use (50%), mechanical safety (30%); also 'noise', zero-rated for overall performance.
  Scores 66–45; price $A50–$A155, top scorer $A59.

Source: Choice, January 1991.

Panel rating is also used for *best car* selections by motoring magazines, although more subjectively and sometimes with commercial overtones. The Australian magazine *Wheels* gave its car-of-the-year award for 1990 to the Toyota Lexus LS 400, which rated seven out of eleven votes from a judging panel that included engineers, racing drivers and a road tester. They used six criteria: value for money, engineering excellence, advancement in design, performance of intended function, utilisation of resources and safety. Motorists may also look for more mundane features such as fuel economy, spaciousness and travelling comfort. The choice of the Lexus was criticised because at a price of about $118 000, even though it may be 'the best sedan money can buy', few people can afford it.

A rival magazine, *Modern Motor*, used a panel of 47 journalists, each with 20 votes to allocate. With 226 votes they chose the Toyota Tarago, which is priced from $A26 000 to $A40 000 for its four models, and they gave the 'best luxury car' award to the Lexus. In an earlier survey of 11 000 people by *Choice* (February 1989), which centred on car reliability, the Tarago only rated just above average with 69.6%, in thirteenth position out of some 75 models of various ages surveyed.

An example of combining subjective with objective assessment is presented by the *Good Statistics Guide* published by the UK weekly *The Economist* (7 September 1991, p. 102). The journal asked statisticians from various countries to rank government statistical agencies in ten large OECD countries by the perceived reliability of their published figures. As criteria the statisticians used the coverage and reliability of the statistics, their methodology, and the integrity and objectivity of the statistical agency. In their judgement Canada has the best statistics in the group, followed by Australia, Sweden, the Netherlands, France, Germany, the United States, Japan, the United Kingdom with Italy coming last.

They then applied two objective-type tests. Firstly, they calculated the extent to which these countries have revised their quarterly GDP statistics in 1987–89, expressed through the mean average deviation between initial and final figures; there Canada again came out on top, with the United States second and Germany last. Secondly, they calculated timeliness by taking the average speed of publication of GDP and some other major economic series; there Germany, the United Kingdom and Italy did much better than Canada. Those two indicators are interrelated to the extent that rapid publication makes subsequent revisions more likely, and for these and related reasons the statisticians did not give much weight to them.

In the final analysis the statisticians reverted to another type of objective reason for excellence. The four top-ranking countries all represent relatively small economies, which makes it easier to collect statistics. More importantly perhaps, they have centralised systems in which numbers are collected by a single agency whose independence is guaranteed by law, at least in Canada, Australia and the Netherlands.

Going from commodity to human competition, we find that in some instances the winning persons or teams are clear champions, well ahead of their competitors whatever the circumstances of the contest or their form on the set day or the situation in which they produced their winning piece of work. In other cases variations in performance are not taken into account for the results of the set occasion—that is, on the day of examination or race, or for a longer period when merit rating is applied to achievements, say over the past year, as discussed in section 5.3 with respect to educational rating. Attempts can be made to even out performances on repeat occasions, by organising round-robin contests rather than knockout competitions or by keeping aggregative seasonal scores for individual players in ball games. To the extent that this method fits into the nature of the game, it can be considered to yield a more comprehensive merit rating than results of single events.

End results depend more or less on the qualifications required for contestants, which can range from minimal preconditions for persons and equipment to specifics about age, sex and previous performances of entrants and to complex rules for equipment, such as the rating rules for yachting adopted for America's Cup matches in 1930, which take '18/100 of length at waterline multiplied by square of sail area and divided by cube root of displacement'.

If the winning conditions are set out unambiguously in terms of specified dimensions such as time, distance, size or frequency, the problems of determining best performance should be mainly peripheral (e.g. geography or weather conditions).

As an example for merit rating by objective or subjective indicators, we can take *games performance*. Judgement is usually sought by the *objective* measurement of wins in games or races in terms of time or points scored. National and international organisations try to establish precise standards for game conditions and scoring, often with built-in weighting systems (e.g. in US football for touchdowns, drop kicks, pass and field goals; or in cricket for hits and runs). These standards concentrate on the outcome of the game; for example, it is immaterial at the end whether the winning point comes from a penalty kick in soccer or the winning time from a repechage race in rowing. Another notable example is lawn tennis, where the majority of sets gained determines the winner, who may have scored fewer points and won fewer individual games than his/her opponent.

However, in the nature of some sports, sole or supplementary *subjective-*type criteria must be applied, presumably because they carry an element of artistic expression. For instance, judges in gymnastics make their decisions for both the compulsory and optional exercises based on the degree of difficulty in performing the exercise, and also take account of the execution of the movement and the form displayed. More elaborately, in aquatic diving championships 37 types of dives are approved from the 1 metre board and 49 from the 3 metre board, arranged in five groups of degree of difficulty (e.g. forward, backward, gainer, cutaway and twisting). Each diver executes six optional and six other dives, within the frame of the degree-of-difficulty table. Five judges mark each dive on a six-point scale, ranging from 0 for complete failure to 9–10 for very good. The highest and lowest scores are excluded from the tally, and the sum or average of the remainder are weighted by the set degree of difficulty.

The subjective element in merit scoring, as in the construction of other indicators, can therefore be reduced by detailed formulation of rules, by weighting and by median-directed averaging that downplays extreme scores at both ends. When scoring is extended from a dichotomy of winners and losers to the determination of *near-winners* or *near-losers*, the scaling becomes uncertain—we might even say idiosyncratic, being often influenced by patriotic attempts to boost the image of the near-losers. It seems to be popular not only to praise the winners but also to extend the halo to unsuccessful finalists, runner-up competitors or those in the top group who did not quite make it to the top.

This applies not only to sports but also to many cultural competitions, where runners-up are often regarded as prizeworthy and therefore praiseworthy (e.g. by publishing names shortlisted for a prize or otherwise as preliminary inclusions for consideration by a final selection panel). This is not to say that such placings need not be regarded as general indicators of meritorious although not top performance by both competitors and the public. However, their value must be judged with caution regarding the scale distance between the top and other performers, unless the judges make specific comments about the relative quality of the entrants.

The significance of contests and prizes also depends on supply. The number of merit awards in many academic, cultural and sporting fields seems to be continuously increasing. This may be due partly to greater public, corporate and private munificence, inspired by a genuine desire to further such activities through rewarding excellence, but to some extent it also reflects the desire to further the names of sponsors. A multiplicity of similar awards can debase the relative merit of each, in particular when the subtleties of more or less firmly laid down preconditions, jury selections and votings are not generally known, or publicised only when disputes arise. Even for that best-known of awards for scientific, literary and pacifist distinctions, the Nobel Prize, few would know the nominating agencies for the six annual awards and the finer points of selection principles and procedures. This applies even more so to the variety of national and international awards that try to imitate Nobel Prize procedures to boost the prestige of sponsors.

A similar situation exists with respect to the *Olympic Games*, where several other contests (e.g. the Commonwealth Games, the Goodwill Games in Seattle) have borrowed some of their lineaments, and the Olympic rating of gold, silver and bronze medals is being applied to many other major and minor contests irrespective of the standard of competitors. The vagaries of differential merit rating of the medals has been discussed in section 2.7 on weighting and equivalence scales, taking alternative overall placings at the 1988 Olympic Games as an example. Reference there was made to the close correlation between gold, silver and bronze medals gained by a particular country. Adoption of a weighting system of 3–2–1 or 4–2–1, rather than 1-1-1 or 1-0-0, would make no difference in the world ranking of top performers (e.g. United States, USSR), although it might move some countries up or down a few places in the lower ranks. This is different if other weights are attached to medals (e.g. population size of countries). However, a high national sporting profile and promotion, or even the chance emergence of one or two good athletes, can put small nations well ahead of large ones.

Finally, it may be mentioned that winning performance scores can be supplemented by partial indicators that rate particular features of the game participants. Examples are bowling and batting averages in cricket; or in tennis, service aces and double faults, forehand and backhand winning strokes, forced and unforced errors, and points gained at net.

5.12 Status

A population can be stratified by status or related concepts in various ways, and the resulting indicators serve both for the description of the population in terms of status and for the structural analysis of the chosen status aspect. For example, a list of occupations, if chosen as status proxy, shows the number of persons in each category, divided by age, gender, training and so on; it also shows the occupational structure of the population overall by skills and, if data are available, matrices of occupational shifts. The relevant indicators can be divided into those based on 'objective' criteria (e.g. income, occupation) and those based on people's perception of status. Such a division is useful for a first approach; but as we shall see, on further consideration the types can overlap and merge.

Demographic data from *population census* collections serve as objective instrumental classifiers for many indicators, which are presented in groups by age, marital status, birthplace, occupation, industry, location or religion. Some census collections also use income, ethnicity, dwelling types and other features. Such classifications and some of their correlative comparisons themselves have many applications, with the practical advantage of being often available in cross-classified detail.

A major application for such data is in *market research*, where the search for indicators of actual and potential markets for particular goods and services has contributed to recent progress in techniques of sampling, classification and correlation. Urban, regional and national *planning* agencies also use single or combined status indicators for their purposes. It can generally be said that in combinations a single indicator (e.g. income) often dominates the index, making the other components redundant, or that such combinations seem to be based on fixed linear relationships of the elements (e.g. income and size of house; occupation and household expenditure), although these may shift over time and between areas. It may therefore be better to use a single series known to be closely related to the status aspect (e.g. age, income or educational attainment).

Surveys of physical characteristics can be useful, such as the historic records of men's height mentioned in section 3.9, or height and weight surveys for school children with details of age, gender and home location. Hospital and other health records and *ad hoc* surveys are also a major source for epidemiological and health status indicators.

Sociologists since Max Weber have been interested in the study of *power, privilege and prestige* (Reiss et al., 1961; Daniel, 1983) and have developed various survey methods of the *perception* type for their identification. One of their major correlates is *occupation*, and research about this connection has been undertaken in many countries. The pioneer study in the United States was done by C. North and P. Hatt at Ohio State University in 1947 for the *National Opinion Research Center (NORC)* (as quoted in Reiss et al., 1961: 40). They tried to obtain a national rating of the relative prestige of a range of about 90 occupations by asking people about the relative desirability of occupations. Informants were given a list of occupations and asked to rate their standing, according to the informant's personal opinion, on a five-point scale as excellent, good, average, somewhat below average or poor. Introductory notes suggested that informants might try to put themselves into the position of being asked for career advice by an outstanding young man, although the list did not refer to career opportunities within occupations.

This type of status identification and rating by a population sample raises many questions about the chosen list of occupations, often over 100, and about the ability of interviewees to pass judgement according to their own predilections or perceived public opinion. Indeed, much of the discussion seems to be concerned not so much with analysis of the power process, manifest in the survey results, as with public perception of the situation and technicalities of the survey, such as the variability of ratings. As much or more attention has been paid to the occupational and locational structure of respondents in relation to their ratings, as to the overall ratings of occupations. This includes claims of sectional convergence in prestige assessment, rather than great variability, and (disputed) views about the invariant nature of prestige hierarchies across time and space (Daniel, 1983: 60–3).

Aggregate rankings in the NORC and similar studies were calculated by working out the frequency of each score, from excellent to poor, multiplying the frequencies by score ratings, from 5 for excellent down to 1 for poor, and dividing the sum by 5 (or corresponding score points with surveys using more or less score categories). This is equivalent to zero-weighting with the assumption of even intervals scales. It has been observed generally that people are less willing or able to make negative rather than positive judgements. In the NORC study there were 52% positive (excellent or good) ratings as against 18% below average and 30% average ratings, and for practical purposes the prestige score was determined by the proportion of excellent or good ratings (Reiss et al., 1961: 118).

The results in the NORC and similar studies give highest rank to judges, government ministers, and physicians and other professionals and lowest rank to unskilled workers. In a few instances top rank was given to otherwise poorly ranked occupations, and more rarely otherwise top-rating professions were downgraded.

In general it appears that such ranking exercises are of interest mainly for the structural details and interrelations rather than for the production of an aggregate indicator, for which the results in this case are broadly predictable anyway. Statistically, power and prestige rating might be on safer ground if based on *objective* criteria such as income, wealth, living space, educational attainment, ownership of cars and household appliances, or similar outward trappings of social position, rather than on the perceptions of friends and foes of the power system. However, conceptually there seems to be a good argument for linking the strong perceptual elements of power, status and prestige with the classification.

As an example of the combination we take Duncan's *socioeconomic index of occupations* (Reiss et al., 1961: chs. 6 and 7), which combines educational and income variables, adjusted for age, with the NORC prestige ratings. Correlative analysis in 1950 pointed to a fairly high degree of 'status disequilibrium'; that is, many men ranking high on one of three variables (status, income and occupation) ranked comparatively low on one of the others. This absence of collinearity suggests that any of these variables by itself does not predict well the levels of the other two.

5.13 Time use

Indicators are usually expressed in terms of money values, number of persons or standard quantitative measures such as weight or number of objects. Time can serve a similar purpose of standardising activities, and can itself represent the indicative purpose when speed becomes the objective of performance measurement, notably in sport, or when a relative indicator is sought for effort and types of activity.

While time, unlike money, is invariant across periods and between regions, it does, like other quantum measures, carry assumptions of the consistency of circumstantial conditions (e.g. that output in a given period is not affected by climate or by workers' capacity), unless these conditions are specified (e.g. in comparing the productivities of skilled and unskilled, or young and old, workers). Indicators expressed in time units are thus presented on a value-free basis with subdivisions, but care must be taken about variable dimensions if these are relevant. One hour of work is not the same now as it was 10 or 100 years ago, inasmuch as workers, tasks and attitudes have changed in many ways since. This aspect of a different meaning of units by the same name over time and between regions applies to all sorts of indicators, whatever the unit. It has been mentioned before but bears repeating here, because some comments on time use statistics seem to neglect the possibility of inbuilt incongruities over longer periods or between different societies.

Thoughts about the division of (human) time between *work* and *leisure* date back to the Greek philosophers, who linked leisure with elitist intellectual pursuits, in contrast to the Calvinists in a later era, who sanctified work and condemned idleness. For the current interest, economic and social approaches can be distinguished.

Firstly, economists apply the time measure in labour analysis, where working hours are used for simple divisions between full and part time work or between ordinary and overtime work and earnings. Labour time is also basic to the calculation of productivity measures, as discussed in section 4.7. More recently attention has been given to the allocation of time in a market setting, in questions such as the effect of wage changes on willingness to work in terms of work and leisure. About the same time the economic notion of work as *paid work* has come under attack from the women's movements, as downgrading, or even degrading, the value of unpaid housework. Secondly, interest has grown from other social sciences investigating the extent and division of non-work time in connection with social needs (e.g. for child care, the provision of recreational and cultural services, and other activities). Apart from public policy, time use has become a significant technique for quality-of-life indication also. We will look here more closely at the use made by economists of time-use analysis and at its social applications, as well as the databases from national and international surveys.

The use of time units for the indication of work effort has already been mentioned, as has the requirement of specifying, where appropriate, the attending characteristics of workers, work effort and work conditions. A more debatable application in labour economics has been the postulate of a dichotomy of time between work and leisure—or preferably, *work* and *non-work* time—where the former is defined on standard economist lines as paid work time and the latter as residual time, obviating the need to define its nature precisely. The analysis is based on the premise that both work, through the income it generates, and non-work, through the spare time options it creates, will yield satisfaction. At some points the two types of satisfaction will be equal, so that a person will be indifferent to the choice between, say, an extra hour's work and $100 wages, or 2 hours' extra work and $180 (or $220). A major advantage of this type of *indifference curve* analysis is that it provides a method, albeit a might-have-been method, of valuing time in money terms. The perils of overstretching this method in estimating unpaid housework on the basis of paid work have already been mentioned in the discussion about the extension of GNP in section 3.2.

Willingness to work is valued by means of indifference curve analysis. If income forgone is regarded as the price of time, a fall in the wage rate will make leisure cheaper and thus more attractive in terms of income, and vice versa for a wage rise. This is the so-called *substitution effect*. However, it can be partly or wholly offset by the *income effect*, operating in the opposite direction, whereby lower wages act as an inducement to work longer hours so as to maintain previous income, and higher wages make extra work more attractive.

It has been claimed that the general postwar trends in developed countries for working hours to decline and wage rates to rise are evidence of a long term substitution effect for individuals. Against this it may be held that the increase in family incomes through the greater workforce participation of married women points to an income effect—or to put it otherwise, that the rising opportunity cost of leisure for women is keeping them at work and has played its part in reducing time spent on unpaid housework.

There is scattered statistical evidence that both effects sometimes operate, as we might expect for workers at different levels of income, age, needs, skill and so on. Account must also be taken of major operational barriers for the full effects either way. Work time flexibility for married workers may be greater than for single workers by variations of full time and part time work and of overtime and multiple job holdings, but the bulk of the labour force have little control over their working hours. We could also quote anecdotal evidence that the substitution effect of tax rises is offset by high levels of consumer debt, which force some workers to seek overtime or a second job in that situation. A more sophisticated analysis on these lines has been initiated by Becker (1965) and his associates at Columbia University, and it has been extended since by segmented labour-market theories.

The income and substitution effects are a useful pointer to the general operation of the labour market—or more precisely, to the reaction of supply to price in the market, excluding reverse reactions of price to changes in supply and the relations of demand to price. However, the simplicity of the assumption about market behaviour and human reactions diminishes the scope for them to be used for analysis of the strength of the opposing forces and for application as indicators to the effect of wage changes on labour supply.

Another restriction is the cavalier treatment of non-working time as a residual that is supposed to be measurable by the opportunity cost calculus. For a more differentiated approach of the division of time, the focus should be shifted from paid/unpaid to *type of activity*, as in the following notional scheme:

- *Paid activity*: by mode of pay, type of product, occupational status.
- *Unpaid activity*: related to paid activity either:
  (a) closely: travel to work, job search, study;
  (b) indirectly: basic rest, household activity; or
  (c) remotely: cultural, educational, spiritual, political, leisure, activities.

This classification retains the major division between paid and unpaid work but acknowledges their interaction. Further subdivisions of unpaid activities could be made on the basis of essential/voluntary or in relation to skill, work milieu, social relations, family duties and so on.

The interest of sociopsychologists has centred on *leisure* activities both as such and in their relation to work. *Work and Leisure* (Smigel, 1963) contains articles by Gross, Wilensky, Berger and Gerstl. E. Gross refers to the instrumental nature but necessary irksomeness of work to supply maintenance needs, in contrast to the intrinsic value of free time for leisure. However, this distinction can become uncertain when work itself is interesting, in particular for professional workers, or is dressed up as being fun or useful for the nation or has similar incentive. H. Wilensky, looking for a sociological explanation of the relative strengths of the income and substitution effects, suggests that, while the affluent society fosters a preference for leisure, a growing minority work very long hours and a majority have an excess of leisure time. B.M. Berger maintains that work and leisure belong to different orders of phenomena—work as a kind of action and leisure as a kind of time—which leads to difficulties in applying normative standards (e.g. good or bad) to free time. This problem arises in attempts to classify work satisfaction and alienation and motivation for leisure time activities. J. Gerstl looks at the fusion and spillovers of work and leisure in terms of the effect of occupational milieu on lifestyle—that is, at the nature of work, its setting and coworkers, rather than at the occupation itself.

This sociopsychological discussion gets away from the economic division between paid and unpaid work. For this we can quote the Marxist view, expressed by Illich, who regards paid and unpaid work as complementary and refers to *shadow work* as the 'shady side of the industrial economy':

> It comprises most housework women do in their homes . . . the activities connected with shopping, most of the homework of students cramming for exams, the toil expended commuting to and from the job. It includes the stress of forced consumption, the tedious and regimented surrender to therapists, compliance with bureaucrats, the preparation of work to which one is compelled, and many of the activities usually labelled family life. (Illich, 1981: 37)

Neither this splendid blast, nor the meticulous analysis of various social scientists, leads to a firm foundation for the construction of a definite classification of activities, and it is not surprising that attempts so far remain beset with methodological problems. They stem in part from the variety of users' interests, which have been listed by R. Andorka as follows:

- measurement of social well-being, quality of life, lifestyle;
- paid and unpaid work by men and women;
- productive activities of households;
- needs of elderly persons and children;
- international and intertemporal comparisons;
- mass media programming;
- production and market planning in leisure goods industries;
- studies of consumer behaviour;
- urban planning

(quoted in Australian Bureau of Statistics, 1988: 2-3).

The impact of technological change on employment has been mentioned as a further use for such data.

A theoretical framework for time use was included by Stone (1973/75) in *Towards a System of Social and Demographic Statistics* for the United Nations Statistical Office as a separate transition stock-and-flow matrix. Attempts to implement it, however, took off only in the mid 1960s, when twelve countries commissioned a *Multi-National Time Budget Research Project* led by Alexander Szalai, whose report on the daily activities of urban populations (*The Use of Time*) was published in 1972.

As an application we can quote a pilot survey conducted by the Australian Bureau of Statistics in Sydney in May/June 1987, using a sample comprising 1000 private dwellings with 1611 adults who completed a 48 hour time diary on designated days. Taking principal activities, 15% of daily time (223 out of 1440 minutes) was spent with the labour force, about the same on household activities, 45% on sleeping, eating and personal care, and 25% on active and passive leisure, including television, reading, sports, socialising and so on. The pattern varied typically by gender: labour force, including travel time, men 21%, women 10%; household, men 8%, women 20%. Labour force activities for both together varied from 20% on weekdays to 4% at weekends. International comparisons suggest that, at least in the 1960s, the share of 'free time' was greater in Australia, Canada and Western Europe than in Eastern European countries.

In an earlier study entitled *How Americans Use Time*, Robinson, of the Time-Use Project of the University of Michigan (1977), referred to time use as a social indicator, because it is connected with a process that indirectly reflects social welfare and because comparisons across time, sections, countries and activities have societal implications. For instance, data from 1965–66 results of the Survey Research Center, based on a sample of about 2000 adults, suggested that, while television viewing is 'dominant' as a leisure activity (2–3 hours a day or 30–40% of free time), it cannot be called 'domineering' because its time is among the first reduced if some more interesting activity is available. There appeared to be some link between free time and life satisfaction, but it was not strong enough to draw generalised conclusions. This area has since been further explored in quality-of-life studies (see section 3.10).

5.14 Urban studies

Urban studies, and the related notions *city studies*, *regional studies* and *urban planning*, operate in a field in which indicators are applied at various levels in connection with demography, economy, ecology, culture, civilisation and similar considerations. Some mention of those applications has been made earlier in connection with economic and social aspects. With reference to status and prestige, for example, Congalton in 1968 ranked 368 suburban areas of Sydney by asking about 4000 people to grade them by what they thought was their social standing on a 1–7 scale, in conjunction with a similar survey of real estate agents (Congalton, 1969). Similar listings on the base of prestige, income and so on have been made elsewhere (see section 5.11).

It may be fitting to conclude with another, more recent, reference that is topical for this domain. It is also a fine example of the effective presentation of economic and social indicators, starting from a well-researched database built up by expert observers and proceeding to rate major elements. This does not mean that the selection and combinations are uncontroversial— they could never be for this type of indicator—but they are presented modestly, with sufficient detail for dissidents to rearrange the basic elements according to their own subjectively preferred choice.

The reference is to a 22″ × 34″ colour-coded wallchart on *Cities—Life in the World's Largest Metropolitan Areas*, issued in 1990 by the Population Crisis Committee in Washington, following a 2 year research study in about 45 countries. It presents a detailed array of statistics, with comments to heighten the impact of the indicative message.

The main table lists about 100 cities by population size, from 29 million (Tokyo–Yokohama) down to about 2 million, and gives each a score out of 10 for different features of living conditions. These scores are added, unweighted, for an aggregate *urban living standards score*, which in the event runs from 86 for Melbourne to 19 for Lagos. The usual provisions were made to compensate for missing data. Indicators used are:

- *public safety*: murders per 1000 people;
- *food costs*: percentage of income spent on food;
- *living space*: persons per room;
- *housing standards*: percentage of homes with water/electricity;
- *communications*: telephones per 100 persons;
- *education*: percentage of children in secondary school;
- *public health*: infant deaths per 1000 live births;
- *peace and quiet*: levels of ambient noise;
- *traffic flow*: miles per hour in rush hour;
- *clean air*: alternative pollution measures.

The final urban living scores are grouped as follows:

- *very good*: 86–75, Melbourne, sharing top score with Montreal and Seattle, followed by other towns in Australia (Sydney), United States (Atlanta), Canada (Toronto), Germany (Essen), Japan, Singapore;
- *good*: 74–60, Europe (many large cities), United States (New York, Los Angeles), London;
- *fair*: 59–45, South America, South Africa;
- *poor*: 44–19, Central and South Asia, Africa, Mexico City.

It appears that the wide divergence between cities is caused largely by differences in food costs, living space, housing, public health and education.

Other factors (e.g. ambient noise, traffic flow, clean air) do not follow the same order.

The survey also recorded the *urban growth rate* in the 1980s, which ranged from between 2% and 5% per year in many of the 'poor' Asian countries to 1% or less in countries with higher living standards. Some comments on changes in 'urban realities' are presented, which can be further studied by statistical analysis of the interrelations of the various factors.

As previously discussed, such aggregative indicators carry a strong element of idiosyncratic views about human values; but against this subjective background, detailed presentation, as in this case, at least opens up the discussion about the substantive issues of urban living.

CHAPTER 6

CONCLUSION

Indicators help us to gain knowledge and understanding. They condense and transform information so that it can be applied to analysis and policy making. They are used in all sciences for their particular purposes. In the case of social indicators, which, broadly interpreted, have been our main subject here, their function has been described as tracing pathways through the maze of society's interconnections (Rice, 1967), or as illuminating the topography of the human landscape (L'Inguiste, 1978). Even monetary or other quantitative indicators should not stand alone as statistical abstractions but should be viewed within a human and social setting that can be described by further indication.

One major theme of this book has been reference to time: what has happened, is happening or will happen. Another has been structure: the analysis of an existing pattern and comparison with other patterns located elsewhere in time or space. A further recurring feature has been the extension of indicative measurement into an ordering function that gives indicators a role in determining and describing what is being measured.

The book has tried to avoid technical obfuscation and to demystify jargon by explaining its meaning. This applies also to the sections on techniques, which select from the general texts a few major processes that are often misapplied or mismatched in their mechanical application to indicators (e.g. averaging, weighting, scaling).

The sections on application represent no more than part of the larger repertory of economic and social types. The list includes areas of current public interest in most of which research into indicative measurement is proceeding at national and international levels, such as the broad issues of development and quality of life, and the more specialised issues of culture, human rights and time use. We have also considered some of the standard fixtures of the economists' armoury of monetary and trade statistics.

Although this has provided only a birdseye view of the specialised research, referred to in the bibliography, it does bring out common features in the endeavour of indicators to show us where we are now compared with other times and places, and where we might be going under alternative directions.

It is emphasised that measurement cannot be divorced from its objective, and that it is therefore important to establish the purpose of an enquiry before choosing an appropriate method. While statistics are generally built on single phenomena, they become indicators when tied to a particular purpose. This can rest on a firm concept such as gross domestic product or consumer prices, or else is built up through the indicators themselves, as applies to the major social areas of health and environment. Reference to this process of 'conceptualisation' or 'reification' leads to the major methodological problems of weighting and aggregation. Lack of logical cohesion there should not be hidden by using elaborate methods in combining disparate elements; nor should the information content of data be overstretched to yield fallacious results.

With indicators we generally look for clear signals of composition, trends or change. Simple directional markings are often preferable to tabular displays loaded up with statistical detail. There is no great difficulty in the presentation of a topic that can be associated, directly or as a proxy, with a single indicator (e.g. stock exchange index, migration statistic). More often, however, we have to deal with notions (e.g. welfare, economic growth) that are composites of disparate elements that run on different scales and trend lines, without certainty about their relative importance.

There is no single sterling solution to the construction of ideal indicators. Various options should be considered in the context of specific uses. This may be an array of subindicators, which can be presented either separately as a checklist to test various dimensions, or as a combined aggregate that gives a limited overall view within a stated horizon such as gross national product. They can be expressed as either linear or non-linear curves, or as rates of growth or decline. They may be directed to the analysis of a single region at a point of time or over time or in comparison with other regions. They may be presented in numerical series with fixed interval scales or in the form of plus/minus signs. This book will have achieved its main purpose if it helps to guide readers to an intelligent choice of the type and construction of the indicator they require.

BIBLIOGRAPHY

The selection largely concentrates on recent texts and articles that provide references to the earlier literature.

Abramson, J.H. (1966) 'The Cornell Medical Index as an Epidemiological Tool' *American Journal of Public Health* vol. 56, pp. 287-98

Ackoff, R.A. (1978) *Art of Problem Solving* Wiley, New York

Adelman, I. and Morris, C.T. (1971) 'Analysis of Various Techniques for the Study of Economic Development' *Journal of Development Analysis* no. 1, pp. 111-35

Afriat, S. (1981) 'On the Constructibility of Consistent Price Indexes' in A. Deaton (ed.), *Essays in the Theory and Measurement of Consumer Behaviour* Cambridge University Press, Cambridge

Ahmad, Y.C. et al. (eds) (1989) *Environmental Accounting for Sustainable Development* World Bank, Washington, DC

Akerman, N (1979) 'Can Sweden Be Shrunk?' *Development Dialogue* no. 2, pp. 71-114

Alexander, S. (1958) 'Rate of Change Approaches to Forecasting' *Economic Journal* vol. 68, pp. 288-301

Allard, E. (1976) 'Dimensions of Welfare in a Comparative Scandinavian Study' *Acta Sociologica* vol. 19, no. 3, pp. 597-607

Allen, R.G.D. (1972) *Statistics for Economists* Hutchinson, London

—— (1961) *State of Economics* Hutchison, London

—— (1975) *Index Numbers in Theory and Practice* Aldine, Chicago

Anastasi, A. (1988) *Psychological Testing* Macmillan, New York

Andrews, F. (ed.) (1976) *Research on the Quality of Life* Survey Research Center, University of Michigan

Andrews, F. and Withey, S. (1976) *Social Indicators of Well-Being* Plenum, New York

Argenti, J. (1980) *Private Corporate Planning* Allen and Unwin, London

Atkinson, A. (1975) *The Economics of Inequality* Clarendon, Oxford

Australian Bureau of Statistics (1979, 1983) *Australian Health Survey* AGPS, Canberra

—— (1988) *Time Use Pilot Survey, Sydney, May–June 1987* Information Paper, Cat. 4111.1, Sydney

Australian Vice-Chancellors' Committee (1988) *Performance Indicators: Report of Working Party with Australian Committee of Directors and Principals in Advanced Education Limited* AVCC, Braddon, ACT

Backstrand, L. and Ingelstam, L. (1975) *How Much is Lagom (Enough)?* Report on development and international cooperation, Dag Hammarskjöld Foundation, Uppsala

Banks, D.L. (1985) 'Patterns of Oppression: A Statistical Analysis of Human Rights' *American Statistical Association Social Statistics Proceedings* pp. 154–62

Baster, N. (ed.) (1972) *Measuring Development* Frank Cass, London

Bauer, R.A. (ed.) (1966) *Social Indicators* MIT, Cambridge, Mass.

Baumol, W.J. and Oates, W.H. (1988) *The Theory of Environmental Policy* Cambridge University Press, Cambridge

Becker, G. (1965) 'A Theory of the Allocation of Time' *Economic Journal* September, pp. 493–517

Beckerman, W. (1966) *International Comparisons of Real Income* OECD, Paris

Bennett, S. and Bowers, D. (1976) *An Introduction to Multi-variate Techniques* Macmillan, London

Berlin, I. (1988) *Russian Thinkers* Penguin, Harmondsworth

Biderman, A.D. and Drury, T.F. (eds) (1976) *Measuring Work Quality for Social Reporting* Wiley, New York

Blackorby, G. and Russell, R.R. (1978) 'Indices and Sub-indices of the Cost of Living' *Economic Journal* vol. 19, no. 1, pp. 229–40

Block, N.J. and Dworkin, G. (eds) (1976) *The IQ Controversy* Pantheon, New York

Bowley, A.L. (1923) *An Elementary Manual of Statistics* Macdonald and Evans, London

—— (1928) 'Notes on Index Numbers' *Economic Journal* vol. 33, pp. 216–37

Bridgman, P.W. (1955) *Reflections of a Physicist* Philosophical Library, New York

Brodin, A. and Blades, D. (1986) *The OECD Compatible Trade and Production Data Base 1970–1983* Working Paper no. 31, OECD, Paris

Brook, R.H. et al. (1979) 'Adult Status Measures in Rand's Health Insurance Study' *Medical Care* vol. 17, no. 7, supplement, pp. 6–53

Brown, A.J. (1948) *Applied Economics* Allen and Unwin, London

Buhmann, B. et al. (1988) 'Equivalence Scales, Well-being, Inequality and Poverty' *Luxembourg Income Study* Working Paper no. 17, Walferdange

Burns, A.F. and Mitchell, W.C. (1964) *Measuring Business Cycles* National Bureau of Economic Research, New York

Caplan, A.L. et al. (eds) (1981) *Concepts of Health and Disease: Interdisciplinary Perspectives* Addison Wesley, Reading

Carley, M.J. (1981) *Social Measurement and Social Indicators* Allen and Unwin, London

—— (1986) 'Impact Assessment: a Policy Approach to Technology Assessment' *Science and Public Policy* April, pp. 77–82

Carlisle, E. and Cazes, B. (1972) in A. Shonfield and S. Shaw (eds) *Social Indicators and Social Policy* Heinemann, London

Chakrarty, S.R. (1990) *Ethical Social Index Numbers* Springer, Berlin

Chenery, H. (1974) *Redistribution with Growth* World Bank, Washington, DC

Chenery, H. and Syrquin, M. (1989) *Patterns of Development* World Bank, Washington, DC

Chouraqui, J.-C. et al. (1990) *Indicators of Fiscal Policy: a Re-assessment* Working Paper no. 78, OECD, Paris

Cliff, N. (1983) in H. Wainer and S. Messick (eds) *Principles of Modern Psychological Measurement* Erlbaum, Hillsdale, NJ, pp. 283–99

Cohen, M.B. (1936) 'The Statistical View of Nature' *Journal of the American Statistical Association* pp. 327–47

Coleman, J.S. (1964) *Introduction to Mathematical Sociology* Free Press, New York

Community Aid Abroad (Oct. 1991) *No Strings Attached* Program Notes, Canberra

Congalton, A. (1969) *Status and Prestige in Australia* Cheshire, Melbourne

Crockett, B. (1988) 'Indicators and International Economic Co-operation' *Finance and Development* September, pp. 20–3

Cronin, B. (1984) *The Citation Process* Taylor Graham, London

Culyer, A.J. (1978) *Measuring Health* University of Toronto, Toronto

Culyer, A.J. and Wright, K.G. (eds) (1978) *Economic Aspects of Health Services* Martin Robertson, London

Daly, H.E. (1987) 'The Economic Growth Debate: What Some Economists Have Learned but Many Have Not' *Journal of Environmental Economics and Management* no. 14, pp. 323–36

Daly, H.E. and Cobb, J.B. (1989) *For the Common Good* Beacon, Boston, Mass.

Daniel, A.E. (1983) *Power, Privilege and Prestige: Occupations in Australia* Longman Cheshire, Melbourne

De Bono, E. (1967) *The Use of Lateral Thinking* Pelican, Harmondsworth

De Caires, B. (ed.) (1988) *Guide to World Equity Markets* Euromoney, London

De Neufville, J. (1975) *Social Indicators and Public Policy* Elsevier, Amsterdam

Deane, P. (1978) *The Evolution of Economic Ideas* Cambridge University Press, Cambridge

Denison, E.F. (1973) in M. Moss (ed.) *The Measurement of Economic and Social Performance* Studies in Income and Wealth no. 38, Columbia University Press, New York

Dews, N. (1986) *Tobin's q* Research Report, Reserve Bank of Australia, Sydney

Diewald, M. (1984) *Das SPES Indikatorentableau 1976, Fortschreibung bis zum Jahre 1982* Arbeitspapier nr. 1950, Sonderforschungsbereich 3, Mikroanalytische Grundlage der Gesellschaftspolitik, Universitæten Frankfurt und Mannheim

Diewert, W.E. (1980) 'The Economic Theory of Index Numbers: a Survey' in A. Deaton (ed.) *Essays in the Theory and Measurement of Consumer Behaviour* Cambridge University Press, Cambridge

Dirn, L. (pseudonym M. Forse et al.) (1986) 'Pour un tableau tendenciel de la société française: un parti de recherche' *Revue Française de Sociologie* vol. 26, pp. 389–408

Dornbusch, R. and Fisher, S. (1989) *Macro-Economics* McGraw-Hill, New York

Doxiadis, C.A. (1968) *Ekistics* Oxford University Press, New York

Drewnowski, J. (1974) *On Measuring and Planning the Quality of Life* Mouton, The Hague

Ducommun, R. (1968) *Measuring Labour Productivity* International Labour Office, Geneva

Edwards, S. (1989) *Tariffs, Terms of Trade and the Real Exchange Rate* Working Paper 3346, National Bureau of Economic Research, New York; also previous papers 2908, 2909, 2950, 3138, 3345

Eisner, R. (1985) 'The Total Incomes System' *Survey of Current Business* January, pp. 1–48

El Serafy, S. (1989) See Ahmad (1989)

Elkana, Y. et al. (eds) (1978) *Towards a Metric of Science* Wiley, New York

Englander, A.S. and Mittelstädt, A. (1988) *Total Factor Productivity* Economic Studies no. 10, OECD, Paris

Erikson, R. (1977) 'Comments on Allard's Having, Loving, Being' *Acta Sociologica* vol. 20, pp. 301–5

Eysenck, H.J. (1962) *Know Your Own IQ* Penguin, Harmondsworth

Ferland, Y. (1976) See UNESCO

Ferris, A. (1969) *Indicators of Trends in Higher Education* Russell Sage, New York

——— (1988) 'The Uses of Social Indicators' *Social Forces* vol. 66, no. 3, pp. 601–17

Fisher, I. (1922) *The Making of Index Numbers* Houghton-Mifflin, Boston, Mass.

Floud, R. (1983) 'A Tall Story? The Standard of Living Debate' *History Today* vol. 33, pp. 36–40

Fox, K. (1974) *Social Indicators and Social Theory* Wiley, New York

Fraser, L.M. (1937) *Economic Thought and Language* A.C. Black, London

Freeman, H.E. et al. (1980) *Evaluating Social Action Projects* Socio-economic studies no. 1, UNESCO, Geneva

Fuchs, V. (1981) in A.L. Caplan et al. (eds) *Concepts of Health and Disease: Interdisciplinary Perspectives* Addison Wesley, Reading

Galtung, J. (1973a) 'World Indicators Program' *Bulletin of Peace Proposals* vol. 4, pp. 354–8

——— (1973b) See UNESCO

Galtung, J. and Wirak, A. (1977) *Human Needs, Human Rights and the Theories of Development* Reports in the Social Sciences no. 37, UNESCO, Paris

Gandevia, B. (1977) 'A Comparison of the Heights of Boys Transported to Australia' *Australian Paediatric Journal* no. 13, pp. 91–7

Garfield, E. (1979) *Citation Indexing* Wiley, New York

Gastil, R. (1978) *Comparative Survey of Freedom* Freedom House, Boston, Mass.

Georgescu-Roegan, N. (1971) *The Entropy Law and the Economic Process* Harvard University Press, Cambridge, Mass.

Gillin, E.F. (1974) *Social Indicators and Economic Welfare* Economic Papers no. 46, Economic Society of Australia and New Zealand, Sydney

Gini, C. (1945) 'The Content and Use of Estimates of the National Income' *Quarterly Review, Banca Nazionale del Lavoro* no. 5, pp. 271–310

Gordon, R.A. and Klein, L.R. (eds) (1965) *Readings in Business Cycles* American Economic Association and Irving, Homewood, Ill.

Gostkowski, Z. (ed.) (1972) *Towards a System of Human Resource Indicators for Less Developed Countries* Ossolineum, Warsaw

Gouiedo, L. (1990) Private communication, SCB Statistics Sweden

Gould, S. (1983) *The Mismeasure of Man* Pelican, Harmondsworth

Grabe, S. (1983) *Evaluation Manual* UNESCO, 1983

Gramlich, E.M. (1990) *Fiscal Indicators* Working Paper no. 80, OECD, Paris

Green, H. (1964) *Aggregation in Economic Analysis* Princeton University Press, Princeton

Griffin, K. (1988) 'Thinking about Development' paper presented at Society for World Development 19th World Conference, New Delhi

Haberler, G. (1941) *Prosperity and Depression* League of Nations, Geneva

Harbison, F.H., Marunhic, J. and Resnik, J.R. (1970) *Quantitative Analyses of Modernization and Development* Princeton University Press, Princeton

Harper's index, copyright 1991, by *Harper's Magazine*, reprinted by special permission

Hauser, P.M. (1975) *Social Statistics in Use* Russell Sage, New York

Hayek, F.A. (1975) *New Studies in Philosophy, Politics, Economics and the History of Ideas* Routledge and Kegan Paul, London

Hazzard, S. (1980) *The Transit of Venus* Macmillan, London

Headey, B., Holmström, E. and Wearing, A. (1984) 'Well-being and Ill-being: Different Dimensions?' *Social Indicators Research* no. 14, pp. 115–39

Headey, B. and Wearing, A. (1988) 'The Sense of Relative Superiority–Central to Well-Being' *Social Indicators Research* no. 20, pp. 497–515.

Heisenberg, W. (1959) *Physics and Philosophy* Allen and Unwin, London

Heller, P. (1988) 'Fund-Supported Adjustment Programs and the Poor' *Finance and Development* vol. 25, no. 4, pp. 2–5

Henry, D.K. and Oliver, R.P. (1987) 'The Defense Build-up 1977–1985: Effects on Production and Employment' *Monthly Labor Review* August, pp. 3–11

Hicks, J. (1942) *The Social Framework* Oxford University Press, Oxford

Hicks, N. and Streeten, P. (1978) *Indicators of Development* World Bank, Washington, DC

Hillhorst, J. and Klatter, M. (eds) (1985) *Social Development in the Third World* Croom Helm, London

Holme, N. and Docter, R. (eds) (1972) *Educational and Psychological Testing* Russell Sage, New York

Holub, H.W. (1983) 'Measurement of Net Economic Welfare' *Review of Income and Wealth* vol. 29, no. 3, pp. 317–21

Horn, M.E.T. (1990) *Electoral Districting: Criteria and Formulation* Information Technology Report, CSIRO, North Ryde, NSW

Horn, R.V. (1971) 'Origin, Quality and Price of Australian Consumer Goods' *Australian Journal of Marketing Research* vol. 4, no. 2, pp. 45–51

—— (1975a) *Australian Labour Market Economics*, Longman Cheshire, Melbourne

—— (1975b) 'Social Indicators for Development Planning' *International Labour Review* vol. 6, pp. 483–506

—— (1980) 'Social Indicators, Meaning, Methods and Applications *International Journal of Social Economics* vol. 17, no. 8, pp. 421–60

—— (1981) *Extra Costs of Disablement* Social Welfare Research Centre Report no. 13, University of New South Wales, Sydney

—— (1983) 'Cultural Statistics and Indicators' *Journal of Cultural Economics* vol. 7, no. 2, pp. 25–40

Horn, S.R.T. and Carrington, G. (1990) 'Development of a National Cultural Statistics Data-base' *Australian Cultural Studies Conference* University of Western Sydney, Sydney

Huff, D (1954) *How to Lie with Statistics* Pelican, Harmondsworth

Human Rights (1986) 'Symposium on Statistical Issues' *Human Rights Quarterly* (Johns Hopkins University, Baltimore) vol. 8, no. 4, November

Humana, C. (1983/1987) *World Human Rights Guide* Pan, London

Hussey, D.E. (1971) *Introducing Corporate Planning* Pergamon, Oxford

Illich, I. (1981) 'Shadow Work' *Social Alternatives* (Australia) vol. 2, no. 1, pp. 37–47

Ivanovic, B. (1974) See UNESCO

Ivanovic, B. and Fanchette, S. (1973) See UNESCO

James, D.E. et al. (1978) *Economic Approaches to Environmental Problems* Elsevier, Amsterdam

Johnston, D.F. (1988) 'Towards a Comprehensive Quality of Life Index' *Social Indicators Research* no. 20, pp. 473–96

Johnstone, J.N. (1981) *Indicators of Education Systems* UNESCO, Paris

Kabanoff, R. (1980) 'Work and Non-Work: a review of Models, Methods and Findings' *Psychological Bulletin* vol. 88, no. 1, pp. 60–77

Kakwani, N. (1980) *Income Inequality and Poverty* World Bank, Washington, DC

—— (1984) 'The Relative Deprivation Curve' *Journal of Business and Economic Statistics* vol. 2, no. 4, pp. 384–90

—— (1986) *Is Sex Bias Significant?* World Institute for Development Economics Research 'Wider' Working Paper, United Nations University, Helsinki

—— (1990) *Poverty and Economic Growth* World Bank, Washington, DC

Kaplan, A. (1964) *The Conduct of Enquiry* Chandler, San Francisco

Kass, L. (1981) in A.L. Caplan et al. (eds) *Concepts of Health and Disease: Interdisciplinary Perspectives* Addison Wesley, Reading

Katzner, D.W. (1983) *Analysis without Measurement* Cambridge University Press, Cambridge

Kendall, M. (1975) *Multivariate Analysis* Griffin, London

Kenkel, J. (1989) *Introductory Statistics* PWS and Kent, Boston, Mass.

Keynes, J.M. (1930) *A Treatise on Money* Macmillan, London

—— (1936) *The General Theory of Employment, Interest and Money* Macmillan, London

Khan, H. (1979) 'International Comparison of Socio-economic Development' PhD thesis, University of New South Wales, Sydney

Koesoebjono, S. et al. (1989) 'Developing Socio-demographic Accounts' *Netherlands Official Statistics* (Quarterly journal of the Central Bureau of Statistics, Voorburg) vol. 4, no. 2, pp. 4–22

Koopmans, T.C. (1957) *Three Essays on the State of Economic Science* McGraw-Hill, New York

Koopmans, T.C. and Tobin, J. (1984) 'Comparative Studies of Income and Prices' *Journal of Economic Literature* vol. 12, pp. 1–59

Koves, P. (1983) *Index Theory and Economic Realty* Akademiai Kiadro, Budapest

Kravis, I.B. (1984) 'Comparative Studies of National Incomes and Prices' *Journal of Economic Literature* vol. 12, pp. 1–59

Kravis, I.B. et al. (1978) *International Comparison Project* Johns Hopkins University, Baltimore

Krupinski, J. and Mackenzie, A. (eds) (1979) *The Health and Social Survey of the North West Region of Melbourne* Health Commission, Melbourne

Kuh, E. and Meyer, J. (eds) (1986) *Model Reliability* MIT, Cambridge, Mass.

Kuznets, S. (1971) *Economic Growth of Nations* Harvard University Press, Cambridge, Mass.

Lahiri, K. and Moore, G.H. (eds) (1991) *Leading Economic Indicators* Cambridge University Press, Cambridge

Lakatos I. and Musgrave, A. (eds) (1970) *Criticism and the Growth of Knowledge* Cambridge University Press, Cambridge

Lancaster, K. (1966) 'Essay on Economic Aggregation and Additivity' in S.R. Krupp (ed.) *The Structure of Economic Science* Prentice Hall, Englewood Cliffs, NJ

Land, K. (1975) 'Theories, Models and Indicators of Social Change' *International Social Science Journal* no. 27, pp. 7–37

Land, K. and Spilerman, S. (eds) (1975) *Social Indicator Models* Russell Sage, New York

Larsen, R. et al. (1985) 'An Evaluation of Subjective Well-Being Measures' *Social Indicators Research* no. 17, pp. 1–17

Lecaillon, J. et al. (1984) *Income Distribution and Economic Development* International Labour Organisation, Geneva

Leontief, W. (1971) 'Theoretical Assumptions and Non-observed Facts' *American Economic Review* vol. 61, pp. 1–17

L'Inguiste, L. (1978) 'Moi Aussi' *Macquarie Annals* (Sydney) vol. 1, pp. 71–80

Lipsey, R.G. (1963) *An Introduction to Positive Economics* Weidenfeld and Nicolson, London

Lisk, F. (1979) 'Indicators for Basic Needs Oriented Development Planning' *Labour and Society* (Geneva) vol. 4, pp. 241–60

McGranahan, D.V. et al. (1972) *Contents and Measurement of Socio-economic Development* Praeger, New York

——— (1979) *Methodological Problems in Selection and Analysis of Socio-economic Development Indicators* UNRISD, Geneva

——— (1985) *Measurement and Analysis of Socio-economic Development* UNRISD, Geneva

Mackerras, M. (1989) *The Mackerras Federal Election Guide 1990* AGPS, Canberra

Machlup, F. (1978) *Methodology of Economics and Other Social Sciences* Academic Press, New York

McWhirter, N. and McWhirter, R. (eds) (1988) *The Guinness Book of Records* Guinness Superlatives, London

Maier, M.H. (1991) *The Data Game* M.E. Sharpe, Armonk, NY

Marshak, J. and Miyasawa, K. (1968) 'Economic Comparability of Information Systems' *International Economic Review* vol. 9, no. 2, pp.134–77

Mazur, A. and Boyko, E. (1981) 'Large-Scale Ocean Research Projects: What Makes Them Succeed or Fail?' *Social Studies of Science* vol. 11, pp. 425–51

Meadows, D. et al. (1972) *The Limits to Growth* Earth Island, London

Melman, S. (1988) 'Economic Consequences of the Arms Race' *American Economic Review* vol. 78, pp. 55–9

Mendenhall, W.S. (1989) *Statistics for Management and Economics* PWS and Kent, Boston, Mass.

Merritt, R.L. and Rokkan, S. (1966) *Comparing Nations* Yale, New Haven

Michalos, A. (1985) 'Multiple Discrepancy Theories' *Social Indicators Research* no. 16, pp. 347–413

——— (1986) 'Job Satisfaction, Marital Status and the Quality of Life' *Social Indicators Research* no. 17, pp. 57–83

——— (1989) *Militarism and the Quality of Life* Canadian papers in Peace Studies no. 1, Samuel Stevens, Toronto

Midzuno, H. (1976) See UNESCO

Moore, G. and Shiskin, J. (1967) *Indicators of Business Expansions and Contractions* National Bureau of Economic Research, New York

Moroney, M.J. (1951) *Facts from Figures* Penguin, Harmondsworth

Morris, L.L. et al. (1988) *How to Measure Performance and Use Tests* Russell Sage, New York

Morris, M.D. (1979) *Measuring the Condition of the World's Poor: the Physical Quality of Life Index* Pergamon Press, New York

Moser C. (1973) 'Social Indicators' *Review of Income and Wealth* vol. 19, pp. 133–44

Moss, M. (ed.) (1973) *The Measurement of Economic and Social Performance* Studies in Income and Wealth no. 38, Columbia University Press, New York

Mukherjee, R. (1975) *Social Indicators* Macmillan of India, Delhi

Nicholas, S. and Shergold, P.R. (1982) 'The Height of British Male Convict Children' *Australian Paediatric Journal* vol. 18, pp. 76–83

Nordhaus, W.D. and Tobin, J. (1972) 'Is Growth Obsolete?' in *Economic Research: Retrospect and Prospect* 50th Anniversary Colloquium, vol. 5, General Series no. 96, National Bureau of Economic Research, New York

OECD (1982) *The OECD List of Social Concerns* OECD, Paris

—— (1986) *Living Conditions in OECD Countries: a Compendium of Social Indicators* OECD, Paris

O'Higgins, M. et al. (1985) *Income Distribution and Redistribution* Centre for Population, Poverty and Policy Studies, Luxembourg

Olenski, J. (1986) 'Meta-information Systems' *Statistical Journal of the United Nations* vol. 4, pp. 31–45

Orcutt, G. (1986) *Living Conditions in OECD Countries* OECD, Paris

Ornstein, R. and Ehrlich, P. (1989) *New World and New Mind* Doubleday, New York

Paglin, M. (1975) 'The Measurement and Trend of Inequality' *American Economic Review* vol. 65, pp. 598–609

Pearce, D., Markandya, A. and Barbier, E.B. (1989) *Blueprint for a Green Economy* Report for UK Department of the Environment, Earthscan, London

Perlman, R. (1969) *Labor Theory* Wiley, New York

Peskin, H.M. with Lutz, E. (1990) *A Survey of Resources and Environmental Accounting in Industrialised Countries* Environmental Working Paper no. 37, World Bank, Washington, DC

Petersen, I.D. (1989) *Unintended War and Nuclear Deterrence* Centre for Peace and Conflict Studies, University of Sydney, Sydney

Phillips, A.H.W. (1958) 'The Relation between Unemployment and the Rate of Change of Money Wage Rates in the United Kingdom 1861–1957' *Economica*, November, pp. 283–99

Poincaré, H. (1913) *The Foundations of Science* Science Press, New York

Popper, K. (1968) *The Logic of Scientific Discovery* Harper, New York

Population Crisis Committee (1987) *Human Suffering Index* PCC, Washington, DC

—— (1990) *Progress toward Population Stabilisation* PCC, Washington, DC

—— (1990) *Cities—Life in the World's Largest Metropolitan Areas* PCC, Washington, DC

Quesera, W. (1990) *Natural Balance: Sooner or Later* Lone Cave, Leura

Read, E.G. and Sell, D.P.M. (1987) 'A Framework for Electricity Pricing' Report from Arthur Young to Electricity Corporation of New Zealand, ECNZ, Wellington, NZ

Reichmann, W.J. (1965) *Use and Abuse of Statistics* Pelican, Harmondsworth

Reiss, A.J. et al. (1961) *Occupations and Social Status* Free Press, New York

Repetto, R. et al. (1989) *Wasting Assets: Natural Resources in the National Income Accounts* World Resources Institute, Washington, DC

Rhodes, E.C. (1937) 'The Construction of an Index of Business Activity' *Journal of the Royal Statistical Society* vol. 100, no. 18, pp. 18–66

Rice, S. (1967) 'Social Accounting and Statistics' *Public Administration Review* vol. 67, pp. 169–74

Riddell, T. (1989) 'US Military Power' *American Economic Review* vol. 78, pp. 60–5

Ridley, M. (1983) 'Can Classification Do Without Evolution?' *New Scientist* pp. 647–51

Robinson, J. (1977) *How Americans Use Time* University of Michigan, Ann Arbor

Rossi, R.J. and Gilmartin, K.J. (1980) *The Handbook of Social Indicators* Garland, New York

Rowe, J.W.F. (1927) 'An Index of the Physical Volume of Production' *Economic Journal* vol. 37, pp. 173–87

Ruggles, R. and Ruggles, N.D. (1982) 'Integrated Accounts for the United States 1947–80' *Survey of Current Business* May, pp. 1–54; November, pp. 36–53

Samson, D., Wirth, A. and Rickard, J. (1989) 'The Value of Information from Multiple Sources of Uncertainty in Decision Analysis' *European Journal of Operational Research* no. 39, pp. 254–60

Samuelson, P.A.. (1952) 'Economic Theory and Mathematics' *American Economic Review* vol. 42, pp. 56–73

——— (1973) *Economics* 9th ed., McGraw-Hill, New York

Saunders, P. (1984) *Inequality: Evidence of Income Redistribution* OECD, Paris

Saunders, P. and Hobbes, G. (1988) 'Income Inequality in Australia' *Australian Economic Review* 3rd quarter, pp. 26–34

Schmid, C.F. (1983) *Statistical Graphics* Wiley, New York

Schroders Australia Ltd (Inc. in NSW) (1990) Circular on economic activity, Sydney

Schrödinger, E. (1952) *Science and Humanism* Cambridge University Press, Cambridge

Scott, W. (1981) *Concepts and Measurement of Poverty* UNRISD, Geneva

Sebriakoff, V. (1965) *IQ: A Mensa Analysis and History* Mensa, London

Seers, D. (1972) 'What Are We Trying to Measure?' *Journal of Development Studies* (reprint) vol. 8, no. 3, pp. 1–13

Selowski, M. et al. (1987) 'Adjustment with Growth' *Finance and Development* vol. 24, no. 2, pp. 3–24

Sen, A.K. (1973) *Inequality* Clarendon, Oxford

——— (1978) *Three Notes on the Concept of Poverty* World Employment Programme Research Paper, International Labour Office, Geneva

——— (1982) *Choice, Welfare and Measurement* Clarendon, Oxford

Sheldrake, R. (1988) *The Presence of the Past* Collins, London

Shonfield, A. and Shaw, S. (eds) (1972) *Social Indicators and Social Policy*, Heinemann, London

Simonis, U.R. (1990) *Beyond Growth: Elements of Sustainable Development* Sigma, Berlin

Smeeding, T.M. (1990) *Poverty, Inequality and Income Distribution in Comparative Perspective* Urban Institute Press, Washington, DC

Smigel, E.O. (ed.) (1963) *Work and Leisure* College Press, New Haven, Conn.

Sneath, P.H. and Sokal, R.R. (1973) *Numerical Taxonomy* Freeman, San Francisco

Soumelis, C.G. (1977) *Project Evaluation: Methodologies and Techniques* UNESCO, Paris

Spautz, M.E. (1977) *The Socio-economic Gap: Project Evaluation* UNESCO, Paris

Stock, J.H. and Watson, M.W. (1988) 'Variable trends in economic time series' *Journal of Economic Perspectives* vol. 2, no. 3, pp. 147–74

Stone, R. (1973/1975) *Towards a System of Social and Demographic Statistics* United Nations, New York

Strumpel, B. (ed.) (1973) *Subjective Elements of Well-being* OECD, Paris

Summers, R. and Heston, A. (1988) 'A New Set of International Comparisons of Real Product and Prices: Estimates for 130 Countries 1950–1985' *Review of Income and Wealth* vol. 34, no. 1, pp. 1–26

Swan, P.L. (1990) 'Real Rates of Return in Electricity Supply' *Economic Record* vol. 66, no. 193, 93–109

Szalai, A. (ed.) (1972) *The Use of Time* Mouton, The Hague

Theil, H. (1954) *Linear Aggregation of Economic Relations* North Holland, Amsterdam

Thirkettle, G.L. (1981) *Weldon's Business Statistics* Macdonald Evans, Plymouth

Tobin, J. (1969) 'A General Equilibrium Approach to Monetary Theory' *Journal of Money, Credit and Banking* vol. 1, no. 1, pp. 15–29

Townsend, P. et al. (1979) *Poverty in the United Kingdom* Penguin, Harmondsworth

Trainer, T (1985) *Abandon Affluence* Zed Books, London

Tufte, E.R. (ed.) (1970) *The Quantitative Analysis of Social Problems* Addison Wesley, Reading

Turner, C.F. and Martin, E. (eds) (1984) *Surveying Subjective Phenomena* Russell Sage, New York

UNESCO extracts reproduced by permission of UNESCO.

UNESCO (1973) J. Galtung *Human Resources* Study 14, SHC/WS/159, UNESCO Paris

——— (1973) B. Ivanovic and S. Fanchette *Toward a System of Quantitative Indicators of Human Resources Development* Study 25, SHS/WS/318, UNESCO, Paris

——— (1974) B. Ivanovic *Social Indicators: Problems of Definition and Selection* Reports in the Social Sciences no. 30, UNESCO, Paris

——— (1976) H. Midzuno *Indicators of Cultural Development* SHC-76/WS/1, UNESCO, Paris

——— (1976) H. Midzuno, Y. Ferland et al., Working Papers on cultural development and indicators for Moscow Conference, June, UNESCO, Paris

——— (1979) *Preliminary Study on the Scope and Coverage of a Framework for Cultural Statistics* CES/AC.4/8, UNESCO, Paris

——— (1981) *Socio-economic Indicators for Planning* Socio-economic Studies no. 2, UNESCO, Paris

United Nations Development Program (1990) *Human Development Index* UNDP and Oxford University Press, New York

United Nations Research Institute for Social Development (1985) D.V. McGranahan et al. *Measurement and Analysis of Socio-economic Development* UNRISD, Geneva

United Nations Statistical Office, United Nations, New York:

——— (1961) *International Definition and Measurement of Standards of Living* E/CN.3/270; refers to (1954) E/CN.179

——— (1974) *System of Socio-demographic Statistics* E/CN.3/449; also E/CN.3/450 and 3/459, and (1975) F/18

——— (1976) *Non-monetary Social Indicators* E/SA/STAT/AC.4/3

——— (1979) *Studies in the Integration of Social Statistics* F/24

——— (1979) *The Development of Integrated Data Bases* F/27

——— (1983) *Framework for Environmental Statistics* prelim, M/75, M/78

United States (1969) *Toward a Social Report* Department of Education, Health and Welfare, Washington, DC

Uno, J. (1988) *Economic Growth and Environmental Change in Japan* University of Tsukuba, Japan; quoted in Pearce et al. (1989)

Van Ginneken, W. (1980) *Socio-economic Groups and Income Distribution in Mexico* St Martin's Press, New York

Van Moeseke, P. (1984) *Measuring Social Position* Massey Economic Papers A8403, Massey University, Palmerston North, NZ

—— (1984) *Two Approaches to Assigning Dollar Values to Social Variables* Massey Economic Paper A8411, Massey University, Palmerston North, NZ

Verwayen, H. (1984) 'Actual and Potential Uses of Social Indicators' *Social Indicators Research* no. 14, pp. 1-27

Vining, A. (1989) 'Performance Measures' *Economic Papers* (Economic Society of Australia) vol. 8, no. 3, pp. 13-19

Weilenmann, A. (1980) *Evaluating Research and Social Change* UNESCO, Paris

White, M.D. (1983) 'A Cocitation Map of the Social Indicators Movement' *Journal of American Society for Information Science* vol. 34, no. 5, pp. 307-12

Wiegand, E. (1988) 'Current Work on the Social Indicators System for the Federal Republic of Germany' *Social Indicators Research* no. 20, pp. 399-416

Wilson, R.W. (1984) 'Health Measures: Are They Health Status Indicators?' *American Statistical Association Social Statistics Session* pp. 565-8

Winch, P. (1958) *The Idea of a Social Science* Routledge, London

Wirak, A.H. (1975) *Human Needs as Basis for Indicator Formation* World Indicator Program no. 13, Oslo University, Oslo

Wolfe, M (1981) *Elusive Department* UNRISD, Geneva

World Bank (1978) *World Development Report* Johns Hopkins University Press, Baltimore

—— (1989a) *Trends in Developing Economies* World Bank, Washington, DC

—— (1989b) *Project Performance Results for 1987* Operations Evaluation Study, World Bank, Washington, DC

—— (1989c) *World Development Report on Poverty* World Bank, Washington, DC

—— (1990) *Social Indicators of Development* Johns Hopkins University Press, Baltimore

World Health Organization (1981) *Development of Indicators for Monitoring Progress towards Health for All by the Year 2000* WHO, Geneva

Wyatt, T. and Ruby, A. (1988) *Indicators in Education* Australian Conference of Director-Generals in Education, Sydney

Young, M., Muenstermann, J. and Schacht, K. (1975) *Armut* (Poverty), Infas Politogramm, Bad Godesberg

Yule, G.U. and Kendall, M.G. (1950) *An Introduction to the Theory of Statistics* Charles Griffin, London

Zapf, W. (1975) 'Systems of Social Indicators' *International Social Science Journal* vol. 27, no. 3, pp. 479-98.

—— (ed.) (1977) *Lebensbedingungen in der Bundesrepublik Deutschland* Campus, Frankfurt

—— (ed.) (1987) 'German Social Report' *Social Indicators Research* no. 19, pp. 5-171 (special issue)

Zarnowitz, V. (ed.) (1972) *The Business Cycle Today* National Bureau of Economic Research, New York

Zimmermann, C.C. (1932) 'Ernst Engel's Law of Expenditure for Food' *Quarterly Journal of Economics* vol. 47, pp. 180-191

Zolotas, X. (1981) *Declining Social Welfare* New York University Press, New York

Zwicky, F. (1969) *Discovery, Invention, Research* Macmillan, Toronto

Some general series with reference to various indicators:

Australian Bureau of Statistics (*ABS*): *Australian National Accounts*, Cat. No. 5201.0 (1989), Household Expenditure Survey, Cat. No. 6528, Canberra

Dun and Bradstreet: *Business Expectation Survey*
Ines News: *International Indicators and Evaluation of Educational Systems*, ORECD-KERI, Paris
Informationsdienst Soziale Indikatoren (ISI), issued by Zentrum für Umfragen, Methoden und Analysen (ZUMA) e.v., Mannheim
Institut für angewandte Sozialwissenschaft: *Ansaetze zu Einem System Sozialer Kennziffern*, Bad Godesberg
National Opinion Research Centre (NORC), University of Chicago
Population Crisis Committee, Washington, DC: Statistical Appendix Series
Review of Income and Wealth, New York
Social Indicators Network News (SINET), Emory University, Atlanta
Social Indicators Research, University of Guelph, Guelph, Ontario
Sonderforschungsbereich 3: *Mikroanalytische Grundlagen der Gesellschaftspolitik*, Universitäten Frankfurt and Mannheim

INDEX

Bold entries refer to sections within chapters.